The #ActuallyAutistic Guide to Advocacy

of related interest

Shake It Up!

How to Be Young, Autistic and Make an Impact

Quincy Hansen

ISBN 978 1 78775 979 4

eISBN 978 1 78775 980 0

The Autism and Neurodiversity Self Advocacy Handbook

Developing the Skills to Determine Your Own Future

Barb Cook and Yenn Purkis

ISBN 978 1 78775 575 8

eISBN 978 1 78775 576 5

Spectrum Women

Walking to the Beat of Autism

Edited by Barb Cook and Dr Michelle Garnett

Foreword by Lisa Morgan

ISBN 978 1 78592 434 7

eISBN 978 1 78450 806 7

The #ActuallyAutistic Guide to Advocacy

Step-by-Step Advice on How to Ally and Speak up with Autistic People and the Autism Community

Jennifer Brunton, Ph.D.
and Jenna Gensic, M.A.

Jessica Kingsley Publishers
London and Philadelphia

First published in Great Britain in 2021 by Jessica Kingsley Publishers
An Hachette Company

1

A CIP catalogue record for this title is available from the British Library and the Library of Congress

ISBN 978 1 78775 973 2
eISBN 978 1 78775 974 9

Printed and bound in the United States by Integrated Books International

Jessica Kingsley Publishers' policy is to use papers that are natural, renewable and recyclable products and made from wood grown in sustainable forests. The logging and manufacturing processes are expected to conform to the environmental regulations of the country of origin.

Jessica Kingsley Publishers
Carmelite House
50 Victoria Embankment
London EC4Y 0DZ

www.jkp.com

To neurodivergent people everywhere and our beloved, proudly neurodiverse families. As our world evolves, may your perspectives increasingly be honored.

Contents

Introduction *11*

Stage One: Building an Advocacy Base by Learning and Listening

Step 1: Emphasize Acceptance **35**

Replace panic with steady growth in awareness/acceptance 37

Reframe autism as a way of being (not a tragedy) 41

Focus on eliminating barriers instead of so-called "bad" behaviors/attributes 51

Work for change in society, cultures, and institutions, not Autistic people 56

Be sensitive to the details but work towards the bigger picture 61

Step 2: Adopt a Balanced Perspective **68**

Avoid assumptions about savantism 69

Take the entire lifespan into account 72

Avoid stereotyping by gender 77

Acknowledge strengths and weaknesses as with all humans 80

Step 3: Presume Competence **86**

Distinguish between autism and other intellectual differences and disabilities 87

Understand that neuro-normalized methods are often used to determine competence 90

Listen, listen, listen—even when someone isn't talking at the speed you'd prefer 92

Be aware that over-sheltering can prevent people from growing 96

Step 4: Advocate for Individuals **102**

Embrace respectful story sharing 103

Be aware of the perils of blanket assumptions 107

Always get to know the Autistic person first 112

Never expect a one-size-fits-all-solution 115

Beware of inspiration porn 118

Honor the diverse aspects of Autistic people 122

Stage Two: Implementing #ActuallyAutistic Advice in Your Own ND Family, Classroom, or Practice

Step 5: Advocate for Things Autistic People Actually Want **131**

Explore only Autistic-initiated therapies 132

Honor diverse relationships 150

Use language carefully—person-first language versus identity-first language 154

Consider the social model of disability 158

Practice neurodiversity-friendly school and workplace advocacy 161

Step 6: Stay Centered on the Autistic Person's Needs and Dreams **176**

Remember that many Autistic people don't want to look or act NT 177

Recognize that a neurotypical's vision of a happy life might not be the same as an Autistic person's vision 184

Listen to Autistic people (and your child) over NT parents and other "experts" 189

Be sensitive to using intent as an excuse 194

Distinguish between meltdowns and tantrums 197

Practice appropriate aspects of independent living at every age 200

Step 7: Include All Autistic People **210**

Defer to Autistic people as the experts in autism 211

Acknowledge and respect the authority of all Autistic people of varying skills sets 218

Remember that while one particular Autistic person may have unique autism characteristics, they may nonetheless have broadly useful insights 222

Stage Three: Public Advocacy for Autism Understanding and Acceptance

Step 8: Connect Respectfully with Actually Autistic People **232**

Reach out to the Autistic community (take the first step) 233

Conduct inclusive research 244

Treat Autistic people as people, not study subjects 248
Learn about the intersection of race and disability 252
Support and/or work with/for organizations that are disability-friendly 259

Step 9: Put Theory into Practice **265**

Be a continual student and implement your own advice 266
Stay on top of technology trends 270
Recognize and acknowledge past flaws, and move forward 271

Advocacy Goals Checklist for Easy Self-Improvement *275*

Interviewee Bios *280*

References *305*

Subject Index *311*

Author Index *316*

Introduction

When Shannon Hughes enlisted the assistance of an autism employment "expert" to help her find a job, she was hopeful this professional would offer useful advice for obtaining meaningful employment. After experiencing chronic invalidation at work and enduring the exhaustion of using all her physical, mental, and emotional resources to function in a neurotypical (NT) environment, Hughes had nothing left over for relationships or developing any kind of support network.

During one of her sessions with the employment expert, they were approached by one of the expert's colleagues. Assuming Hughes needed help introducing herself to other adults, the expert spoke to Hughes as if she was "a shy first grader," asking if she was willing to introduce herself to the man who had approached them. Hughes was immediately offended. "I have decades of experience in interacting with people in a professional environment, introducing myself, and promoting myself professionally," she explains. She says her social skills are well-rehearsed and better than those of many NT people, although they are exhausting for her to practice. Hughes explains that if she was around two people who didn't know each other, she would introduce both of them instead of asking only one person to introduce themselves.

But Hughes didn't want to be rude, so she introduced herself, and the colleague left. Then the employment expert thanked her in the most patronizing tone for allowing her to "challenge" Hughes. Hughes says, "I wanted very much to 'challenge' her with a lesson on what social behavior she was practicing, which was downright insulting to someone with autism, but it had already been a long day, and I wanted to go home."

During her time working at a disability resource center in Missouri, Hughes realized that everyone, no matter how well informed they are, makes mistakes about what disabled people are capable of. Even in that presumably inclusive context, she witnessed medical professionals who work every day with people on the spectrum making incorrect assumptions about competence. "It's important not to make assumptions, and to treat people with disabilities with the same respect and consideration as you would anyone, unless you have concrete knowledge that they need anything else from you," Hughes notes.

Hughes' story is one example of the importance of presuming competence for people on the spectrum. But the employment expert's mistake is not an isolated incident. Like most neurodivergent (ND) people, this book's co-author, Jennifer, remembers numerous similar incidents throughout her own life, as well as her Autistic son's childhood: the time a neighbor congratulated her on her son's "normal interaction," teachers and special educators assuming he needed modifications instead of accommodations, and so on.

The point is, like all human beings, every Autistic child or adult has their own strengths and weaknesses. Yet most

Autistic people regularly encounter generalized assumptions around their competence and capacities long before they reach adulthood. When well-meaning parents and family members, care providers, friends, partners, and schools lack a holistic awareness of neurodiversity, they may treat children, teens, and young adults on the spectrum in ways that can have far-ranging, long-lasting repercussions for the Autistic people in their care. Likewise, a lack of awareness on the part of the people and institutions around them has significant and ongoing negative consequences for Autistic adults.

But we can learn, grow, and do better—together. This book is designed to lead the reader through a series of incremental, manageable steps towards truly aware and respectful advocacy and allyship. We start with small-scale, personal-level insights, move on to families, schools, and other institutions, and gradually widen our scope to a broad societal focus. At each stage, we offer opportunities and suggestions for both proactive reflection and practical actions that are conducive to the amplification of #ActuallyAutistic viewpoints (the #ActuallyAutistic hashtag was created by the Autistic community to identify and celebrate Autistic voices and expertise as distinct from the #autism hashtag). Proceeding from the personal to the political, we propose a comprehensive, holistic, and respectful approach to autism advocacy. The book is also clearly organized by topic, so readers can easily locate those sections that feel most useful at a given time.

Jenna interviewed more than one hundred Autistic people, and nearly all of them had advice to improve autism advocacy and NT allyship. Jenna has been soliciting advice from the Autistic community since 2013 (as the mother and sibling of people on the spectrum), with a mission to connect parents, caregivers, and educators with #ActuallyAutistic voices and help Autistic people reclaim the autism narrative. Jennifer's ND perspectives (both as a parent and as an individual) and extensive advocacy experience round out this rich trove of #ActuallyAutistic wisdom. In the pages that follow, you'll hear from the Autistic community about the most productive and respectful ways to advocate for Autistic people.

About the authors

At this point we'd like to tell you a bit more about ourselves.

Dr. Jennifer Elizabeth Brunton is an academic turned freelance writer and editor. She has a B.A. in sociology and anthropology from Bryn Mawr College, Pennsylvania, and earned a Ph.D. in sociology from Columbia University, New York.

A longtime professor, Jennifer taught ethics, bioethics, comparative religion, and philosophy, as well as sociology.

Having identified as Autistic after reading Donna Williams' *Nobody, Nowhere* (1992) in her twenties, Jennifer's advocacy efforts only grew after it became clear that her son was also ND. Her teaching and writing have always included an explicit orientation towards civil rights and social justice.

Jennifer's writings include a wide range of articles about culture, wellness, science, travel, tech, food, and business, as well as a literary mystery and other diverse publications. Her editing projects cover the gamut as well, with working as the editor of the Americans of Conscience Action Checklist being a particular point of pride. Her most beloved project, however, is her neurodiverse parenting and advocacy blog, Full Spectrum Mama (fullspectrummama.blogspot.com).

An ND mother of two, and a fierce advocate for equality and inclusion for all, she currently lives in western Massachusetts.

Jenna Gensic is a freelance writer, disability advocate, and mother of four from northern Indiana. She has a B.A. in English and Secondary Education and an M.A. in English writing.

She is the author of *What Your Child on the Spectrum Really Needs: Advice From 12 Autistic Adults* (2019) and manages the Learn from Autistics website (www.learnfromautistics.com).

Jenna has an Autistic brother and son, which is where her interest in autism advocacy began. Her studies of autism advocacy and the neurodiversity movement eventually led to the development of the Learn from Autistics website, where she regularly engages with the Autistic community and shares Autistic expertise with NT parents, caregivers, and others, whether NT or ND.

Jenna writes and speaks about parenting issues related to prematurity, cerebral palsy, and autism.

We feel it is important to acknowledge that we finished the final drafts of this book during a global pandemic which has had untold impacts on all of the planet's inhabitants. For many, perhaps especially in the ND community, the coronavirus has increased isolation, poverty, depression, and anxiety. For some, the opportunity to stay close to home (and family, where applicable) and interact largely via the internet, among other elements of quarantine fallout, may have in some ways improved quality of life. Only time will tell. The advice in this book will help advocates build a foundation of healthy support options for the Autistic people in their lives (both during times of routine and in the uncertainty of the pandemic) and build a more inclusive and equitable world.

Redirecting our fervor

Are your advocacy efforts aligned with the desires of the

Autistic community? Who are the experts you have reached out to for help determining what is best for your Autistic child, loved one, student, friend...? There will surely be variations in opinions, but a commitment to continual engagement with the Autistic community is the best way to make sure our advocacy efforts are creating powerful, positive change for the Autistic people in our lives.

Despite good intentions and strong efforts, we sometimes do not advocate in the most effective ways. Why do we fall short? *The Real Experts* contributor Nick Walker (2011) explains that one of the reasons it's difficult for parents to help their children thrive is because their children's sensory experience of the world and the way their children's minds work is often fundamentally different from their parents'. This holds true for others who do not share a similar neurology.

But even neurodivergent parents and educators, such as Jennifer, face advocacy challenges. Neurodivergent people are just that: neurologically diverse. We must all listen to a range of ND voices (not just our own) if we seek true understanding. Autistic parents with Autistic children grapple with both the intricacies of their own child's specific ways of being and the difficulties of attempting to function and advocate successfully as Autistic adults in a world that is largely designed to suit NT people.

NT or Autistic, our advocacy shortcomings are not for a lack of effort. Those who work with Autistic people naturally want to do their best by their clients and students, keeping up with the latest research, participating in workshops, and so on. As caring parents—or grandparents, guardians, partners, friends, family members—we spend our days doing research, consulting with "experts," and trying to follow their advice for help raising our Autistic children or advocating/allying with our Autistic young adult and/or adult loved ones. We love our children/loved ones, and we'd sacrifice anything for them. When it comes down to it, most people with an Autistic person in their life are eager to learn about autism.

But if we aren't integrating a diverse range of perspectives from the Autistic community, *we're falling short*. We have the best of intentions, but are sometimes criticized for our efforts, especially when they are centered on "expert" NT advice rather than #ActuallyAutistic counsel. Rather than feeling attacked when faced with new information that may contradict NT-driven ideas and advocacy strategies, would-be advocates and allies who are able to integrate ND perspectives will grow in ways that may well benefit themselves, the (other) ND people in their lives, and the entire Autistic community. Good intentions are more valuable when they are not used as excuses in the faces of our critics but are instead redirected with the same fervor to more positive advocacy strategies that many Autistic people endorse. This book is full of compelling information and proactive strategies that will help you to better channel your energy and efforts.

You may be reading this book because you are interested in how you can contribute to an autism advocacy movement that will improve the life of your Autistic child, family member, partner, student, client, or community member. The passion you have for supporting the Autistic person or people in your life is integral to helping them develop a positive Autistic identity and achieve a variety of life successes. If you are a parent or guardian, know that your child needs you. Your child will benefit from your love and support their entire lives. Whatever your role, you may also be interested in what the Autistic community has to say about the advocacy efforts they are witness to. The diverse and evolving population of

Autistic people houses the real experts on autism, and they are full of advice for helping you better advocate for your child and/or advocate with the Autistic people you care about. This book is about making you a more powerful advocate with the assistance of the Autistic community.

Advocate identity

When it comes down to it, advocacy isn't about us. Advocates serve those they advocate with or for. This book is in part about learning how to do so. It's about awakening you to your passive or active role in a system that suppresses marginalized voices. It's about removing yourself from the spotlight society has placed on parents, teachers, therapists, doctors, or other NT experts and learning how to best serve the people and community you care about. The best way to do that is to respect, trust, and promote the expertise of the Autistic community.

Questions about #ActuallyAutistic advocacy

So many autism parents (grandparents, guardians...) consider advocacy as part of their identities. They spend a great deal of time and energy fighting for what they believe is best for their Autistic loved one(s), so anyone who tries to reshape what this behavior looks like is certain to be met with some resistance. Autistic neurodiversity advocates have been feeling this resistance for years.

Common arguments from NT parents aimed at the Autistic community run along the lines of statements like "You are so high-functioning. You have the ability to advocate. You can't possibly speak for my low-functioning child" or "Your experiences are entirely different from my child's. If you were as disabled as my child, you would want a cure for Autism."

When Jenna asked Julia Bascom, Executive Director of the Autistic Self Advocacy Network (ASAN) about this common opposition, she responded:

> It's important to point out that many self-advocates do, in fact, experience significant disabilities, and that many parent supporters of the neurodiversity movement have high-needs children. There's a belief that anyone, or any family, who says they experience both autism and happiness must not really be disabled, and that's just demonstrably not true.
>
> I think one of the factors leading to this false dichotomy is that a lot of people don't know of many examples of people with intellectual disabilities or intense support needs who are leading self-determined lives. It's hard to imagine possibilities for your child that you haven't seen before yourself.

Bascom offers some advocacy tips for parents and loved ones of children exhibiting the most disabling autism symptoms, encouraging them to join inclusive support groups like the Thinking Person's Guide to Autism, the Arc, or The Association for Persons with Severe Handicaps (TASH). She also stresses that children should have access to an effective way to communicate. ASAN has a guide for families trying to navigate alternative communication called *Everybody Communicates* (2018).

Other common questions are: "Shouldn't I be able to determine what therapy is best for my child?" Or "Shouldn't I be able to determine which educational setting/approach is best for teaching my child/student? My child is too young to decide for herself." Or "My child does not understand the importance of therapy."

When children are young, they rely on their parents to choose the best course for their development. Part of determining the most appropriate therapy for your child is doing your due diligence to research the recommended therapies before trying or committing to any kind of schedule. Investigating what the adult Autistic community has to say about these therapies is an essential (but often overlooked) part of this process. This is discussed in more detail in Step 5.

Identifying as an ally

Parents and providers often want to be allies to their children/clients. As an autism parent or specialist, it is a natural extension to want to be an ally for any Autistic person, or to support autism-related causes, both locally and nationally. But Autistic self-advocates have insisted there is a lot to be learned as an NT autism advocate if you want to be a true ally. Additionally, neurotypicals really shouldn't designate themselves as allies. This is a title they can strive for, but validation comes from the Autistic community. Neurotypicals must constantly strive to be allies but be humble enough to recognize that the title isn't theirs to claim. It's a little more complicated for Autistic parents, but we all have a lot to learn about neurodiversity, advocacy, and being a true ally. This book will help you earn that title in the eyes of the Autistic community (if that's important to you), but, *much more importantly*, it will help you advocate in the ways that make the most positive change for the Autistic person in your life.

Scope

Advocates support and promote the interests of a group (Merriam-Webster 2020). We believe that if you are not a member of the group you are trying to support, you have a special responsibility to engage with this community as often as possible to learn about their interests and goals. We also want to be very clear that this book is explicitly inclusive of Autistic autism advocates, whether they are advocating for themselves, and/or for their children, students, partners, clients... We can all improve our advocacy efforts and allyship by integrating extensive and varied Autistic viewpoints.

This book initially came out of Jenna's efforts to engage with the Autistic community around the topic of advocacy: What mistakes are neurotypicals making? Where can we improve? The 100+ interviews she conducted to answer these questions took place via email or Skype. This book is a compilation of insights and advice gleaned from those interviews, as well as from other Autistic writers and speakers on the topic of advocacy. All of the people quoted, cited, or paraphrased here are Autistic, unless noted otherwise. There are only a few exceptions where an article has been cited and not authored by someone on the spectrum.

Looking to add a neurodivergent perspective to her book from the outset, Jenna invited Jennifer—a writer and editor who was originally an interview subject—to collaborate on the project. Building on subject matter that arose from Jenna's interviews, and informed by both authors' experiences as NT (Jenna) and ND (Jennifer) parent advocates, our step-by-step format addresses a series of related advocacy topics, with each step building upon the previous ones to create an advocacy framework that spans all sectors of daily life, from the personal to the political. Each step concludes with specific summary guidance for advocates.

A note on vocabulary and capitalization

We want to be very clear about the language we use. This section is intended to serve as both an introduction to our use of several key terms and a reader reference.

Ableism

"Ableism" refers to discrimination against somebody based on a disability. It is a set of beliefs that identify people as socially, physically, mentally, or morally inferior, based on their physical, emotional, developmental, or psychological disability. Ableism can be hidden in a person's subconscious. Ableism can lead to the inferior treatment of Autistic people and pressure them to hide or attempt to "cure" autism.

Asperger's Syndrome

Prior to the publication of the *Diagnostic and Statistical Manual of Mental Disorders, 5th Edition (DSM-5;* APA 2013), Asperger's Syndrome was a diagnostic label given to people who met autism criteria and had typically developing language. Today Asperger's Syndrome is no longer a subcategory of autism, and all Autistic people are categorized under the same umbrella of Autism Spectrum Disorder. Some of the people quoted in this book received a diagnosis prior to the *DSM-5*, and they sometimes refer to this label. The controversial history of the historical figure after whom this diagnosis was named has caused many to actively avoid this label. However, some positive and #ActuallyAutistic uses of the term have endured.

Autistic

In order to respect the existence and identity of the Autistic community, we have chosen to use a capital 'A' in the word "Autistic" to identify it as a proper adjective. Exceptions occur within quotations from an Autistic contributor if the person has chosen to use lowercase. Because much of the correspondence with the contributors was written, lowercase usage is common within quotations.

The Autistic community

The phrase "the Autistic community" is often used throughout this book to refer to the diverse group of Autistic people with unique personalities, skills, needs, and desires. This phrase does not refer to a unified or homogenous group. While many people within the Autistic community have similar desires and passions for equal rights, opportunities, and dignified living, the authors of this book do not suggest that all Autistic people believe and want the same things nor that they agree with the approaches to achieving the goals we share. This book is based on the authority of personal experience and the power of personal storytelling.

"High-functioning" and "low-functioning"

Although "high-functioning autism" is not an official diagnostic label, the mainstream public often uses this term to describe people on the spectrum with average or above average intelligence and a range of NT-relevant capabilities. Most people also use this term to indicate the degree to which Autistic people can exhibit behaviors that make them appear to function similarly to neurotypicals in the mainstream environment. There are many problems with the widespread usage of high- and low-functioning labels, including the fact that they suggest a false sense of identification and don't do justice to the unique skill sets of people all over the spectrum. The overly-simplistic labels of high-functioning and low-functioning inaccurately divide Autistic people. These and other problems with the widespread usage of these terms will be explored in more depth in Step 7. Most of the Autistic people quoted in this book condemn these terms, and we have avoided using them.

Identity-first language

This book uses identity-first language (IFL: "Autistic person") rather than person-first language (PFL: "person with autism") when referring to people on the spectrum. This decision mirrors the strong preference of many people in the Autistic community, including a significant majority of those quoted in this book. Exceptions occur if an Autistic contributor has a preference for PFL. A more in-depth discussion of the preference for IFL can be found in Step 5.

Individuals versus people

Some Autistic people condemn the use of the term "individuals" to describe them. Many neurotypicals use this word to express that every person is different and that no one is interchangeable, which is true. However, the conscious semantic adjustment to *continually* emphasize individuality (when "individuals" is not emphasized in common speech) can signify a subconscious negative association. The term "individuals" can be othering and is often openly used to describe hyper-stigmatized groups. Thus, many dislike this usage. We have avoided using this term for these reasons. Exceptions include situations where individuality is generally discussed or specifically emphasized (rather than referring to groups of people, for example) or when this phrasing is used in quotations.

Neurotypical/neurodivergent/neurodiverse

Sometimes we use the term "neurotypical (NT)" to refer to a person who is not Autistic, and "neurodivergent (ND)" to someone who is Autistic. These are labels used within the Autistic community for this purpose as well. ND is a term that could also apply to anyone with an atypical neurology (including dyslexia, attention deficit hyperactivity disorder [ADHD], or bipolar disorder, for example). In this book, there are many instances when either we or a contributor have used NT to signal a reference to someone who is not on the utism spectrum, and ND to signal someone who is on the autism spectrum. Because much of the advice in this book can benefit both Autistic and non-Autistic members of the ND community, we sometimes use the term ND to signify advice that may be relevant to all members of the ND community. When referring to Autistic people specifically, we use IFL as mentioned above. "Neurodiversity" refers to the natural existence of varied neurologies, making for an inherently neurodiverse human race.

On the spectrum

Referring to an Autistic individual as "on the spectrum" elicits a variety of responses from the Autistic community. Some Autistic people dislike this reference because it is sometimes used as a slur, casually equating social awkwardness with autism. Others dislike the phrase because it suggests neurology is like an accessory rather than a way of existing, and others dislike it for entirely different reasons. Yet other Autistic people have neutral or even positive associations with this language because they believe it most accurately describes autism. In this book, we have respected the individual preferences of the contributors and avoided usage of this phrase around the quotes of people who dislike this language. However, we have used this phrase in other sections of the book, especially with individuals quoted who preferred this language or had neutral associations with it.

Pronouns

Cisgender and trans people are referred to using "he/she" and "her/his" pronouns, while nonbinary and gender-fluid people are identified by "they" and "their."

Spelling

Both Jennifer and Jenna live in the U.S.A. and have used the North American "-ize" spellings throughout this book (e.g., "realize," "specialize," "recognize"). However, several of the Autistic individuals who are quoted live outside of the U.S.A. where "-ise" spellings are customary. Within quotations that were submitted in writing, we have chosen to leave the native spellings of these "-ise" words as is.

Quotation/source policy

All quotations are from Autistic people and all source materials are written by Autistic authors unless otherwise specified.

All quotes that are attributed to people but do not mention additional reference details are from Jenna's blog interviews with Autistic people. More details about each person can be found in the extensive biography section.

When we mention simple facts, statistics, and so on, we will not necessarily indicate the ND or NT status of the researchers and/or authors referenced.

The authority of personal Autistic experience

This book is based on the authority of personal experience and the foundational assumption that Autistic voices should be respected and valued. Autistic input is powerful and useful because of the intimate familiarity Autistic people have with this way of being. The opinions and advice in this book should be esteemed as uniquely useful, not flawed because of where they come from. Accessing Autistic expertise is important, not only because it helps us uncover the truth but because it is the right thing to do.

As Julia Bascom explains in the Foreword to *Loud Hands, Autistic People, Speaking*, the Autistic community has a lot to say. Moreover, she contends that there is "something beautiful and powerful about a community of people who are routinely silenced, abused, neglected, and murdered, yet who continue to survive, finding and nurturing one another and growing in strength and sense of purpose, year after year" (Bascom 2012a, p.7).

For these reasons and many more, Autistic perspectives are deeply worthwhile for other Autistic people, whether adults, parents, and/or children. In addition, they are profoundly necessary and useful for neurotypicals, whether parents, grandparents, educators, service providers, friends, and so on. But Autistic people do not exist merely as a resource for neurotypicals; they should be valued as nothing less than full and equal members of the human race. This book is an engagement with human experts exploring different facets of the human condition and is intended as a resource for all autism advocates and would-be allies.

Everyone makes mistakes

The advice in this book is meant to motivate positive, effective advocacy behaviors that engender accountability and result in improved autism acceptance and Autistic success in a variety of forms. Many of the contributors to this book spoke about the positive efforts of autism advocates and how they are happy to have anyone with good intentions on their side. Former Michigan State basketball player and public speaker Anthony Ianni says, "Every advocate that I've met or presented with has been great and has had a lot of great knowledge." Poet/author Gretchen McIntire says, "I try to focus on gratitude that others are trying." Many contributors said advocates do amazing work and achieve great progress as a result of their efforts.

At the same time, there is much division in the autism advocacy community over terminology, education, research funding, and general advocacy behaviors. This is natural, given the many unique human beings, relationships, and viewpoints encompassed by that large and diverse group. But it's also because it is split in two, says advocate Emma Dalmayne: "There is the autism community which is primarily parents of autistic children, and the autistic community which is made up of autistic adults." Some advocates insist that putting different advocacy behaviors under the microscope is a distraction from the primary shared goal of helping people on the spectrum; however, the Autistic community has insisted this introspection is important. Dalmayne articulates some of the reasoning behind this stance:

> These [advocacy] choices may be anything from depriving their children of screen time, to using ableist language to describe them. We should always correct parents if they are stating that they are using supplements, diets, or quack therapies in an attempt to heal/purge or cure their autistic child of their neurological difference. We should, however, also try to educate them on their terminology and attitude towards their children. They need to be guided, encouraged, enlightened, and given the choice to listen to us willingly.

These advocacy differences are still important because not all "help" is truly helpful, and, in truth, some advocacy strategies can unknowingly cause damage. Dalmayne's desire for hopeful education sets the tone for this book.

Several contributors stressed that everyone makes mistakes, so parents and other advocates shouldn't be overly self-critical, but, rather, continue their drive to do good. Australian writer and parent Rochelle Johnson extends this sentiment, saying: "Just like everyone, advocates make mistakes. Everyone makes mistakes, and the most important thing is to learn from them, acknowledge them, and sincerely apologise and aim to move forward in a positive way."

Marriage and family therapist Bob Yamtich recommends advocates reflect on the ways they participate in the world while actively acknowledging their own inner states. "I see self-connection to feelings and needs as the foundation of effective participation in the world," he says. "Every breath of mindfulness contributes to self-connection, which, in turn, contributes to those individuals you want to support."

Knowing when to back off

Sometimes would-be advocates and/or allies may need to back off at the request of an Autistic person or group. Not everybody wants or needs someone to advocate or ally with them, however sincere, heartfelt, or well-meaning your efforts may be. This holds true for all allies and advocates of any neurology. When someone doesn't want your intervention or participation, you may want to direct your energy towards more general neurodivergent causes or self-advocacy.

Of course, figuring out how best to proceed can be trickier when dealing with a resistant child or teenager (either NT or ND) who does not yet fully understand their own best interests or the long-term implications of certain actions (or the lack thereof). Families, other caregivers, and professionals in such situations will need to find their own balance of respect, trust, and support. This can be particularly hard when it comes to NT or Autistic teens (and transition-age young adults, who are no longer children but may still benefit from some scaffolding as they grow more independent). Integrating other ND perspectives, such as those in this book, can provide invaluable input throughout this process.

A fruitful journey ahead

The following chapters take an in-depth look at nine key elements of effective, respectful, inclusive advocacy and allyship. Every topic was chosen, shaped, and informed by #ActuallyAutistic perspectives. Each step outlines one important aspect of advocacy, examines related actions and attitudes, and integrates wisdom from diverse Autistic voices. These wide-ranging chapters contain crucial details for anyone who aspires to be a genuine autism advocate.

We also explore typical advocacy pitfalls linked with each chapter's subject matter. If you find that you have participated in any of the advocacy behaviors condemned by some of these Autistic contributors, resist the urge to defend your behavior or look for exceptions that justify your actions. Instead, just listen. Just. Listen. Absorb this advice and imagine the feelings behind the words. Search for opportunities to promote positive attitudes towards autism with new advocacy strategies on small or large scales. Your interest and commitment to reading this book are a wonderful beginning to positive change. Your efforts are important, so thank you. We are grateful for your support of the Autistic community.

STAGE ONE

Building an Advocacy Base by Learning and Listening

The steps that make up this first stage introduce some basic tenets of neurodiversity that are crucial to supporting Autistic people. The concept of neurodiversity frames autism as a natural neurological variation and not a problem with nature that needs to be solved or eliminated by selective abortion. The neurodiversity viewpoint is rooted in the desire for equal rights and treatment in society. This section addresses some of the basic beliefs and behaviors associated with autism acceptance to build a foundation for positive change in the lives of those you care about.

This foundational stage presents information intended largely for personal growth. It assumes that truly valuable advocacy is rooted in extensive knowledge, as well as in genuine empathy that stems from both familiarity and wisdom. Naturally, such shifts and deepening insights on the parts of individuals will have important reverberations in the larger world, but these chapters ask us to first take a critical look at our own thought processes and assumptions.

Step 1

Emphasize Acceptance

> *Love and appreciate your kids for who they are right now, not as some distant future adult. They are worthy and valuable and amazing, right in this moment. If you can understand this deeply, not as some wish, but as something you feel and know – this is a pathway to thriving children.*
>
> — ALLY GRACE

Autism acceptance is the latest civil rights movement. Autistic people everywhere have spent decades advocating for their right to be treated with dignity and respect, and the world is finally taking notice. Stories about autism and Autistic people are common in the media, and Autistic representation is improving in literature, television, and movies. Although not all Autistic people may approve of the public discourse on autism, especially if it lacks Autistic input, it's now possible to find conferences and educational events led by Autistic people, and, at the very least, follow public Autistic advocates on social media and read articles about advocacy that are authored by people on the spectrum. The Autistic people who are speaking and writing publicly about autism overwhelmingly advocate for acceptance.

This chapter explores different ways families, educators, and others can work towards autism acceptance, beginning with positive changes in their own minds and a commitment to truly—and primarily—listen to Autistic people when it comes to autism. These shifts will, ultimately, lead to a reframing of how autism is traditionally discussed in society and bring a more positive perspective into homes, schools, practices, and beyond. This attitude of acceptance is a critical foundation to any advocacy efforts that would be endorsed by the Autistic community. The ideas discussed in this section challenge would-be advocates and allies to commit to changing themselves and their surroundings rather than focus on changing the Autistic person.

As parents, we (Jenna and Jennifer) find this perspective refreshing, critical to positive emotional development, and most effective in achieving desired results. It's much easier to control your own attitude and environment than to force your child, student, spouse, or other Autistic person in your life to become someone they are not. Once the focus is placed on supporting the Autistic person rather than on the impossible task of eliminating their autism, it's much simpler and more effective to begin making small adjustments that have a potentially large impact on that person's social/emotional development, not to mention their daily life.

This approach has particular resonance for Jennifer, as it may for many ND parents. As ND children (and throughout our earlier lives), we may have suspected—or been told—that there was something "wrong" with us. We may have fought to "pass" in NT society, in an earlier, more ignorant era. And we may have at some point tried to force our children to do the same. In some ways, acceptance, for us, may need to start with fully accepting ourselves.

Acceptance is something we can all work on, whatever our neurology. Here are five ways to boost acceptance in yourself, your family, your community, and beyond.

Autism acceptance behavior, No. 1: Replace panic with steady growth in awareness/acceptance

Why is this needed?

Author and theology professor Ron Sandison says the "experts" told his parents he "would never attend college, have meaningful relationships, or excel in athletics." Given the common myths and lack of awareness around autism that can prevail even among medical and other professionals, this sort of prognosis is all too common upon diagnosis. And families may also be frightened by what they hear about autism on social media or in their communities. But no one interested in real progress—for an individual and/or for Autistic people in general—should remain paralyzed by panic. And it is particularly incumbent upon therapists, teachers, and others who work with Autistic people and their families to help mitigate such negative reactions by actively seeking out more positive perspectives and encouraging families to meet their children where they are.

Autistic people understand that an autism diagnosis can come as a shock to a family, even one that includes neurodivergent members (who may have been traumatized by a lack of awareness and acceptance during their own childhoods). Instead of panicking and despairing over the warnings of doomsday prophets, it's important to commit to steady progress towards autism awareness and understanding. This means reaching out to the Autistic community for guidance on how to best serve the Autistic person (or people) in your life.

For families: understanding your grief

Activist Jim Sinclair is well known for awakening parents to addressing their grief after first hearing about their child's diagnosis. In the Autism Network International Newsletter, *Our Voice*, Sinclair explains that some parental grief is natural. This grief, however, doesn't actually stem from the child's autism. Instead, it comes from the loss of the "normal" child the parents originally anticipated. Sinclair warns that parents need to eventually move past these feelings:

> [T]his grief over a fantasized normal child needs to be separated from the parents' perceptions of the child they do have: the autistic child who needs the support of adult caretakers and who can form very meaningful relationships with those caretakers if given the opportunity. Continuing focus on the child's autism as a source of grief is damaging for both the parents and the child, and precludes the development of an accepting and authentic relationship between them. For their own sake and for the sake of their children, I urge parents to make radical changes in their perceptions of what autism means. (Sinclair 1993)

Sinclair adds that autism cannot be separated from the child, so trying to rid your child of autism is like wishing for a completely different child.

Setting the right tone

ASAN emphasizes that upon first receiving a diagnosis for their children, parents should be given positive resources about autism and the journey they will go on with their children. Jenna notes that this wasn't the case for her and her husband after her son was diagnosed. While their families were supportive and positive, medical professionals warned about the need for intense early intervention. This all-too-typical example highlights the crucial role autism-aware medical, educational, therapeutic, and other professionals can play in nurturing inclusive, hopeful autism-aware families from the moment of diagnosis and beyond.

Parents and other caregivers are often bombarded with an enormous amount of new information upon diagnosis. While it's natural to feel overwhelmed, families must also take some initiative, carefully weighing information to ensure that NT biases and discouraging messages are seen for what they are: discrimination. Later diagnoses bear similar potential pitfalls, so Autistic people who are diagnosed after childhood will generally still have to contend with a barrage of NT-biased information, as will those around them, whether family, friends, partners, or professionals.

Even seemingly well-meaning organizations and efforts can display an insidious and damaging lack of awareness. In 2019, ASAN ended their partnership with *Sesame Street* after the show created a public service announcement (PSA) featuring their Autistic character, Julia, to promote Autism Speaks' "Screen for Autism" initiative. *Sesame Street* had consulted with ASAN for several years during the development of its Julia Muppet. But according to ASAN, the new PSA promoted a discriminatory "100 Day Kit" resource for parents of newly diagnosed children. A statement from ASAN (2019) explains:

> These PSAs use the language of acceptance and understanding to push resources that further stigma and treat autistic people as burdens on our families. The 100 Day Kit encourages parents to blame family difficulties on their autistic child...and to view autism as a terrible disease from which their child can "get better." It recommends compliance-based "therapies" and pseudoscientific "autism diets," but fails to educate families about communication supports. It even instructs parents to go through the five stages of grief after learning that their child is autistic, as they would if the child had died.

ASAN (2019) explains that parents are often bombarded with negative messages about what their lives and their child's life will be like. They are also pressured to enroll their children in therapies that mask Autistic traits in order to help them succeed. ASAN calls on organizations to instead promote content to families that carries messages of inclusion and acceptance. Late-diagnosed Autistic people and their loved ones may experience a range of emotions upon diagnosis, from relief to surprise to devastation, but one thing is certain: seeking out more positive information and Autistic-inclusive viewpoints will facilitate a more balanced, helpful perspective. When we focus on awareness and acceptance instead of fear, we are building a better world for Autistic children and adults—now and into the future.

Autism acceptance behavior, No. 2: Reframe autism as a way of being (not a tragedy)

Why is this needed?

How would you feel if people felt sorry for you for being yourself? Jennifer has had this experience, both as an individual and a parent. And so have many other Autistic people.

As Sinclair (1993) explains, autism isn't something a person *has* or is trapped inside:

> Autism is a way of being. It is pervasive; it colors every experience, every sensation, perception, thought, emotion, and encounter, every aspect of existence. It is not possible to separate the autism from the person—and if it were possible, the person you'd have left would not be the same person you started with.

Reframing autism as a neutral way of existing, a condition inextricably linked to one's identity, is important in helping Autistic people develop self-confidence and improving autism acceptance in society. Conversely, viewing autism as a tragedy can lead to the dangerous pursuit of autism "remedies," place additional stress on families, limit opportunities for Autistic people, and reinforce stereotypes about autism.

Avoiding autism "remedies"

Many well-intentioned advocates identify as "Autism Warriors," portraying themselves in constant battle with their child's autism. In her article "How 'Autism Warrior Parents' Harm Autistic Kids," Shannon Des Roches Rosa (an NT parent advocate and creator of the website The Thinking Person's Guide to Autism) explains:

> Autism Warrior Parents (AWPs) insist on supporting their Autistic kids either by trying to cure them, or by imposing non-Autistic-oriented goals on them—rather than by trying to understand how their kids are wired, and how that wiring affects their life experience. (Des Roches Rosa 2019)

AWPs might emphasize the need for an autism cure or support research that searches for a cure. They believe autism is a human flaw they must help their child overcome or circumvent in order to succeed in society like they do, on their terms. They view autism as a constant enemy that has robbed them of an otherwise normal child.

Morgan Giosa, a web developer and blues guitarist, has experienced first-hand the dangerous consequences of the zealous pursuit of a cure for autism. At the age of five, his family took him to see a psychiatrist who diagnosed him with Asperger's Syndrome. Giosa says that while the early diagnosis was beneficial in helping him develop self-awareness, the psychiatrist "completely destroyed" his early life and hampered his cognitive development by prescribing him Risperdal, an anti-psychotic medicine. He says:

> Giving a 5-year-old a daily regimen of Risperdal is the equivalent of giving that same 5-year-old a small amount of bleach to drink every day. This medicine had a profound negative impact on my fine motor skills, on my intellectual development, and the physical side effects for me included fine

motor tics (mild tardive dyskinesia), excessive weight gain, heart problems such as arrhythmia, and other life-threatening medical consequences.

Giosa discourages psychiatric professionals from immediately prescribing psychotropic medication as the go-to acceptable solution for those on the autism spectrum. He says that he is disheartened when he sees overmedicated Autistic people "who are such bright, shining stars and can so often achieve genius within our society." He wonders how often overmedication is the result of people wanting to cure autism rather than adapt their own behavior to accommodate those with ASD. Giosa explains:

> We should indeed adapt to accept and embrace the strengths and brilliance of those with autism and Asperger's and even those with bipolar or schizophrenia, instead of immediately jumping to the idea of trying to "cure" or "fix" these people, as if they're damaged or deviant from the "norm."

He believes that the cognitive side effects of antipsychotic drugs don't justify their use for the majority of Autistic people.

"I don't think it's appropriate or realistic to focus on finding a 'cure' for autism. I understand that life can be difficult for parents of autistic children, but it's not feasible to cure it," he says. He also challenges the need for society to cure autism, basing his reasoning on the prevalence of this common way of being:

> It's now the case that 1 in 59 children are diagnosed with autism. That doesn't seem deviant or divergent to me. It seems to me like autism is the new "normal." So, given that this is the case, I think civilization should adapt to accept autism quirks as part of the process of the autistic individual achieving creative genius, rather than medicating to attempt to lessen behaviors viewed as undesirable.

The emphasis on finding a cure for autism is a manifestation of viewing autism as a tragic disease. Misguided parents have resorted to dangerous methods to treat their Autistic children, including feeding them non-FDA-approved products with serious side effects, such as severe vomiting, diarrhea, and low blood pressure from dehydration (Scutti [NT] 2019). For anyone who views autism in this way, it's important, at the very least, to understand that not everyone on the spectrum is on board with this line of thinking. In "They Don't Want an Autism Cure," Julia Bascom asserts that autism isn't a disease or injury, but rather, a neurodevelopmental disability that shapes brains differently. She continues:

> If I can't talk, does it make sense to look for a pill for that, or should my speech therapist help me learn how to type or sign instead? Is flapping my hands or intensely and obsessively loving something "weird" or wanting to be by myself the psychological equivalent of diabetes, or is it a natural and beautiful part of human diversity? (Picciuto 2017)

Megan Amodeo, a writer and mother on the spectrum, shares this sentiment and warns that many autism "cures" are dangerous and ineffective. She explains: "Autism advocates often make the mistake of trying to 'cure' autism. While their intentions may be admirable, not everyone with autism wants to be cured. Many in the autism community are perfectly happy the way they are."

Often, neurotypicals attempt to "cure" Autistic loved ones by discouraging their intense interest in very specific subjects or activities. Jennifer remembers how her parents tried to dissuade her son from his focus on Pokémon. They felt strongly that he should be broadening his interests and learning about other toys and games, and even went so far as to refuse to buy him Pokémon cards for his birthday as a "remedy" for his perceived obsession. Her own experience with the comforts and satisfactions of deep exploration and involvement with certain foci over the course of her life allowed her to firmly express to her son's loving grandparents that their actions were a form of discrimination. Fortunately, they were able to listen and learn, and thereby become truly supportive in this area.

Avoiding additional stress

Another problem with a laser focus on autism as a lifelong tragedy that needs to be cured is that it inflicts additional stress and emotional pain on Autistic children and adults. Children will pick up on a parent's fear and negativity, according to marriage and family therapist Bob Yamtich. Yamtich understands that passion is sometimes necessary, but says, "All that adult care, all that parental love, can often come off as panic to a young one." He acknowledges this is a difficult line "because sometimes there is urgency to access more resources to improve quality of life." He stresses that if parents could become more confident in their support plans, they might not appear desperate in the minds of the Autistic people around them.

"One domain where there may be room for improvement is self-doubt. If you can find somebody you trust to consult with, you may be able to rest assured in your efforts," Yamtich suggests. Connections with, and perspectives from, Autistic people are integral to this process of parental growth. When parents understand autism as an equally valid way of being human and seek out resources that aid them in nurturing their unique child as a worthwhile person, they're able to foster confidence in their children as well.

Furthermore, building self-confidence is a critical aspect of healthy identity development (for both neurotypicals and Autistic people) that impacts virtually every aspect of children's lives. Writer Kmarie reminds us that accepting and celebrating individuality is a loving behavior for any adult playing a role in an Autistic child's life: "Concentrate on education from other autistics, support their differences, and celebrate ALL that they are...the struggles, the gifts, and the ordinary... so they know they are worthy of being loved."

The alternative can be bleak. Autistic children can develop poor self-esteem when they believe there is something fundamentally wrong with them. Yenn Purkis, an author and public speaker, says a deficit emphasis "can become a self-fulfilling prophecy and can follow the child into adulthood and impact their potential." Furthermore, continual focus on a child's autism as a source of grief hinders the potential for an accepting and authentic relationship between parents and their Autistic children (Sinclair 1993).

For all of these reasons and many more (some detailed below), educators and other professionals, too, must shift away from the idea that autism is inherently tragic or negative and move towards a more inclusive perspective that frames autism as simply a way of being human. Only the latter will be genuinely helpful to the families and people in their care.

Expanding opportunities

If people view autism as a tragedy, how high is the bar for Autistic people? How do others view Autistic potential? What are the trickle-down effects of this worldview? Buying into the autism tragedy paradigm is a poor foundation on which to base an advocacy strategy, says Australian blogger and mother Ally Grace. She explains that the media unfortunately feeds parents ableist assumptions about autism. Ableism is a set of beliefs that discriminates against disabled people by devaluing them via the belief that they need to be fixed in some way (Smith n.d.). Grace says of most NT advocates:

> [They] see disabled people through a lens of sadness, despair, grief, lost chances, dashed hopes, medicalisation, othering, and pathologisation. There are social factors at play that feed directly to parents of disabled children, which give these messages and which also give the entitlement to feel this way and to complain about it. They then, using this paradigm, attempt kindness and compassion. So, unfortunately they are just not coming from the right place to begin with!

Grace goes on to explain that the autism tragedy paradigm is especially damaging because it prevents Autistic people from gaining access to the same opportunities as neurotypicals:

If someone advocates that we should be tolerant of the damaged, socially inept, emotionally bereft, autistic people that are unfortunately in this world—this is really damaging and unhelpful! Not the part where they believe we should be kind to autistic people, of course. But the part where they assume we are less-than and that we should be tolerated instead of seen as equal and instead of actually being given things that will allow us to get the same opportunities that nondisabled people get.

Amy Sequenzia, a nonspeaking Autistic advocate, agrees that negative portrayals of autism can limit Autistic rights: "There is an assumption that we are suffering and that our lives are not really fulfilling. This can lead to a lack of interest in investing in us, in giving us equal rights and accommodating our needs" (Sequenzia 2011, p.94).

Breaking stereotypes

An emphasis on autism as a tragedy also leads to people focusing on the most disabling of autism symptoms, and not giving attention to the broad range of both needs and strengths of people on the spectrum. Writer J. R. Reed encourages people to recognize Autistic strengths. "We're unique individuals with unique skill sets, and if people took the time to learn about us, and accept us as we are, I think they would be shocked and amazed at what we can accomplish." According to Angela Andrews, a data analyst and mother, a lack of attention to both the needs and strengths of Autistic people results in misconceptions about Autistic abilities. She says that although some

Autistic people do indeed have significant challenges with verbal communication and other elements of NT-dominant society, a large segment of the Autistic population has gifts that aren't celebrated often enough. Andrews asks:

> Why are our abilities not celebrated, such as the ability to memorize music simply through playing it a time or two, or remember what was read after only glancing through it? What about the abilities to visualize things perfectly within the mind, as though an artist has painted a gorgeous oil behind one's eyes, or the uncanny ability to see patterns where others cannot? These are extremely valuable in many different facets of life, and yet no one hears of them.

Graphic designer Robbie Ierubino sees the artistic benefit of an Autistic lens. He says, "For me, Autism is not just any condition. It's a gift that can give me different points of view and imagination."

Irish author Frank L. Ludwig attributes several of his strengths to autism:

> I certainly attribute my creativity to my autism, be it in writing, developing ideas or problem solving, because autism enables us to think originally ("outside the box"). My ability to focus intensely on something of interest, such as researching a topic or writing a poem without taking a break for hours on end, is also undoubtedly a result of my autism.

Ludwig says he possesses a unique attention for the needs of children, which was another strength when he worked in the childcare field:

> I found my attention to the individual child an advantage. For example, I usually was the first to spot if a child got upset while many of my colleagues were happy to have a functioning group and only became aware when the child burst into tears.

Ludwig says that a common mistake in society is for people to emphasize Autistic weaknesses and ignore their strengths.

Andrews adds that such a polarizing focus in the media leads to stereotyping:

> By portraying all autistic individuals in a negative manner in order to garner support, it leaves many feeling as though we are either not "true" autistics or, worse, leaves people assuming we have equal difficulties and thus cannot work, cannot communicate effectively, and cannot function in society appropriately.

That Autistic people often find ways to function and even thrive in NT society does not negate the fact that some on the spectrum sometimes find the challenges posed by that society overwhelming, even insurmountable. But in any case, society itself—and not some inherently tragic or lesser way of being—is at the root of the issue. Anna Nibbs, a British academic developer and mother, wants neurotypicals to reframe the autism-as-tragedy paradigm and explains that the "suffering" of autism usually comes "as a result of being Autistic in a world that isn't built for us and isn't very accepting of us."

Autism acceptance behavior, No. 3: Focus on eliminating barriers instead of so-called "bad" behaviors/attributes

Why is this needed?

The autism tragedy mindset focuses on the negative aspects of autism, specifically negative behaviors that need to be eliminated. If autism is always viewed through a negative lens, it's easy to see it as a collection of negative symptoms that must be dealt with. Sometimes families are so distracted by behaviors they want to curb that they fail to identify and address the underlying causes. Focusing on negative behaviors rather than addressing their causes is problematic because it delays the discovery of real solutions to everyday barriers and ignores Autistic attempts to communicate and self-regulate. Because neurotypicals perceive the world and react to their environment differently than Autistic people do, it's sometimes difficult to understand exactly what each behavior communicates. However, determining what these problematic behaviors are expressing and then figuring out how to change the environment that causes them is a more respectful and effective approach to addressing negative behaviors.

Finding real solutions to real barriers

Jamie Knight, a writer and developer from London, explains that some neurotypicals mix up cause and effect when it comes to addressing Autistic behaviors. He explains an alternative way to view negative behaviors that allows for them to be addressed in simpler, healthier ways:

> Many NT advocates think that autism causes behaviours. In my experience, that's backwards. Badly designed environments cause barriers, and barriers cause behaviours. Badly designed environments disable everyone. Because most environments don't consider my needs, I encounter more design errors than other people do. Remove the environmental barriers, and I thrive. I live with autonomy, hold down a good job, and have fun adventures because we have fixed the design mistakes in the environments around me. I think good autism advocacy focuses on removing barriers in the environment. Barriers may be built things, attitudes, expectations, or assumptions. The good news is environmental barriers are much easier to change than people, and every small change adds up.

There are many different kinds of barriers Autistic people face (overwhelming sensory input, pressure or impatience from non-Autistic people, and physically limiting environments, to name a few). Understanding a person's barriers is key to helping address negative behaviors (which are forms of communication) and reducing anxiety and stress. It's common for therapists to focus on negative social behaviors rather than understanding why they exist, says Australian blogger and comedian Jodie Van de Wetering:

> I feel there is perhaps too much emphasis—in terms of both research and therapy—on the social skills aspect of the condition, because that is what other people can

> see. They can't see the pain caused by our sensory sensitivities, for instance. But from personal experience, the social skills stuff is much easier when the sensory sensitivities are under control, because it's hard to be sociable when you're in pain. (Van de Wetering quoted in Gensic 2019, p.38)

Jennifer can attest to the enormous impact her environment has on her social functioning, as well as to the lack of awareness many neurotypicals have in this area. There are times, for instance, when her neurology is so overburdened by her surroundings that even looking at a bright color can cause agony; or when interaction becomes virtually impossible due to internal meltdown caused by sensory-social overload. Awareness around the varied but very real barriers neurodiverse people face can drive positive changes in environments and interactions, and thereby contribute to increased acceptance of neurodiverse ways of being.

Understanding stimming

Some Autistic behaviors are seen as negative by neurotypicals when, in fact, they are harmless and neutral. Robbie Ierubino explains, "When people stim, it can make others confused, afraid, and even angry."

Katie Oswald, Executive Director of Full Spectrum Agency for Autistic Adults, describes how stimming—or engaging in repetitive, self-stimulating actions, movements, or sounds—is a common Autistic behavior that neurotypicals misunderstand. She says:

> Occasionally stims can be harmful or a sign of an impending meltdown and need to be dealt with, but most often these stims are how we manage our intense anxiety, and it helps to soothe us. That way we are less likely to have a meltdown.

Stimming has become more widely understood in society, but many parents and therapists nevertheless prioritize its elimination to serve a socialization goal of "not standing out." Oswald advises:

> Please get to know each individual person to understand when a stim might be a sign of trouble and when it is harmless, so you don't try to correct behavior that doesn't need correcting. Stimming is an important method for managing our anxiety.

Despite the need for this method, it's unfortunately commonplace to discourage stimming in relation to other adaptive behaviors. Kim (2011, p.39) says: "Who would tell a Deaf person not to sign in public, or a paraplegic not to use their wheelchair in public? But people tell autistic kids not to stim in public all the time."

In *The Real Experts,* Maxfield Sparrow, writing as Sparrow Rose Jones (future citations will refer to Jones, as indicated in the cited text, but we will use their current name of Maxfield Sparrow in our writing), also addresses stimming, articulating that the goal of therapy should be to help someone lead a happier, more functional life—one that may well include stimming! Nonetheless, therapists often focus on behaviors that make neurotypicals uncomfortable rather than acknowledging them as a means of communicating. Sparrow says it is unethical to try to eliminate these behaviors without first addressing why they exist:

> Taking away things like hand flapping or spinning is not done to help the child. It is done because the people around the child are uncomfortable with or embarrassed by those behaviors. But those are coping behaviors for the child. It is very important to question why a child engages in the behaviors they do. It is very wrong to seek to train away those behaviors without understanding that they are the child's means of self-regulation. (Jones 2011, p.54)

In *Loud Hands, Autistic People, Speaking*, Bascom explains that her sister is able to read her hand flapping and understand her feelings much better than she would have by trying to read her facial expressions. Her sister notes that Bascom actually has "one [a type of hand flap] for everything;" and Bascom herself says, "I wish everyone could look at my hands and see *I need you to slow down* or *this is the best thing ever* or *can I please touch* or *I am so hungry I think my brain is trying to eat itself*" (2012b, p.179). Unfortunately, when the public sees Bascom's hands, she doesn't feel safe or understood. Her sister explains: "They watch your hands...and you might as well be flipping them off when all you're saying is *this menu feels nice*" (2012b, p.179).

Canadian writer C. L. Lynch agrees that therapists need to see and understand stimming behavior as communication and not a strange problem to fix:

> If my husband sees me stimming more than usual in the middle of the day, he frowns and asks if my day is going okay. But many times he mistakes my emotions based on my facial expressions. My stims are better at translating my emotions than my face is, unless I'm actively animating my face in an allistic way for the benefit of my allistic audience. Which is exhausting, by the way... Grabbing my hands when I stim the way ABA recommends would NOT help my day go better. It would be an excellent way to piss me off and make me feel frustrated and anxious, though. (Lynch 2019a)

Autism acceptance behavior, No. 4: Work for change in society, cultures, and institutions, not Autistic people

Why is this needed?

Always expecting Autistic people to change is an extension of the deficit paradigm. When this paradigm is the norm, society expects Autistic people to mimic neurotypicals in order to be fully accepted. Autistic people must constantly find workarounds to live and work in spaces that assault their sensory systems and/or don't accommodate their communication needs. Additionally, some places of employment, for example, might be open to inclusivity changes, but they expect the Autistic person to be the one to lead the effort. This often comes from a lack of understanding of autism and causes extreme exhaustion for Autistic people living in a world not built for them.

Placing the burden of change on the Autistic person isn't helpful, because it ignores the inherent injustice Autistic people experience on a daily basis, and it perpetuates the deficit paradigm. Furthermore, it creates more stress, anxiety, and fatigue for the Autistic person. It also denies the world the benefits of rich, diverse experiences and voices. A more supportive approach is to consider how society, institutions, and individuals can adapt to be more inclusive to Autistic people.

Leading the change

When neurotypicals expect Autistic people to do all the work in order to have a seat at the table in various social contexts, they aren't respecting the sensory overload, discrimination, and other burdens people on the spectrum invariably experience in their day-to-day lives. This expectation also perpetuates the stereotypes that everything associated with autism is negative, and that Autistic people need fixing.

Canadian writer and presenter Maxine Share explains that communication is one area where neurotypicals often place the burden of change on the Autistic person:

> One of the most wrenching realities in the autism world is the number of children, teens and young adults who have never been taught to be fluent in a communication method that works for them. I wish I could tell you why this is. I suspect it is because we have far too few professionals who know how to gain the trust of autistic students, who understand the unique learning profile that can accompany the identification, or who understand autistic culture enough to propose effective approaches. What I do know is that the onus for not learning how to communicate with non-autistics is often placed on the vulnerable autistic child, not on the professionals. I have heard from professionals that the child wasn't interested, refused to engage, would run, would stim, would lash out...but never,

> ever did I hear: "I think we are getting this wrong. Let's try another way, because it is so important to find what will work for this child."

Communication Specialist Eric Evans recalls how he witnessed a formal presentation on autism in which the presenter assumed the burden of change rested with Autistic people:

> I remember in my senior year of undergrad, I attended one of my teammate's final science presentations. Other students presented as well before him, so I sat through a few. One in particular was about people on the spectrum's communication "shortcomings." Her whole presentation was about how difficult it was to "teach" a group of students on the spectrum how to "properly" communicate. It was the most insulting and self-observed presentation I had ever sat through at a higher education entity. I wanted to leave, but I couldn't stop being amazed at how serious and confident this presenter was. After the horrific conclusion, I raised my hand and asked this presenter, "Instead of trying to get people on the spectrum to communicate your way, have you ever thought about trying to communicate with the spectrum?" The answer I received, in short, was a confused and puzzled "No?"

Elizabeth Boresow, a public speaker and music therapist, offers another example from her life to illustrate this problem:

> NT advocates too often place the burden of creating change on autistic adults. For example, I've been trying to impress on our local community the need for an autistic adult support group for those of us with autism and additional mental health conditions. I can't even tell you how many times a well-meaning NT advocate has said, "Oh, you would be perfect to lead that," when what I'm asking for is for someone to take charge and care because those of us who are advocating get tired. I think NT advocates often forget that autistic adults have limited spoons.

Avoiding additional stress and fatigue

Elizabeth Boresow's reference to spoons comes from a widely circulated article, "The Spoon Theory" by Christine Miserandino (2020), which explains the fatigue disabled people experience on a daily basis. Miserandino (who is not Autistic) used the theory to explain how she lives with Lupus, but the article and its main concept have been widely adopted within several different disability communities, including the Autistic community. Miserandino explains that while able-bodied people start the day with endless "spoons," disabled people begin the day with a fixed number of "spoons." Each activity that expends energy during the day (getting out of bed, preparing a meal, dressing for work, socializing, etc.) uses up a spoon. Disabled people must choose what activities to use spoons on, because when they run out, they can no longer function for the day.

In addition, disabled people are essentially forced to use more spoons *from the outset,* since their differences can make everyday functioning in an ableist world a challenge. The combination of limited spoons and the need to deploy *more* spoons for basic daily activities can be debilitating for many. This might sound very daunting. But Jennifer and others have personal experience of the ways that, in the right context, an awareness of this paradigm can actually be quite liberating. This idea of spoons can be used to inform our choices in order to better schedule our days, design our environments, and more. Parents, friends, family members, educators, therapists, and other professionals can also integrate this spoon idea vis-à-vis external environments and activities. Sometimes, such measures can even allow us, our loved one(s), and/or those we work with to "grow" additional "spoons" with which to tackle life.

In order to help preserve spoons, Alix Generous (a psychologist and public speaker) explains it's important for parents to be reflective with how they can change their own behavior to help accommodate their child. Generous says that some parents tend to emphasize negative aspects of dealing with autism, when, in fact, they might be contributing to the difficult behavior. She says it may take a third party, such as a therapist, to help identify how parents might be unintentionally contributing to—or hindering potential remedies to—the challenges they experience with their children. She explains:

> It's also important to be open to improving yourself in your own mindfulness. It's always a tragedy to see that the child has to do all the work to change and then the parents feel like they don't have to, when, in actuality, the child's success depends on their ability to be a good parent. And being a good parent means you have to step outside of your comfort zone to improve yourself so you can improve the environment around you.

Although Generous was speaking specifically to parents, this #ActuallyAutistic wisdom is relevant to *anyone* hoping to be a positive force in Autistic people's lives.

Recognizing the benefits of diversity

While Autistic people may decide to mask or make behavior modifications to fit in, as a society, we must recognize that these efforts to conform to mainstream culture (no matter how supportive or collaborative they might be) might not always be advantageous to all involved. Frank L. Ludwig suggests that nonconformity has important benefits for societal progress:

> It's our failure to conform to society, it's our failure to think the way others think, it's our failure to subscribe to group dynamics and groupthink, it's our failure to give in to peer pressure, it's our failure to blindly follow tradition, it's our failure to unquestioningly obey authority, and it's our failure to accept the status quo that have driven human progress for tens of thousands of years, thanks to autistic individuals who successfully resisted attempts at being mainstreamed.

Autism acceptance behavior, No. 5: Be sensitive to the details but work towards the bigger picture

Why is this needed?

While an emphasis on shaping specific advocacy behaviors is important, advocates must nevertheless keep their focus on the broader goal of autism acceptance. An overemphasis on the politics around terms, approaches, and the like leads to different advocacy groups attacking one another at the expense of spending energy on improving the lives of people on the spectrum. Some people interviewed expressed their frustration with others prioritizing the politics of autism advocacy over all other advocacy efforts or stressing that there is only one way to be a good advocate. One Autistic blogger known as "Old Lady With Autism" stresses that it's a good idea to gather insight from many different groups of people "representing many sides of ongoing arguments surrounding autism and its issues." She says she is grateful for these different perspectives: "I decided some of the ideas presented did not seem viable to me, others I embraced wholeheartedly. I think it is up to the individual to decide for themselves." Overemphasizing politics or upholding unforgiving standards for advocacy can distract from more important issues affecting the Autistic community and alienate those who are only trying to help and would gladly adjust their efforts to serve more people on the spectrum.

Identifying the important issues

Australian professor Sandra Jones says that the conflict and negativity between different groups of advocates is disturbing. She's seen Autistic people criticizing parents for speaking on behalf of their (young or nonspeaking) children. She's also seen parents criticizing Autistic people for speaking on behalf of the entire autism spectrum. She says her Autistic son feels similarly:

> I was talking to my oldest son...about the debates regarding person-first versus identity-first language and how heated the

> conversations can get. He made the very valid point that the energy we use up arguing about language between ourselves (autistics and allies) would be far better spent advocating for greater acceptance and inclusion for autistic people.

Writer Kmarie agrees that while the politics of advocacy and identity language is important to some, it shouldn't be the primary advocacy focus. She says:

> I know it is an important part, and for some autistics, it is especially crucial for their healing, but overall, I feel this should be later on the list of importances, and first and foremost, it should be about support. Support, understanding differences, and validating before improving. Most of all, they need to know they are loved for whom they are, not for what they could be. Their souls deserve to know that being accepted is part of their parents' choice.

When NT and ND people work together for positive social transformation in an atmosphere of unconditional acceptance, individuals and society both benefit.

Bringing together advocacy communities

Speaker and trainer Paul Isaacs believes that autism politics can become unhealthy and even militant among people both on and off the spectrum, and becoming overinvested in this space can deteriorate mental health. He says:

> My personal opinion is that everybody has a story and that their realities are just as valid as anyone else's—there should not be a single representation, but a more egalitarian outlook where all person hoods and realities are taken into account. It is my opinion that autism isn't culture, but a "culture" has been created around autism.

When Isaacs feels overwhelmed with autism politics, he takes a note from late Autistic advocate Donna Williams, who advised him to "take a step back, regain healthy boundaries, find yourself, and do socially binding things."

Katie Oswald emphasizes that even though nuances of autism advocacy are important, Autistic self-advocates should be patient and understanding with neurotypicals as they learn different Autistic preferences:

> I see people in the autism community getting angry and defensive sometimes, and I think this can cause people to resent us. Although I do sometimes get angry, too, I try not to lash out at neurotypicals. I understand that they do not hate autistic people and want to hurt us but are just ignorant about autism.

Oswald offers advice to other Autistic people who might see a situation that could be an opportunity to teach a neurotypical. She recommends taking that opportunity to do so but being polite instead of accusatory so they will be more receptive and willing to learn. Oswald says, "If you are nice and they still don't want to learn, then they are not worth your time."

We shouldn't lump all human beings of *any* specific "type" (female, Asian, tall, etc.) into a monolithic, homogeneous group, and we (both neurotypicals and Autistic people) must be mindful that we don't do so for Autistic people either. If we can seek to avoid universally offensive terms and one-dimensional portrayals of autism, honor the rich variety of potential language preferences and advocacy approaches, and align our words and actions respectfully, we'll be able to spend most of our energy furthering autism acceptance.

SUMMARY GUIDANCE

- Upon first hearing about someone's autism diagnosis, recommend resources authored by the Autistic community.
- Avoid participating in advocacy campaigns or supporting organizations that emphasize finding a cure for autism. The idea of curing autism is a complex issue and most Autistic people are not in favor of it. Understand that when you place an emphasis on finding a cure or portray autism in a negative light, you are likely to damage your child's/client's/student's self-esteem and cause additional stress for both the Autistic person and Autistic people in general.
- Ask yourself why an undesirable behavior is occurring in order to address it.
- Take responsibility for adjustments and accommodations, rather than placing the burden of change on the Autistic person.

- Work with other people's desires to do good for others on the autism spectrum. Don't disregard someone who doesn't use the advocacy language you do. Patiently educate when you can, and try to work together to make a difference.

REFLECTION QUESTIONS

? How might my friends and family identify me? As an Autism Warrior who fights hard to eliminate autism? As a supportive advocate who promotes autism accommodations and societal acceptance? Something different? What actions have I taken to adopt this identity?

? Take an inventory of the behaviors you are trying to correct in light of the following questions: What is the cause for each? What ways can I address the causes of these behaviors in order to limit their frequency by honoring the need they express?

? Make a comprehensive list of the most essential support needs of the Autistic people in your life, and then ask yourself: What expectations for change do I have for these people? In what ways can I help reduce the burden of change for them so that their needs can be met more efficiently?

? NT compliance- and conformity-oriented therapies and changes are discriminatory. What does true acceptance mean to me and my Autistic loved ones—and how can I best and most sensitively promote this ideal?

Step 2

Adopt a Balanced Perspective

> *I'm nothing like Rain Man or Sheldon. I'm not a math genius, computer programmer or anything like a Vulcan. It also bothers me how most autistic people in media tend to be white, male, and heterosexual. I'm none of the three.*
>
> —EMMALIA HARRINGTON

Many Autistic people want parents and other aspiring advocates to be aware of the polarizing autism portrayals that tend to dominate the media and encourage stereotypes. It's common to find stories about autism in social media news feeds, and more awareness events and fundraisers are popping up on a regular basis. It's easier than ever to pass along click bait. But some of what is celebrated about autism can become problematic when it reinforces stereotypes.

It's important to be aware of several underlying assumptions that can shape the ways autism is portrayed in mainstream media outlets, social media, and some autism-focused groups. These pervasive, often unconscious beliefs may eclipse the very real needs of particular people and prevent parents and others from perceiving and promoting autism in an unbiased fashion. This chapter explores six different ways to adopt a balanced autism perspective that respects Autistic people and is inclusive to all autism families.

Balanced perspective example, No. 1: Avoid assumptions about savantism

Why is this needed?

One common stereotype pervasive in contemporary culture holds that most Autistic people are savants and, further, that this is the only redeeming quality of autism. The Academy Award-winning movie *Rain Man* brought savantism to the public eye, portraying the exceptional abilities some Autistic people possess. Savants commonly exhibit remarkable skills in the areas of art, mathematics, music, mechanics, or spatial awareness. Approximately 10 percent of Autistic people have savant skills (Wisconsin Medical Society n.d.). The conscious or unconscious expectation that all Autistic people have a savant skill is problematic because it objectifies Autistic people by suggesting they are only valuable or interesting if they have some kind of special talent. In addition, doing so perpetuates stereotypes about autism.

Avoiding objectifying portrayals

These frequent portrayals of Autistic savantism can distract from a more inclusive and realistic perspective, in which Autistic persons are seen as human beings, valuable because of their humanity alone. Writer Ada Hoffmann explains that a common advocacy problem entails "assuming that autistic people are all good at the same things and that being good at these things is what makes our existence worthwhile." Since only 1 in 10 Autistic people has savant skills, perpetuating the belief that most Autistic people are savants holds many diagnosed people to an unrealistic standard, and de-emphasizes or completely disregards other worthwhile aspects of their identity. Regardless of whether or not an Autistic person is a savant, an overemphasis on savant skills highlights Autistic people as unidimensional "one-trick ponies" who are valued because of their special talents rather than their intrinsic human worth.

Writer Joey Murphy says there is an emphasis on uncovering special talents, skills, or productivity levels in order to demonstrate an Autistic person's worth. As a result she is hesitant to talk about her own talents and how she uses them "because it really places emphasis on the NT paradigm of productivity within a capitalist framework":

> A huge part of the stigma that ASD folk face is around productivity—our energy levels keep us from being as "productive" in work or school; there's a lot of cultural bias against the ways that we need to take care of ourselves: rest = laziness, quiet = antisocial; ABA [Applied Behavior Analysis] therapy is driven by the goal of achieving uniformity of behavior and communication because normalizing/standardizing is more conducive to commodifying human labor. These preconceptions are always hanging over the heads of ASD [autism spectrum disorder] folks: we will never be fast enough, good enough, productive enough to keep up. It reinforces the idea that we are failures by most measures in a society that only values earning power.

Even assuming that we have a "Talent" also promotes the myth that ASD folks are likely to have some sort of savant-like ability that makes us more palatable to NT society.

Breaking stereotypes

Expecting savantism in Autistic people perpetuates stereotypes, since it simply isn't an accurate standard for all people. In an article by disability lawyer Lydia X. Z. Brown written early in their advocacy work, they explain that assuming that Autistic people are exceptional at math or computers is a mistake. Brown says:

> If there's one thing that's sure to offend an Autistic, it's seeing them in terms of common stereotypes about autism. A very small minority of Autistics are also savants. Many Autistics have higher than average measured IQ, and many Autistics have measured IQ that falls right into the median, while still others have an intellectual or cognitive disability. Some Autistics have dyscalculia or similar learning disabilities, and actually find math to be extremely difficult. Other Autistics, including those who might be good at math, simply don't like it. And yes, some Autistics happen to be excellent with math and enjoy working or studying in related fields. There are Autistics who are relatively computer illiterate as well as Autistics who thrive in the IT world and community. Asking if we like math, computers, or numbers because we're Autistic is like asking me if I like/am good at math because I'm Asian. (Brown 2012a)

Balanced perspective example, No. 2: Take the entire lifespan into account

Why is this needed?

Massive growth in our understanding of autism has led to high-quality diagnostic tools and the potential for more accurate diagnoses at younger ages. But support is still needed across the lifespan. Advocates and allies can best serve the Autistic population by bearing in mind that autism doesn't end at 18. In fact, if we truly want a more just and inclusive neurodiverse society, taking more mature Autistic perspectives into account and working for related progress for Autistic people of all ages will be key.

While many young adults and adults on the spectrum struggle to find resources, it's easy now to find information about many facets of childhood autism, from different kinds of autism assessments to the importance of early intervention. Setting aside for the moment the genuine concerns many Autistic people have about many or most interventions (please see Step 5), this accessibility does nonetheless have its downsides. An emphasis on early diagnosis and intervention implies that Autistic children must be labeled and "treated" at the earliest possible opportunity. It also creates a context in which infancy and childhood take center stage, to the detriment of Autistic people in all other age brackets. The widespread focus on curing autism can lead to aggressive therapies implemented for Autistic children at very young ages. Additionally, many people Jenna has interviewed believe that the colorful puzzle piece symbol often used to represent autism is suggestive of a childhood condition, and they dislike this association (along with the symbol's connection to the autism-deficit model).

Autistic children grow up to become Autistic adults. An

overemphasis on childhood autism can be a distraction from the needs of Autistic teens and adults, impacting such areas of concern as transitions into the workplace and care for the Autistic elderly.

Supporting adult transitions

Many Autistic advocates assert that while attention to any age is good, there is room for improvement with addressing some of the needs of the adult population on the spectrum. There is so much "advocacy around childhood that we don't have appropriate supports in place for emerging adults," says Elizabeth Boresow. Writer David Gray-Hammond agrees Autistic adults have a different set of needs than Autistic children. Adulthood for independent citizens demands "considerable responsibility" with "various sources of stress," says Gray-Hammond. "We must pay bills and rent (or mortgage payments), food costs seemingly more money every year, and for some of us, we have the stress of work (sadly many autistic adults are either under-employed or not employed at all)." Author and speaker Dr. Daniel Wendler acknowledges that children are "crucially important," and interventions, *if/when appropriate*, are most effective when they are applied early, but too many adults are struggling today, and their needs are being overlooked by the mainstream media. He says:

> I know many autistic adults that have aged out of the school system and are struggling to find their way in the world, and I wish there were more resources available for them. I especially wish there was a way to mentor adults with autism to become

the leaders for the next generation of autism—providing them with purpose would go a huge way towards helping them find their way in life.

Autistic adults have many overlooked needs. Michael Scott Monje Jr. describes some of these issues in his essay "Not That Autistic" (Monje Jr. 2011). Not only do Autistic people have difficulty transitioning into the workforce; they can also struggle with maintaining a liveable wage in comfortable working conditions:

> Being Autistic got me into a low-paying academic job, because it gave me the extra edge when it came to commitment, perseverance, and memory retention, but it also became the reason I never left the low-paying part behind, since my ignorance of my situation led to my not knowing that I should pursue certain resources or work to improve skills in areas where I lacked them. (Monje Jr. 2011, p.64)

Jennifer notes that she had the almost exact same experience, spending many years working hard as an adjunct for very little pay and no job security only to realize that she—despite her Ivy League doctorate—was trapped in a cycle of academic impoverishment that she'd unfortunately lacked the life skills or residual mental bandwidth to properly evaluate.

Supporting the mental health needs of adults

A crucial component to supporting adult transitions (or any stage of Autistic adulthood) is taking care of mental health needs. David Gray-Hammond says it's likely the Autistic adult in your life is experiencing a deficit of support. He says this is especially critical because many Autistic people have had traumatic life experiences, including abusive therapy and bullying. "The world is not designed for autistic people, and this puts an extra level of stress on autistic adults." Autistic people are often denied control over their environments, and are thus deprived of the right to feel safe in their environments. Gray-Hammond says these are the reasons Autistic adults are diagnosed with anxiety disorders such as obsessive compulsive disorder (OCD) at a higher rate than the general population. "We find ourselves regularly in situations that are highly distressing, and are often met with ignorance or even abject hatred of our needs. This, perhaps, is why so many of us experience mental health problems."

Gray-Hammond warns families to be vigilant of addiction, especially substance addiction, which he has suffered from. He describes how his substance abuse resulted from a desire to make sense of his place in the world:

> Having spent a number of years in the Autistic community, and having experienced addiction myself, I am very aware of the regularity with which autistic people will self-medicate themselves. For me, substance misuse was an attempt to replace my own identity with one that I felt fit into the world better. I could not cope with the world as an autistic adult, and I knew that people found me difficult and weird to be around, so I sought to change that the only way I could find. That way was drugs and alcohol.
>
> Addiction compounded my mental health problems and led to me spending time in psychiatric hospitals. This was my

> truth as an autistic adult. There was no support for me, and so I turned to darker means of survival.

Gray-Hammond explains that when advocates speak about supporting "all Autistic people," we must consider the nature of that support. He contends that:

> - Appropriate housing is support.
> - Appropriate access to physical healthcare is support.
> - Appropriate access to mental healthcare is support.
> - Appropriate welfare benefits are support.
> - Safe and reciprocated socialisation is support.

Gray-Hammond suggests pushing for these supports by lobbying researchers and institutions to conduct studies into things that affect quality of life for Autistic adults, such as addiction. "Until autistic adults have their needs met, there is no acceptance of 'all autistics,' and no, our needs are not special; they are human needs."

Focusing on the needs of the Autistic elderly

The blogger known as "Old Lady With Autism" is on a mission to advocate for late-diagnosed Autistic people as well as the Autistic elderly who may not have received a diagnosis. She wasn't diagnosed until September of 2019, three days before her 68th birthday. Awareness of her own neurodivergence was revelatory:

> Knowing about my own autism helped me understand all the ways I struggled in my life, and allowed me to understand myself and others, make adjustments and accommodations to help me live a fuller life without as much distress due to neurological issues. It has been a relief to know and understand that all that pain and strife was not "all my fault."

But she says it's difficult to find information about the elderly Autistic population:

> When I was searching for how autism expressed itself in older people, and particularly in elderly women, there was very little information available. I would eagerly turn to articles online titled "Late diagnosis in Autism" or "What it feels like to have a late diagnosis of autism," and these were articles written by people in their late 20s or early 30s.

She works now to balance out the overemphasis on childhood and aims to speak with nursing homes, senior centers, police and fire departments, and caretakers to raise awareness of the role autism can play in difficult behavior patterns and social struggles in elderly people who have not yet been diagnosed.

Balanced perspective example, No. 3: Avoid stereotyping by gender

Why is this needed?

Research suggests girls on the spectrum might be better at

camouflaging both at home and in social circles, which may be one reason why three to four times as many boys are diagnosed with autism (Wright 2015). The common understanding of autism as a "boys' disorder" might explain why so many girls who are struggling socially are not considered by clinicians for an autism diagnosis (Russo 2018). Only addressing how autism manifests in males overlooks the unique ways it presents in the female population, thus increasing the likelihood of delayed diagnosis or misdiagnosis, and, increasing exhaustion, anxiety, and stress for Autistic girls and women.

Preventing delayed diagnosis or misdiagnosis

Even when a girl is identified as possibly needing attention, current diagnostic measures may fail to accurately assess her. Researchers have questioned the validity of some autism assessments since they were designed to detect the condition in boys (Russo 2018).

Kirsten Lindsmith, a writer and artist, explains that the ideas that autism is less common in women and that Autistic women present at the extremes of the spectrum (either very "high-" or very "low-functioning") are common misconceptions. She says, "It's my experience that the social rules that govern gender, and how we teach gender to children, result in autistic women and girls being better able to 'pass' as neurotypical." Lindsmith adds that because the classical image of autism is built around the male presentation, even professionals overlook Autistic girls. She explains:

> I once saw a paper about how professionals who do autism assessments say that autistic girls are less likely to display obsessive interests, yet when these girls were reassessed, they have the same prevalence of obsessive traits as their male counterparts. They're just obsessed with things like makeup or celebrities—culturally encouraged girl interests—instead of trains and cars.

Some autism tests that screen for intense interests fail to recognize this trait in girls. In her article "The Costs of Camouflaging Autism," Francine Russo (2018) cites research illustrating how

> boys with Autism tend to obsess about things such as taxis, maps or U.S. presidents, but girls on the spectrum are often drawn to animals, dolls or celebrities—interests that closely resemble those of their typical peers and so fly under the radar.

Jennifer's successive interests in dinosaurs, cats, and tropical fish, for instance, were viewed by her family as related to her love of animals and science, rather than indicative of her being on the spectrum. Other Autistic qualities were written off as extreme versions of typical "girlish oversensitivity," "moodiness," and "awkwardness."

Researchers may not even understand how little they know about autism in girls. Kevin Pelphrey, a leading NT autism researcher at Yale University's Child Study Center who is studying the differences in Autistic males and females, says he is discovering that "everything we thought we knew in terms of functional brain development is not true" (Szalavitz 2016). He continues, "Everything we thought was true of autism seems to only be true for boys," and explains that "their brains process social information differently."

Avoiding exhaustion and stress

The effects of camouflaging or "passing" and misdiagnosis include exhaustion and additional stress. A 2017 British study suggested exhaustion was a near-universal effect of camouflaging, with one participant explaining how she needed to curl up in the fetal position to recover (Russo 2018). Other girls and women obsess over how they can fit in socially. Society tends to steer a focus on social success onto body image, a trend that unfortunately often results in the development of eating disorders (Geggel 2013). This was the case for Asperkids founder Jennifer O'Toole. In an article for *Brown Alumni* magazine, she explains that "Perfectionism, anxiety, eating disorders—these often mask autism in girls and women" (Murphy 2019).

Balanced perspective example, No. 4: Acknowledge strengths and weaknesses as with all humans

Why is this needed?

Most people agree that progress made towards respecting, supporting, and accepting Autistic people in society is worthwhile. But both opponents and proponents to the neurodiversity movement sometimes take issue with an overemphasis on positive autism portrayals at the expense of addressing the real issues Autistic people face on a daily basis. Different Autistic people describe autism in different ways. Some would gladly welcome a cure, others are proud to be Autistic and view autism as a "superpower," and many are somewhere in between.

This section describes the problem with strictly discussing autism in positive ways and recommends that advocates and allies take a more nuanced approach. It explains why it's important for parents to acknowledge the strengths and weaknesses of their Autistic children in a balanced fashion, just as they would with any NT child. It's absolutely vital to view autism in positive ways, not only because of its very real positive aspects, but so that society can become more accepting and inclusive of people on the spectrum. However, if we only discuss the benefits of autism, we may alienate some Autistic people, non-Autistic family members, and allies, and/ or overlook deficits and opportunities for support.

Avoiding alienating some autistic people, non-autistic family members, and allies

Kirsten Lindsmith warns that "being too positive and sweeping the disabling aspects of autism under the rug can alienate non-Autistic family members/allies, and create feelings of frustration and despair in more disabled Autistic people." She admits that it's not acceptable to portray autism only as a tragedy either, but too many advocates make autism into a black or white issue. She explains:

> Autism isn't a fate worse than death, or a hopeless sentence of mediocrity and misery. But many adult autistic people I know are fans of slogans like "I don't suffer from autism, I enjoy every minute of it." As a reaction to the long history of autism being

> treated as a disease to be eradicated, instead of an adjective to describe a common type of person, the pendulum in the autism community has swung towards autism pride. Which is a great thing! But acceptance at the price of improvement shouldn't be the goal, and there's a big difference between "cure" and treatment.

Lindsmith explains that only emphasizing the positive aspects of autism can be troubling to families and people who deal with more severe challenges. She says that while Autistic people who need significant support deserve love and acceptance, "they don't deserve to be pushed under the rug and ignored in favor of putting a spotlight on only the positive things about autism."

Finding opportunities for support

Kirsten Lindsmith explains that autism is inherently disabling to various degrees, making her life more difficult than it would be without it: "Acceptance is wonderful, and I'm proud to be autistic and love the positives of my autistic traits, but I also need access to accommodations, treatment, and help." She recommends that Autistic advocates meet and work with more "severely challenged" Autistic people and pay more attention to their blogs and books.

Gillan Drew, a British author and father, agrees, and says that he's seen NT autism advocates portray Autistic people as far more capable than they actually are:

> I've been to talks encouraging businesses to recruit autistic people where advocates have sung our praises and spoken about us purely in terms of how great we are—we're not ordinary, we're extraordinary; we're not human, we're superhuman; we're better than neurotypical workers because we're more punctual, reliable, honest, conscientious, which is one step short of peddling the myth that we all have savant skills. In short, we're utterly awesome. Why wouldn't you want to be autistic?

He explains that it's wonderful to see people portray the positive traits of autism, especially when so much in the media is negative; however, it's important to be realistic. Drew says that while some Autistic people are exceptional and great workers, some aren't. Some have social deficits that mean they're not team players. He explains: "This is not to denigrate us, but I think it does more harm than good to pretend we're all great when we are, in fact, all individuals."

Dr. Daniel Wendler encourages parents to find opportunities for their Autistic children to use their talents and celebrate them for what they can do: "No matter how much support they need, a person with autism is always far more than their struggles. Help them to realize that." In other words, autism advocates and allies can seek to amplify each person's strengths and gifts, while also situating support as part of the legitimate and basic human needs of many Autistic people—and looking for opportunities to institute that support in targeted, specifically useful ways.

Autistic people have strengths and weaknesses just like non-Autistic people. Some, even most, of their autism-related weaknesses are weaknesses primarily because of the NT world in which they find themselves and might otherwise simply be experienced as neutral (or even positive) traits. But that doesn't negate the fact that such NT-world weaknesses can pose major challenges. Pretending that all Autistic people are remarkably gifted, that autism is solely a superpower, and so on, can be alienating and disempowering for Autistic people and advocates alike. Instead, it's best to acknowledge and approach each person as a whole, complex person within an exceedingly diverse larger population.

SUMMARY GUIDANCE

- Emphasize the inherent dignity of all Autistic people, regardless of savant status.
- Encourage support for Autistic adults and elders, including programs to help manage college workload, transition-to-employment programs, job training, workplace autism education initiatives, improved access to support workers or home health aides, etc.
- Learn about different gender identities on the spectrum and how each experience is unique.
- Avoid solely promoting autism-positive messages.
- Stress that autism has positive, negative, and neutral traits so that it can be celebrated, supported, and accepted without minimizing anyone's life experiences.

REFLECTION QUESTIONS

- **?** What kinds of autism awareness/acceptance swag do I have? What are the specific messages behind these items and what does the Autistic community have to say about them?
- **?** In what ways does my NT or ND status affect the way I think about autism?
- **?** How might I integrate a more genuinely inclusive view of neurodiversity?
- **?** Which aspects of the above examples of balanced perspectives felt surprising or challenging to me? Taking those aspects into account, how might I grow in my attitude and actions, going forward?

Step 3

Presume Competence

> *We do not measure intelligence in those who cannot communicate with spoken word. We don't, and so schools conclude that they lack cognitive ability—though anyone who works in this field can tell you that many non-speaking people are interested, intelligent, and curious.*
>
> — MAXINE SHARE

Presuming competence means "to assume an autistic person has the capacity to think, learn, and understand—even if you don't see any tangible evidence that such is the case" (Stout 2020). Teacher/author Laura Nadine compares the presumption of competence to self-esteem and describes it as an expression of love:

> It's an inner idea one holds that permeates through everything we do. In fact, the amount of self-esteem a person has is often proportional to our capacity to presume competence. It's that idea that we can believe in the potential of people. Only with presuming competence we must have a longer sight than with

seeing our own potential. Self-confidence is like using the stars to navigate the oceans; while presuming competence means we're navigating those same oceans by our memory of the star map rather than our sight of the stars themselves. Once you arrive at your destination, you'll know it worked. Many people struggle with this concept of seeing potential in others and that being enough to keep teaching them. I do not struggle with this. It is the deepest version of love I can give.

Presuming *incompetence* for people on the spectrum is common and leads to damaging stereotypes that Autistic people have difficulty escaping. Daily encounters with people who have low expectations of you can be continually traumatizing. Many Autistic people have this daily experience in overt and subtle ways.

This chapter explores a variety of different behaviors that exemplify presuming competence. We can communicate a presumption of competence in the ways we talk about autism, the ways we talk to Autistic people, and the ways we help our children grow. A humble approach to learning about autism with a willingness to listen is an essential foundation to a presumption of competence.

Presuming competence behavior, No. 1: Distinguish between autism and other intellectual differences and disabilities

Why is this needed?

Assuming intellectual disability and/or other mental health differences inevitably and inextricably accompany autism is a strikingly common misconception. If more people were aware of this misconception and had the courage to clarify the different ways autism presents itself, this would profoundly further the movement to establish Autistic people as the real experts on autism. Autistic people do not need neurotypicals to give them the authority of expertise—they already possess it; nevertheless, NT allies can certainly help others to recognize Autistic expertise and encourage their families and peers to presume competence.

Autism is a neurological difference, and not an intellectual, psychological, or mental health condition. Correcting the misconception that mental handicap or other intellectual differences and disabilities are inevitably present in Autistic people is important because this belief leads to the perpetuation of stereotypes about autism, and it causes unnecessary suffering among Autistic people.

Correcting misguided assumptions

Ada Hoffmann says one mistake advocates make is "assuming that an autistic person, especially a higher-support autistic person, doesn't have knowable opinions." The assumptions that all Autistic people are intellectually disabled in some way and that intellectual disability is a symptom of autism are simply untrue. Writer C. L. Lynch says a big mistake people make is assuming that the outside reflects the inside: "If an autistic person does not appear to understand, they are assumed not to understand. Big, big mistake."

Nonetheless, the assumption that intellectual disability is tied to minimally verbal (speaking) people is common. Angela Andrews says that although some Autistic people have some mental health conditions, this is not a symptom of autism, but rather a separate condition. The same is true of any other differences and disabilities a given person may experience. "In fact, most autistic individuals are extremely intelligent, including those without speech," Andrews says. "Autistic people exhibit a broad range of abilities and disabilities."

Presumptions of incompetence tend to dominate formal therapy and learning plans, which is why actively including ND people in goal-making is especially important. Ensuring that ND people have the opportunity to be present, involved, and heard (via whatever medium they are most comfortable with) in individualized education program (IEP) meetings or any discussions about goal setting demonstrates an assumption of competence and helps build self-advocacy skills that will help them throughout their lives.

Avoiding stereotypes

According to C. L. Lynch, "The pervasive belief that 'severely autistic' people are intellectually disabled and oblivious to their surroundings – incapable and uninterested in communicating – is incredibly harmful to all autistic people." Lynch explains that these people suffer by being treated like children throughout adulthood. They listen to conversations about them happening in front of them, and they are sometimes denied the ability to communicate. But even speaking Autistic people with less visible symptoms also suffer from these stereotypes, says Lynch. The reverse assumptions can also be harmful. "It's also harmful to people like me, who are assumed to be doing just fine because we LOOK like we are doing just fine," she adds. "I'm really not doing just fine."

Another dangerous effect of presuming incompetence (whether it be through intellectual or emotional capability) is stereotyping about the ability to form relationships and have families. Anna Nibbs says:

> I think there's also a huge misconception or a stereotype that autistic people wouldn't ever be fit to become parents, that we couldn't be trusted to have children. You only have to look at examples such as the recent book *To Siri, With Love*...to see parents believing that it would be better to deny an autistic person's autonomy and even forcibly sterilise them than ever risk them becoming a parent.

Presuming competence behavior, No. 2: Understand that neuro-normalized methods are often used to determine competence

Why is this needed?

As the previous sections have outlined, ND people tend to have different ways of experiencing and navigating the world, which impacts their life path and definition of "success." The NT vision of competence might be different than the Autistic vision. Similarly, even if the definitions of success are the same, the assessment criteria might be based on NT assumptions about competence that don't accurately reflect the skill sets of ND people. Developing neurodiverse competency models is necessary in order to accurately determine strengths and support areas.

Investigating formal competence assessments

Too often, neurotypicals use neuro-normalized methods to

evaluate ND people, determine successes and failures, and encourage changes in behavior. Brent White explains that neurotypicals often use normalized communication methods such as emphasizing eye contact or engaging in small talk. He also says that neuro-normalized methods of competence are often used to evaluate success. As an example, a 2016 study of 1,470 school-aged children demonstrated how cognitive abilities vary even among minimally verbal (MV) people on the spectrum (Zeliadt 2016). The study also revealed that cognitive results varied depending on the assessment that was administered.

Assessment tools in studies like this one can be inaccurate or subjective. In this study, the assessments used varied criteria to classify children as minimally verbal. However, regardless of the assessment method used to classify children, 43–52 percent of those studied had significantly higher nonverbal than verbal intelligence scores. The scores from MV children on the former test are similar to what typically developing children achieve on the verbal and nonverbal sections of intelligence tests (Zeliadt 2016). White explains that using neuro-normalized methods to determine success is problematic and can lead to valuing NT expertise over ND expertise.

Giving too much weight to test results is risky for ND people for so many reasons. It seems self-evident that divergent brains will often manifest different skills and strengths than those found and valued in the NT population. As neutral and objective as people who develop assessments may try to be, they are still almost inevitably operating from a neuro-normalized perspective. In addition, even many NT people don't "perform" well on some or all assessments (think: standardized testing). And sometimes certain ND competencies serve us well in some assessments and not others: Jennifer, for example, regularly tested in the 99th percentile on academic standardized testing but would barely reach the single digits in most social skills assessments, such as "inference" or "facial recognition." Given these factors, individuals, families, and professionals alike would do well to consider NT bias as a significant factor, along with general variance in testing "performance," when evaluating assessment results—and err on the side of assuming competence whenever possible.

Presuming competence behavior, No. 3: Listen, listen, listen—even when someone isn't talking at the speed you'd prefer

Why is this needed?

"Sometimes the mistake of advocates is speaking before listening," says Elizabeth Boresow. Practicing patience with everyone we communicate with is an important part of presuming competence. It's tempting for neurotypicals to step in and fill silence gaps in an effort to move a conversation along and "help" others communicate. But when you take the time to listen, even when someone isn't talking at a speed you prefer, this demonstrates a willingness to assume competence and meet the communication needs of the person you are speaking with. Active listening also honors the dignity of Autistic people by offering them a chance to speak for themselves.

Being respectful of communication needs

So many Autistic people have expressed their frustration with being talked over or not given the proper wait time they need to formulate responses. Autism consultant, author, and Autistic advocate Kieran Rose says a common problem is "silencing, dismissing, and speaking over Autistic voices." Sometimes people may believe they are being helpful or supportive when they finish someone else's sentences, but many Autistic people have said this is not the case. Author Jennifer Brozek explains that we need to take the time to listen to the person on the spectrum.

> Impatience and assumptions are our worst enemies. Sometimes, we lose our words. Words are my life, and I still have mental train wrecks that don't allow me to convey what I'm trying to say. Getting impatient with me makes it worse. We can't always give a coherent, concise answer to what is wrong or what we need. Advocates need to be aware of this.

Respecting that Autistic people have a voice

Savannah Logsdone-Breakstone says that neurotypicals often assume they know what she means before she finishes her sentences, and they tend to speak over her, whether to preemptively dismiss her or support her. Similarly, she says neurotypicals sometimes assume it's acceptable to speak for people on the spectrum instead of "acting as a megaphone for autistics, especially when the autistic has an atypical or idiosyncratic communication style." This is especially important for advocates to reflect on since many believe they speak for their children or are the "voice for the voiceless" and that this kind of behavior is helpful, supportive, and praiseworthy. "Don't talk over us," says writer Emmalia Harrington. "We may need allies to help amplify our message. This is not the same as being center stage."

Terra Vance (consultant/writer/NeuroClastic founder) believes that neurotypicals sometimes think Autistic people aren't capable of speaking up for themselves or that they need someone to speak on their behalf. "We don't," she clarifies. "We need neurotypical people to use their positions of privilege to bring us to the table and allow us to speak for ourselves. We need them to share their platform with us so that we can be advocates for ourselves." Vance explains that when neurotypicals speak for Autistic people, they take away an opportunity for them to speak for themselves. She says Autistic people need neurotypicals, but not to speak for them about what they need:

> They filter our perspectives through a neurotypical lens, thus removing from our self-advocacy the rawness and authenticity of our experiences and perceptions. They take from us an opportunity to be heard, to show the world that we are sentient and independent thinkers. We definitely need them and their efforts, but not to take us on like a project. We need them to use their advantages and invite us into the conversation. Without them, we will never gain parity and tolerance, both in the mainstream and in academic literature.

Jennifer agrees that being spoken over is a serious concern among Autistic people. When receiving a lot of emotional, intellectual, or sensory input, she herself tends to struggle with verbal interaction and can be taken for someone with little to contribute to a conversation or classroom. That's not the case at all—for her or for other Autistic people: "Very few of us are 100 percent unable to communicate in some fashion, and, trust me, we all have plenty to say."

She finds that a habit of speaking for Autistic people and not listening to Autistic advocates can carry over into other advocacy behaviors:

> If a neurotypical person has ZERO IDEA what it feels like to be neurodivergent, how can they be in charge of designing spaces, educational materials, etc. for someone whose brain responds very differently from theirs in ways they might not even be able to fathom? At the very least, neurotypical people advocating for or involved with neurodivergent people should really, truly listen to them—and believe them. Then act/advocate/design/scaffold/step away accordingly...

Honoring the dignity of those on the spectrum

Not only can the wrong message be conveyed when people speak over or for Autistic people, but Anna Nibbs points out that this behavior is troubling because it demeans the Autistic person, infantilizing them or reducing them to a study subject to be observed and talked over. Nibbs says the assumption is that "we have no inner life and thus no reason to complain because we're not actually proper people." Nibbs recalls that she even used to believe this before she knew enough about autism to recognize it in herself. Speaking to Autistic people as adults and avoiding baby talk is another way to respect their authority and presume competence, says NT co-founder of The Art of Autism, Debra Muzikar (2018).

Listening to Autistic people means acknowledging, respecting, and managing communication differences in a way that is inclusive of Autistic voices. Katie Oswald says she knows that NT advocates mean well, but sometimes they speak for Autistic people when Autistic people don't need them to. "I think sometimes people, even advocates, can forget that just because we may communicate differently, doesn't mean that we don't have a voice."

Oswald explains that while there are a variety of different ways to communicate using augmentative and alternative communication (AAC), there is definitely still room to grow as far as acceptance and usage. Examples of AAC technology include voice augmentation devices, eye gaze technology, or iPads with communication apps. AAC could also encompass a need for increased wait time or the use of sign language. "I think people are getting better at letting deaf and hard of hearing people speak for themselves," Oswald notes, "but I don't see the same level of respect given to autistic people who use AAC methods. Reminding people to pause and give us the time we need to speak for ourselves is one thing that advocates can do to help." Oswald reminds us—and Jennifer heartily concurs—that even speaking Autistic people need time to organize their thoughts before they speak: "Often people interpret this as an opportunity for someone else to speak. Please don't talk over us when we are trying to contribute to a conversation."

Presuming competence behavior, No. 4: Be aware that over-sheltering can prevent people from growing

Why is this needed?

Parents act with the best intentions: They want to protect their children from ridicule; they want to see their children succeed; or they just want them to be happy. Other family and community members, including professionals, generally feel similarly. However, Angela Andrews warns that over-sheltering can prevent children from learning and growing. Author/speaker Tom Iland says, "It hinders the progress of the young person or, in some cases, can even result in learned helplessness for the young person."

On the other hand, safe, gradual exposure to challenges demonstrates faith in Autistic worth and potential and encourages continual growth. Parents, teachers, therapists and other advocates who presume competence in the Autistic people in their lives understand that this principle guides every opportunity they offer them. This demands a regular commitment to equal opportunities throughout their lives and resisting the temptation to over-shelter them from the world.

Demonstrating faith in the value and potential of Autistic people

Many allies believe they know what's best for the Autistic people in their lives. Tom Iland says this is only somewhat true: "Advocates have good intentions and they should; however, they cannot live the life of the person with autism...only the person with autism can do that." Iland asserts that the focus of all advocacy efforts should be on "discovering the kind of life the person with autism wants to live and helping them live it," rather than changing them to fit the life others want for them. "There may be a variety of reasons parents coddle their children," says Iland, "whether it be underestimating the young person's potential, letting fear be the main motivator behind decisions, or having an undying need to be right, just to name a few." But a focus on the Autistic person and their potential will give parents the courage to push their children to develop in healthy ways.

Writer and public speaker Courtney Johnson says she always knew her mother loved her and had high expectations for her. "She accepted me and loved me unconditionally for who I was, always," she explains. "She never made me feel like I was less-than for being autistic, or that normal was something I should strive for. Even if I couldn't connect well with others, I knew no matter what that I was loved."

Johnson says that her mother expected her to be successful, which is sometimes different from the expectations of autism organizations who are trying to help Autistic people. Johnson says she had a friend in high school who worked at an autism organization where his job was making "simple crafts," despite the fact that he was "smart, creative, talented, brimming with potential." As Johnson points out, these programs often underestimate and undervalue Autistic people: "What people with autism need isn't special jobs; it's to work in an environment that can accommodate unique sensory needs and to be treated with respect, humanity and compassion for who they are."

Encouraging growth

"One of the biggest mistakes I've seen neurotypical autism advocates make is to argue we are uniquely vulnerable individuals who need wrapping in cotton wool," says Gillan Drew. Drew says parents and siblings (and others) who have an intimate understanding of how difficult it is for their loved ones to navigate the world at times are "understandably sensitive to limit the stresses and strains" placed upon them, but this stance is ultimately a destructive and limiting one:

> The problem is that by fighting our battles for us, emphasising our difficulties, and preventing us from undergoing challenges, they prevent us from growing as people and experiencing the good as well as the bad. While it is true that we have problems, we need to be given the opportunities to find solutions and discover what we can do, in addition to what we can't. Protection and imprisonment can be two sides of the same coin.

Angela Andrews underscores that while it's important to acknowledge opportunities to make accommodations for Autistic people, it is nevertheless critical to help them learn to cope in mainstream society. "If you shelter an autistic, cater to their negative symptoms, and keep them apart in a false environment, you are writing a recipe for their failure" (Gensic 2019, p.80). Morgan Giosa says his mother didn't protect him from social failure. He says his social skills aren't inhibited, and his mother's approach to teaching him social skills was immersion in social contexts with neurotypicals, "regardless of whether or not I fell flat on my back." She didn't hold him back. But there is also a lot neurotypicals can learn from Autistic people, according to Giosa. He explains:

> I firmly believe it isn't a one-way street. So, now, I'm reading original poetry and playing original music at open mics, in crowds of neurotypicals, interacting with other musicians and artists, most of whom are neurotypical. So, I've learned a lot from neurotypicals, and I hope they can learn from me as well.

Self-expression, whether through the arts, speech (in whatever medium), or chosen activities, career, habits, and so on, is an essential facet of being human. When we presume competence, we avoid conflating autism with a lack of consciousness or a reduced right to self-determination, and we avoid the incorrect assumption that Autistic people necessarily live with other disabilities and/or differences. Furthermore, we build on approaches that benefit all concerned, including intentionally taking some testing with a grain of salt, listening openly, respecting the need for freedom and growth, and facilitating two-way learning and understanding.

SUMMARY GUIDANCE

- Practice wait time in each of your conversations. Be cognizant of how often you are speaking, and avoid interrupting or talking over others.
- Resist the temptation to complete people's sentences.
- Avoid speaking negatively about someone in front of them (or behind their back!).
- If someone is nonspeaking, presume they are fluent in AAC, and determine how you can adapt your communication style to meet the needs of the person with whom you are interacting.
- Question NT-designed competency tests and try to incorporate ND input on similar tests whenever possible.
- Speak to Autistic people as adults. Avoid baby talk.
- Create regular learning opportunities to help the Autistic child(ren), teen(s), young adult(s), and/

or adult(s) in your life gain independence. Avoid over-sheltering.

REFLECTION QUESTIONS

- **?** In what ways have I listened to the voices of those on the spectrum before using my own voice to amplify what they need and want?
- **?** Do I speak for Autistic people with my own voice/agenda or do I amplify Autistic voices? How do I know?
- **?** Parents and other caregivers: In what ways do I shelter my child? What are my biggest fears for my child's future? How can the Autistic community help me overcome or manage these fears?
- **?** Professionals: Do I see myself in some of these limiting attitudes and behaviors? How can I learn from the Autistic community to presume competence in my interactions with Autistic people?

Step 4

Advocate for Individuals

> *We need to make sure that we avoid diagnostic overshadowing...so that everyone's support needs are adequately met. For example, I'm also diagnosed with an anxiety disorder, but if someone were to simply attribute my anxiety to autism ("you're just anxious because you're autistic"), I may not be getting the appropriate help I need to manage anxiety, as it requires separate supports from other things that could be considered "autism."*
>
> — QUINCY HANSEN

This chapter asks both NT and Autistic advocates and allies to remember that every Autistic person has unique interests and needs. Thus, there are no simple, unilateral solutions to all of the challenges faced by this diverse group of people. As you gain confidence as an autism advocate, it's important to keep a nuanced balance between communicating the needs of the general Autistic community and stressing individualized solutions. This chapter explores different ways we can keep the spotlight off ourselves and remember that advocacy solutions are individual and personal. This includes avoiding parent-centered story framing, avoiding generalized assumptions about autism, and spending time getting to know the person you are advocating for or speaking about.

Advocate for individuals tip, No. 1: Embrace respectful story sharing

Why is this needed?

The way parents, other family members, teachers, etc. frame their life stories and those of the Autistic people in their lives influences societal perceptions of autism and Autistic self-worth. Many parents seek to share their stories as caregivers in both formal and informal ways. Parent memoirs are easy to find. Talks or professional development workshops led by parents of children on the spectrum are also common. Parents also share their stories and experiences in support groups, on social media, and with other family and friends. At times, such sharing can eclipse genuine advocacy and center parents (or grandparents, or teachers...) as the most important element in an Autistic child's journey.

While parental advocacy stories are important, some Autistic people warn that these experiences tend to be the ones that dominate the conversation online and in the media. That makes the way this story sharing is framed all the more important, because Autistic people have asserted that respectful story sharing makes all the difference in creating constructive communication that celebrates and supports Autistic living. On the other hand, story sharing that is too parent-centered or negative can damage an Autistic person's self-worth and distract from the ways society can accept and embrace autism.

Stealing the spotlight

Ally Grace wants parents to consider whether they are truly advocating for disabled people or whether they are advocating for themselves and their own agendas. If they see disabled people "through a lens of sadness, despair, grief, lost chances, dashed hopes, medicalisation, othering, and pathologisation," Grace explains, they aren't advocating from the right place. "Ableist support is not useful."

Speaker/writer Chris Bonnello readily admits that he is wary of generalizing and doesn't want to be interpreted as "besmirching the efforts of parents who fight tooth and nail for their children with very real and honest resolve." But he warns that sometimes, although parents never mean to do so, they may phrase their advocacy efforts in a way that makes them draw more attention to themselves than their children. "I don't think any parent intends to do this," he says, "but if your advocacy sounds like 'how difficult it is to raise an autistic child' rather than 'how my autistic child is struggling,' others may interpret your advocacy wrongly."

Eric Evans agrees that parents sometimes steal the advocacy spotlight:

> I hate it so much sometimes when I read certain articles, mostly from parents that indirectly insult their child's potential. From my point of view, it often appears that people on the spectrum are hopeless without their oh-so loving and perfect mother who saves them from the big bad world. It often turns into a community of pats on the back from other mothers about how good a mother each one is. It becomes about them and their struggle. Something about it just really rubs me the wrong way sometimes.

Respecting that only Autistic people really "get it"

Daniel Bowman Jr. says that it's okay for parents to share their experiences, but they should avoid telling stories that aren't theirs to tell: "Where it goes off the rails for me is when they [parents] more or less pretend that they get it. They don't. They can't." Being an autism parent doesn't mean you are an expert on autism. Bowman hopes that society will someday elevate the status of Autistic people as true experts on the Autistic condition:

> On Twitter these days, we call it the #ownvoices movement. If I want to read fiction about the Igbo people of Nigeria, I don't read white people who aren't from there. I read Chinua Achebe or another #ownvoices writer. I hope that people someday afford the same status to autism—that they'll seek out our stories first and foremost. As we say: "Nothing about us without us." Yet critics dole out accolades quite regularly to allistic people attempting to write the autistic experience.

This holds true for educators, therapists, and other professionals who work with ND populations. While sincere efforts to understand will go a long way, assuming you "get" another person's neurology—especially when publicly sharing information or anecdotes—is both alienating and negating to many Autistic people.

Asking for permission and practicing empathy

Anyone seeking to disseminate details about someone else's life should be extremely careful to ask permission where appropriate: "While all kids are at risk, this oversharing especially impacts the privacy and dignity of children with disabilities, including those on the autism spectrum, because it can reveal struggles or challenges that should remain private" (Moss 2020).

We must all be careful when determining what stories to tell. Parents' lives are especially intertwined with their children's, and this complicates storytelling. Sharing stories without permission can humiliate Autistic people, and, if done on social media or published elsewhere on the internet, the damage can be permanent. After all, "the Internet might preserve stories in a sort of virtual permanent marker, but the real permanency should be in a trusting and loving bond between parents and children who treasure and respect that relationship" (Moss 2020).

Avoiding communicating burden

Speaking publicly about the difficult life of raising an Autistic child is likely to have a negative impact on the Autistic person. The perception of Autistic people as burdens to society or to a family can have dangerous, violent consequences and, in extreme cases, is used as justification for the murder of Autistic people. Many Autistic people have spoken about their frustration and anger that other people make them feel this way. Lydia X. Z. Brown (again, early in their advocacy career) writes in an open letter to ND people who feel like a burden:

> You are not a burden to society if you need any form of accommodation to navigate this world. The society in which we live was not constructed around the needs and experiences of people like you and me. In fact, it

> ought to be the basic, minimum standard of human decency to ensure that you and I have equal access as everyone else. And sometimes that means making accommodations for us. (Brown 2012b)

Brown goes on to explain that society's true burden is to compensate "for its long train of abuses, disenfranchisement, marginalization, discrimination, dehumanization and paternalism perpetrated and perpetuated against those who have been denied power, equal rights, and self-determination."

Poet Marie asks for people to emphasize positive storytelling and focus on strengths, with special consideration for how Autistic people might feel. Positive storytelling will help build confidence:

> Let's focus on the positive, that is to say, what we can do. Neurotypicals wouldn't like to be constantly reminded of what they cannot do either. Self-confidence is very important, and it certainly doesn't boost the self-confidence of autistic people to constantly be told that they should be something or someone else.

Advocate for individuals tip, No. 2: Be aware of the perils of blanket assumptions

Why is this needed?

Many NT and ND people alike take pride in being an individual, thinking for themselves, and having free will. But there are numerous stereotypes for different roles we fill in our lives. We might be able to think of stereotypical behaviors associated with being a scientist, a professional athlete, a single parent, an exotic dancer, a teenager, or a kindergarten teacher. But we enjoy the freedom to accept whichever of those stereotypes we identify with and to reject the others.

We don't want people to assume that we fit all of the common stereotypes, and we certainly don't want others promoting those stereotypes as universally accepted so that it forces others to view us in different ways than how we choose to identify. The same idea applies to the ND community and having an ND diagnosis. We should avoid overgeneralizing autism, because it denies people the opportunity to identify as they wish, and it encourages misleading stereotypes about autism.

Understanding Autistic variability

Many Autistic people have spoken out against making generalizations about autism. Bob Christian says it's a mistake for parents to think "that because they know their autistic child, they know all autistic people. That's not the case, because the spectrum is so wide, really every autistic person is different." Author/editor Austin Shinn says that many NT advocates "generalize us, not noticing that refusing generalization is our hallmark." In addition, Terra Vance says that neurotypicals often use confirmation bias to make judgments about Autistic people, taking what they know about one Autistic person and applying it to all of the spectrum. Vance clarifies: "We are as diverse as the term 'human,' but our differences from NTs are vastly different."

"I think the biggest mistakes I see are forgetting Autistic people are just as unique and varied as neurotypical people are," says Alex Earhart, the blogger known as Autistically Alex. Writer/photographer Braydon Keddie says it's true Autistic people share similarities, but there is incredible variation among them: "We have a lot of similarities, no doubt; social anxiety and habitual routines just to name a few. The truth is, because we belong to an entire spectrum, the way we are wired can be very different." Some advocates tend to think about (and talk about) autism as a collection of symptoms. But Autistic advocates ask us to understand that Autistic people also possess the same human variation as neurotypicals. Advocacy geared towards individualized support needs is more beneficial than trying to group Autistic people under the same umbrella of symptoms, feelings, and needs.

Talking about Autistic people as though they are all the same, with the same problems and solutions isn't helpful, adds Gillan Drew:

> The reality is that we're unique individuals and should be treated as such. I knew one well-respected autism advocate who promoted the view that people with autism cannot understand sarcasm and so to use it around a person with autism is a form of abuse—which belies the fact that some of the most sarcastic people I've ever met have been on the spectrum. We are not better or worse than neurotypical people—we are simply different. And that's fine.

Beware of conflating comorbid medical and physical conditions with autism, and/or autism "severity"

Autism is not a medical condition—it is a neurological way of being. Quincy Hansen says it's easy for people to lump different physiological behaviors and symptoms into the same label of autism, but this can be dangerous and unhelpful if it overlooks specific support needs and/or impacts the apparent "severity" of an autism diagnosis. Hansen explains that co-occurring conditions need to be treated, recognized, and diagnosed as separate conditions so that they can be appropriately addressed:

> An autistic person with co-occurring conditions may have additional needs that must be met, so saying, for example, "autism and a seizure disorder," rather than (inaccurately) lumping in seizures with autism allows additional potential support needs to be accurately determined because it is made clear that they have these additional support requirements related to their seizure disorder.

Understanding her comorbid conditions helped Rochelle Johnson change her attitude on autism and gain self-acceptance:

> I think perhaps what has changed my attitude and developed my acceptance and celebration the most is the realization that, in large part, the difficulties and struggles that we as autistics can have are largely the result of comorbid conditions. Not entirely, but largely.

Conflating comorbid conditions with autism can result in the tendency to label autism severity. C. L. Lynch explains that breaking down an Autistic person's needs makes much more sense than trying to describe the severity of their autism. "There are many different flavours of autism, and some are much more visibly disabling than others." Lynch says that some people who can't control their muscle movements are often labeled as having "severe" autism.

> But really, it isn't that their autism is more severe. It's that they have motor control issues—called "apraxia"—that I do not have. But if you ask any autism specialist if autism is, at heart, a motor control problem, they will tell you "no." Maybe they're wrong—certainly all autistic people have strong feelings about the world around them and how they interact with it—but for now, apraxia is considered a side-order to the main dish that is autism.

Lynch proposes avoiding these labels that conflate different medical and physical conditions with autism and don't accurately depict a person's needs: "It just makes more sense to talk about what particular struggles the autistic person has and not try to compare us as being better or worse off than someone else who also has autism." Grouping autism and co-occurring physical and/or medical conditions together, and/or judging people based on their "symptoms" reduces people to "cases," rather than seeing them as unique and worthy of respect and personalized attention. Autism advocates can instead take measures to avoid severity labels in their rhetoric and emphasize specific areas of need rather than broad, undefined categories of people.

Advocate for individuals tip, No. 3: Always get to know the Autistic person first

Why is this needed?

It might seem like simple advice—get to know the person you are advocating for. People often claim some level of expertise with autism because they have to study it to learn how to best support the Autistic people in their lives. But some Autistic advocates remind us to keep the focus on the Autistic person and learn about their specific needs before recommending any support strategies, never mind offering any other sort of advice or assistance. It's important to get to know the person first because the autism stereotypes we hear about are often untrue, and standardized, unspecified advice can distract from the discovery of useful support strategies, not to mention the furtherance of genuine acceptance, awareness, and inclusion for that person and others in their life.

Jennifer agrees that generalizing is a universal issue and stresses the importance of getting to know each Autistic person in order to determine their specific interaction and advocacy preferences, as well as their support needs, where applicable:

> Parents, teachers, helpers, therapists: make sure you are really addressing the person in front of you! We are all different. If you've read or heard something, let's say that "Autistic people don't have empathy," investigate for yourself whether the unique individual in your life actually lacks empathy. This is actually a huge pet peeve for me, because what some ND people *do* lack is the ability to easily discern how people feel, or process their responses quickly or easily, but I have

> *never* met an Autistic person who didn't care—deeply—once they understood.

Similarly, Braydon Keddie says that treating people as individuals is essential to understanding who they are:

> Where are we strongest? Where do we need to grow? What are we scared of? What are we excited about? What are our dreams? When you start to see these traits in a person, you start to see how you can help them best.

Keddie adds that it's important to understand where people are with their understanding and acceptance of autism because this will likely guide your priorities, and you'll be better able to support them. "Maybe they are absolutely okay with being on the spectrum. Maybe, like I was at a point in my life, they are trying to just be accepted as a person on the spectrum." You will likely have different advocacy priorities depending on whether those closest to you desire research into alleviating disabling symptoms, autism acceptance, both—or another approach entirely.

Interests vary widely

Interests vary widely among people on the spectrum, just like they do among neurotypicals, yet many Autistic people report that they frequently see interest stereotyping. Austin Shinn said he sees that neurotypicals "push us hard in places where we're overrepresented, such as in STEM fields, while ignoring those of us drawn to liberal arts heavy fields who still need help." Autism specialist and author Lana Grant explains that these interests can cross into the realm of socialization preferences. Parents, for example, may want their child to have friendships:

> This is because in society we measure happiness by popularity and being liked. It is a myth that all autistics have little interest in other people and friendships. Some autistics don't need friendships in the way many NTs do. But some autistics do want friendships, but they're just not sure how to go about making and keeping those relationships.

A given Autistic person may or may not share the goal of forming friendships, and they may or may not want or appreciate intervention (support) in that process. Either way, getting to know the Autistic person and their specific interests (which will change as they grow and develop) is paramount to helping them succeed.

Later, in Step 6, Temple Grandin expresses the importance of exposing Autistic children to a variety of experiences in order to determine their interests or discover areas they might enjoy developing skills in. As an advocate for the greater autism community, it's important to work towards offering a variety of opportunities for Autistic people, especially those that might be currently underrepresented. As a start, consider your current area(s) of expertise. Are ND people offered equal opportunity in this space? If not, what are the barriers to making this happen?

As with so many other external limits and stereotypes imposed on children and groups—such as those arising from poverty, racism, xenophobia, homophobia, transphobia, and so on—when more traditionally privileged or abled people ally with those less privileged or non-typically abled to question those barriers, great progress can be made. More opportunity and greater exposure to choices pave the way for overcoming obstacles by building knowledge and awareness of the many possibilities ND people can pursue.

Advocate for individuals tip, No. 4: Never expect a one-size-fits-all-solution

Why is this needed?

The logical next step after getting to know the Autistic people in your life is to understand there will not be a simple solution to everything they might be having difficulty with. Autistic people have varying interests and needs, which means that they will have varied solutions and ways of addressing the areas in which they struggle. Understanding there is never a one-size-fits-all-solution helps advocates to avoid stereotypes that might not be helpful for the Autistic people in their lives, and to keep a positive and hopeful attitude about finding solutions that work well, where appropriate.

It's also important to note that many Autistic people do not feel that they need anyone to offer them solutions. As a would-be autism advocate, truly following Tip No. 3 (above) may mean abandoning a need to "help" the Autistic person or people in your life, if that is their wish. There are still plenty of ways to serve as an advocate or ally, as we will explore in later steps.

Finding positivity in complexity

"Everyone is different," says Jennifer Brozek. Everyone has individual issues, she adds, and some people become frustrated because of this: "They want an easy answer, and there isn't one." When advocates understand and accept this, they can more efficiently work to find ways that will serve those closest to them. In fact, both neurotypicals and Autistic people may find it helpful to bear in mind that every human being faces unique barriers and must forge their own path, and that for some it is longer and harder than others. This is all the more true when basic human diversity is coupled with neurodiversity. Developmental differences, which are generally present in most Autistic people, can also play a role in lengthening the journey towards desired goals, whatever they may be.

And if indeed a given Autistic person does seek support, remember to be patient if you/they have a hard time finding the perfect resource(s). Author/ultrarunner/educator Tracey Cohen suggests that advocates keep in mind that autism is not a "one-size-fits-all" issue and thus stresses that positivity when looking for support solutions can be helpful:

> We are all so very different, but I would suggest that every advocate...keep things as positive as possible, and if advocating for a specific person, respect that person's needs and wishes as sometimes our good intentions can allow us to forget to learn what someone might really need and want for themselves.

Throughout this process, we need to not only get to know the Autistic person and understand that their needs will be very specific, but also understand that while the Autistic community is a wonderful place to look for guidance, we still need to look for experts who have broad knowledge within this community. Terra Vance says that not every Autistic person needs to be an autism ambassador or exemplar of the Autistic experience:

> In the same way that having graduated from high school does not make a person an expert on education or developmental science in adolescence, being autistic doesn't mean that a person is an expert. Neurotypical people need to champion the voices of autistic people who have spent years in advocacy and put in the work to have collected and assimilated enough information from autistic voices to be a fair representative of our collective voice.

Each person on the spectrum is an expert on their unique experience as an Autistic being, but there are many Autistic advocates who have broader expertise on the Autistic condition as it impacts others, because they have years of experience in the autism advocacy space. Just as we should never expect to apply a one-size-fits-all solution to every challenge faced by Autistic people, we should never attempt to advocate for any person or group without consulting the appropriate person and/or expert voices.

Advocate for individuals tip, No. 5: Beware of inspiration porn

Why is this needed?

Several Autistic people interviewed warned neurotypicals to avoid creating and sharing inspiration porn. Inspiration porn is a term used to describe the reduction of disabled people to objects of inspiration (Disability Marketing 2021). This might take the form of: objectifying a disabled person (for example, a "What's your excuse?" meme of a person in a wheelchair) in order to guilt or inspire an NT and/or able-bodied person to work harder or be more productive; celebrating disabled people for commonplace activities; praising an incredible feat as inspiring because of a person's disability (and not because most of the general population couldn't do it); or commending able-bodied and/or NT people for acting with simple, human kindness towards those with disabilities (Brown 2016). Former Autistic Self Advocacy Atlanta president and web developer Bennett Gaddes explains:

> One of the worst mistakes is demanding that neurodiverse/disabled people be "inspiring." This often takes the form of sharing "inspiration porn" through social media. The most common kind of inspiration porn is clickbait articles or memes in which a disabled person has their privacy violated while performing some routine task such as eating in a restaurant, or otherwise praising a non-disabled person for assisting a disabled companion.

Lydia X. Z. Brown has written several articles about inspiration porn and ableism. In "Disabled people are not your feel-good back-pats" (Brown 2016), they reference Ari Ne'eman, former President of ASAN, who describes the "Very Special Episode syndrome," an advertising term originally used in American television promos to indicate discussion of a highly emotional topic (TV Tropes n.d.). This term is also widely used by other disabled critics. Ne'eman applies this term to the type of inspiration porn that praises the nondisabled for simple acts of kindness, or objectifies disabled people for the instruction of the non-disabled. Brown (2016) explains:

> Very Special Episode syndrome—where a disabled character is newly introduced for one or a few episodes of a long-running series (in a book or film, this could easily be adjusted to a single chapter, single scene, or background plot) to teach the main characters (of course not disabled themselves) a very important lesson about tolerance before going back to the institution or special needs school where they "really belong."

Creating and/or sharing inspiration porn is harmful to the disability community because it objectifies Autistic people, destroys Autistic privacy, and hides important social justice questions.

Yes, people today do tend to regularly share about their children, students, clients, friends, loved ones, communities, and so on—whether NT or ND, disabled or not—on social media and elsewhere. So, if an advocate or ally wants to join in this common activity in a way that includes an ND person, what is the best way to respectfully do so? The distinction lies in several areas. The guidelines in the following sections offer examples of when sharing should definitely be avoided.

Avoiding objectifying portrayals

Many in the Autistic community, as well as in other disability communities, assert that the problem with inspiration porn is that people with disabilities shouldn't exist only to inspire others. They have intrinsic value as humans, regardless of whether or not they are doing anything "inspirational." Because so much of society equates disability with daily suffering, people assume that merely existing is inspirational (see "How to Avoid 'Inspiration Porn' When Talking About Disability" by S., 2016). This is an ableist assumption that discriminates against disabled people and disregards disabled voice, authority, and expertise. In an article titled "Inspiration porn: How the media and society objectify disabled people," Kit Mead (2019) describes this type of objectifying classification as toxic to mental health, making people feel like they have no control over their lives or their stories.

Respecting privacy

Mead (2019) explains that another consequence of inspiration porn is that it destroys privacy. Disabled people might be fearful of being filmed "for someone's feel-good story":

> We already face enormous pressure to not ask for help—to be the "supercrip" and "overcome" our disabilities—and the risk of being a viral story is yet another reason we might avoid asking for help when we need it.

Names, pictures, and video are often shared without consent in these situations. "The instantaneous destruction of privacy tells society that it is acceptable to sacrifice our privacy to make a feel-good news story, and to do it to any disabled person...over and over again," Mead (2019) notes. Advocating for, and allying with, Autistic people as fully human and thus entitled to the same basic rights as everyone else means never violating their right to privacy by recording or sharing their image or activities without explicit permission.

Putting the spotlight on social justice issues

Inspiration porn also hides issues of social justice, writes non-Autistic writer David M. Perry in an article titled "Inspiration porn further disables the disabled" (2015). While there is nothing wrong with promoting acts of kindness, the way they are often presented conceals critical issues the disability community faces. For example, a story made the news in 2015 when a Kentucky woman in a wheelchair was helped inside a Qdoba restaurant and filmed when she asked an employee to help feed her. The media praised the employee who assisted her. Perry (2015) questions the media attention surrounding this story: "Did Jones [the person who filmed the incident] ask permission before objectifying this woman in his quest to praise Quarles [the Qdoba employee]? Do people with disabilities have the right to expect privacy?" He continues with legal and policy questions:

> Why is Qdoba not accessible to disabled patrons in the first place? No one should have to wait outside a door to be let in. And shouldn't Kentucky provide appropriate community-based supports for this person so a disabled woman can lead a more independent life rather than rely on the kindness of strangers? (Perry 2015)

When nondisabled people are praised for simple acts of

kindness, it allows the conversation to be about what should be an obvious, basic sense of decency rather than real issues that create social change and human equality.

Advocate for individuals tip, No. 6: Honor the diverse aspects of Autistic people

Why is this needed?

Have you ever heard someone say, "Well, we're all somewhere on the spectrum," describe someone as "a little Autistic," or suggest everyone has problems with socialization or difficulties with change at times? Well-intentioned neurotypicals sometimes minimize Autistic symptoms in an effort to be more inclusive. Unfortunately, these good intentions of inclusiveness usually have the opposite effect. Overstating the ways in which Autistic people are just like everyone else belittles the Autistic experience, dilutes the authority of a diagnosis, and closes the conversation to learning more about autism.

Respecting rather than trivializing the Autistic experience

Gillan Drew explains that "while it might be nice to claim we're 'just like you,' it can be quite patronizing to somebody with autism as it belittles the reality we face and our lived experience." He adds:

> While many behaviours might resemble autistic traits, the root cause and the degree to which they impact our lives is not comparable to neurotypical society. It is like saying to a person

with anorexia that you understand what it's like because sometimes you don't feel like eating—it's not the same at all!

Jennifer concurs. Years of having certain NT friends and family insist that their or their NT child's social and other struggles are "just the same" as those she and her son encounter ultimately resulted in her decision to stop discussing related concerns. This, in turn, reduced her social connections, making her feel doubly alone. Increased awareness of the truly diverse/divergent aspects of autism can help us avoid the kinds of interactions that further the isolation of Autistic people.

Chris Bonnello (2017) explains: "When you tell an autistic person that 'we're all a little autistic,' I can almost guarantee that their first reaction will be to feel like you're trivialising their difficulties." He goes on to explain that he understands it is not the intention of the neurotypical to belittle anyone on the spectrum or trivialize their experiences, and that they are only trying to offer support or show they are not alone in their struggles. However, he counteracts this with the suggestion that there are better ways to show this type of support than by falsely claiming a shared experience. He says:

> If you want an autistic person to feel less alone, don't use a misleading statement that means "we're all just like you," when all our life experience tells us it's simply not true. Instead, ask them for their perspective, and listen attentively to it. Listeners kill loneliness. (Bonnello 2017)

Motivational speaker and poet Russell Lehmann suggests, "When I reach out for comfort, instead of trying to identify with me, all I need is for you to listen. Just lend your ear, heart and soul. No words needed."

Validating the autism diagnosis

As Gillan Drew notes, if we are all on the spectrum somewhere, it makes the diagnosis of autism meaningless. "Autistic and Unapologetic" U.K. blogger James Sinclair (2019) adds another important point: "If we were all a little bit autistic, then why would autistic advocates need to fight for awareness?" Russell Lehmann agrees that misguided sympathy is a common NT behavior, explaining:

> When I hear people tell me "It's alright, I've had a bad day too," I feel that it minimizes my struggles. I don't have bad days, I either have a great day or an absolutely horrific day. I can't explain the pain I go through on a weekly basis, but I would not wish it on anyone. It's a beast.

Michael John Carley, a public speaker and author, says admitting an Autistic person is different is important to helping support them. He tells parents that "he [the Autistic person] is different, and you have work to do." The same advice could be applied to anyone else who interacts with an Autistic person. Autistic people are different from neurotypicals, and neurotypicals can strive to create a more inclusive environment by validating their feelings, opinions, and experiences and meeting the Autistic person's specific needs in whatever ways they can.

Being open to learning opportunities

In speech-language pathologist Kat Muir's past romantic relationships, she always waited until after she had been on a few dates with someone before disclosing that she was Autistic, in order to allow the person to get to know her without the label first. Whenever she did disclose her autism, she said the news was usually received with neutrality or positivity. But she explains that those reactions didn't translate into long-term understanding and support, perhaps because the people she dated preferred to assume she was just like them. She describes this disconnect:

> All would be well until several months in, by which point my significant other would have contacted me to tell me about something that was bothering them: difficulty at school, something upsetting that a friend had said, or just your average bad day. I thought I was doing my best to be comforting, but I would often be told (either at the time or in a later moment of calm) that I wasn't "emotionally engaged" or "open enough." I'd feel like I was being scolded, but I couldn't really understand what I needed to do differently, even when they tried to explain it to me. I have ended more relationships than not, but when I was on the receiving end of a breakup, that was almost always the reason.

Muir goes on to explain that she received the best insight into her dating experience by watching an episode of *Star Trek* in which android Data attempts to date a fellow crew member. She says, "Some of the dialogue might be accused of being a caricature of a person with autism, but it is nearly an exact depiction of me attempting a romantic relationship." Some neurotypicals might think they are being polite by acting as if Autistic people are like everyone else, but that stance can undermine NT comprehension of genuine divergences. Muir explains that she doesn't disclose a diagnosis as an excuse for behavior, but rather a request for understanding. She says, "I shared my diagnosis not as an excuse for leaving others feeling unheard, but to give context. I may not respond in the typical way, but it doesn't mean I don't care."

James Sinclair underscores this desire for acceptance as long as needs are acknowledged and supported, explaining that most Autistic people who object to overstated similarities dislike it because it feels like the second people say these words, they are closing their minds to the possibility of learning more about autism. He explains: "After all, to them all 7.5 billion people who are both on the planet and on the spectrum are doing just fine, so why do adjustments need to be made for the few diagnosed autists who are calling out for change?" (2019).

Sinclair (2019) adds that even though many Autistic people object to this type of comparison, that doesn't mean neurotypicals shouldn't try to show empathy:

> But maybe next time, instead of saying "We are all on the spectrum," try saying something like "I see where you're coming from" or "I've experienced something similar." It still sends the same message (and is equally as presumptuous) but it doesn't carry the same risk of backfiring and causing more harm than good.

Step 4 is essentially based on the elementary acknowledgement that Autistic people are fundamentally human, which status confers certain basic rights around privacy, personal experience, diagnoses, labeling, and more. Developing a holistic perspective on the many facets and diverse demographics of autism is conducive to respectful, inclusive, effective, empathetic advocacy and allyship, along with improved communication that's based on genuine mutual understanding.

SUMMARY GUIDANCE

- Understand Autistic people are just as unique and varied as NT people are (avoid overgeneralization of traits).
- Get to know the unique needs of the person you are working with.
- Avoid interest stereotyping.
- Avoid using the experience of Autistic people to emphasize "feel-good" messages about life.
- Maintain a positive outlook about the future.
- Search for Autistic advocates to follow who have experience in advocacy and have assimilated enough information from Autistic voices to be a fair representative of a collective voice.

REFLECTION QUESTIONS

? What kinds of opportunities have I helped create for my Autistic child, family member, student, or client? Are any of these based on stereotyped interests? Are there ways to help that person build on specific interests and turn them into potential career pathways?

- ? What barriers exist in my current employment or interest areas to offering ND people equal opportunity? How might I make headway on eradicating such barriers, in my profession and beyond?
- ? In what ways have I overgeneralized about autism to the potential detriment of someone else?
- ? Do I tend to share stories about neurotypicals treating ND people in positive ways? Do I also share stories that raise questions about societal inequality for people on the spectrum? Have I ever shared stories about Autistic empowerment or acceptance? How might I ensure that any public sharing, where appropriate, is respectful to all people involved?
- ? How can I better get to know the Autistic person or people in my life? Where applicable, how might I better support their unique needs?
- ? In what ways do I claim autism expertise? If NT, how can I relinquish that expertise or slip into the background and use my privilege to serve as a platform for elevating Autistic voices and expertise? If Autistic, are there other voices I might incorporate into my advocacy efforts?

STAGE TWO

Implementing #ActuallyAutistic Advice in Your Own ND Family, Classroom, or Practice

As we learn more about the desires of the Autistic community, we have a responsibility to do what we can in our own little corner of the world to act in ways that uphold the dignity of the Autistic people in our lives. Parents, family members, partners, and/or friends will find it's natural to start implementing what they've learned in their own homes and daily lives; teachers will likely do the same in their classrooms, as will doctors and therapists in their practices. The advice in Stage Two reveals ways you can keep your advocacy efforts alongside what Autistic people are asking for and that all voices are included and valued.

The foundational steps undertaken in Stage One will support genuinely inclusive approaches and meaningful, effective actions as, in Stage Two, our advocacy and allyship expand beyond personal reflection and information gathering.

Step 5

Advocate for Things Autistic People Actually Want

> *If you try to get me to stop making my lists and offer me some sort of therapy for my "perseveration," guess what? You're discriminating. If you suggest better tools for designing those lists and great strategies for addressing list content, now we are talking!*
>
> —JENNIFER BRUNTON

Autism advocates are well-intentioned, without a doubt, but sometimes we, especially those of us who are NT, miss the mark. Sometimes we think we know what is best for the Autistic people in our lives, but without responsible engagement and active efforts to identify this, it's easy to stray from the right path or miss it entirely. We know there are big life areas where allies are needed and voices need to be amplified to better support the Autistic community. But our advocacy responsibilities go beyond merely identifying the support areas we believe are important. We also need to ensure we are advocating for things the Autistic community wants (and in the right ways).

If you are NT, this is especially important to be aware of. Not only do Autistic people sometimes have different needs and desires; they also have different preferences for how these needs and desires are supported or obtained. But whether NT or ND, respecting specific needs and preferences is necessary to supporting healthy identity development. This chapter highlights five different areas advocates tend to be loud and passionate about, and notes where Autistic preferences sometimes differ from the loudest or most public voices.

Much of the below is addressed to parents, since adult-driven (generally NT adult-driven) decisions around advocacy behaviors are often made by parents during an Autistic person's childhood. However, autism advocates and allies in other roles will also find much to think about, so we hope they will feel included as well.

Advocacy behavior requested by #ActuallyAutistics, No. 1: Explore only Autistic-initiated therapies

Why is this needed?

When children are diagnosed with autism at young ages, it's common for parents to seek the advice of doctors or therapists for direction. But for now let's overlook the scores of medications, treatments, and "cures" that have circulated throughout society, and instead focus specifically on autism therapies. NT medical experts have recommended all kinds of therapies and treatments for those on the spectrum: occupational therapy (OT), speech therapy (ST), physical therapy (PT), Floortime, applied behavioral analysis (ABA), and cognitive behavioral therapy (CBT), to name a few. When children are young, parents have the critical role of helping them navigate through life (with or without therapy), making decisions about their daily routines and how to manage their needs, desires, and emotions.

Today, many parents and others in a position to make choices for children are in the fortunate situation of being able to easily obtain advice from those who have lived through these therapies. Many Autistic people have spoken out about what they liked or didn't like about particular autism therapies. And while everyone has different needs and preferences, and thus what works well for one will not be guaranteed to benefit all, there is nevertheless plenty that adults can glean from listening to these different perspectives on therapy. Often the crux of the ethics or efficacy of therapy isn't the particular type of the therapy but the way that therapy is approached and implemented. Understanding Autistic perspectives to therapy and helping pursue and support Autistic-initiated therapies is necessary in order to achieve the intended results and treat Autistic people with the dignity they deserve. When Autistic people initiate the therapy, the motivation to succeed increases. This freedom of choice allows them to be in control of their goals and routines and doesn't make them feel like they are constantly in need of fixing in ways they don't understand or care about.

Emphasizing positive/healthy personal development (rather than indistinguishability from peers) as a therapeutic goal

Autism therapy that emphasizes NT accepted behaviors, communication styles, sensory preferences, and emotional regulation techniques at the expense of developing healthy ways to navigate the world as an Autistic person is unhelpful.

Differences are embraced in so many areas of modern life, but when it comes to social norms, people aren't cut a lot of slack before being cast to the sidelines. Often, minor behavioral differences lead to misunderstandings on the part of the NT observer, resulting in negative interpretations of actions that are neutral or even proactive as far as the Autistic person is concerned. For example, a typical NT person might think that staring at the floor or frequent checking of the time signals disinterest in the conversation. Or a neurotypical might interpret an Autistic person's behavior as stoic and insensitive if, after news of a tragedy is announced, they don't process the situation in the same way the NT person would have done, whether because they don't cry, or because they follow up with repetitive questions or exclamations of sympathy.

Other times, Autistic behavior might be interpreted as odd, silly, or repulsive—not because it is misinterpreted as rudeness or another character flaw, but simply because it is *different*. These are neutral behaviors that are condemned because they are not common. Some examples are rocking back and forth, carrying sensory toys around, talking at length about the same topic, laughing "too hard" at a joke, staying home instead of choosing to go out with friends every weekend, or avoiding eye contact during a conversation.

Some therapies, including ABA, encourage indistinguishability from peers (Lovaas Institute 2020). Autistic people warn that using therapy to encourage sameness and cater to the comfort of neurotypicals puts an unhealthy and unnecessary burden on the Autistic community and stifles the rich benefits of uniqueness, creativity, and human diversity. Emphasis on sameness and NT behavior encourages masking, an exhausting and detrimental daily reality for many Autistic people. Maxfield Sparrow explains that while ABA is often under the radar as a highly controversial autism therapy, varied approaches to this therapy exist and the label ABA might be implemented in very different ways. Because ABA is covered by insurance, therapies are sometimes called ABA in order to obtain insurance coverage even though they do not strictly follow ABA principles (Jones 2011). As with any therapeutic modality, the approaches taken to goal setting and implementation are crucial to whether or not the therapy will be positive or create long-term damage.

Sparrow explains that ABA reinforces a daily fatigue because it emphasizes the importance of "intensive, saturated therapy," up to 40 hours a week for very young children.

> Think for a moment how exhausted you, a grown adult, are after 40 hours of work in a week and you will begin to understand why we get so concerned about putting a three-year-old child through such a grueling schedule. Being Autistic doesn't give a three-year-old child superpowers of endurance. (Jones 2011, p.52)

Sparrow also explains that often the goals of ABA favor NT expectations of behavior and societal norms: "Worse than the exhaustion of so many hours of therapy, though, is the heavy focus on making a child 'indistinguishable from his peers.' The main goal of ABA is to make a child LOOK normal." Sparrow says that parents can be fooled into believing the effectiveness of the therapy when their children end up eventually meeting "milestones," such as saying "Mommy" for the first time or sitting through a meal without fidgeting. However, Sparrow asserts that this apparent progress is misguided and comes at a great cost:

> But if your child is getting classic ABA therapy, what you are seeing is an illusion. And what looks like progress is happening at the expense of the child's sense of self, comfort, feelings of safety, ability to love who they are, stress levels, and more. The outward appearance is of improvement, but with classic ABA therapy, that outward improvement is married to a dramatic increase in internal anxiety and suffering. (Jones 2011, p.53)

Furthermore, a well-rehearsed layer of training does not change the underlying neurology: "Underneath the performance is still an Autistic brain and an Autistic nervous system, and it is very important to remember that" (Jones 2011, p.56).

Therapy should improve your child's life, not traumatize them.

> A therapist might tell you that "a little crying" is a normal thing, but I was once an Autistic child and I can tell you that being pushed repeatedly to the point of tears with zero sense of personal power and knowing that the only way to get the repeated torment to end was to comply with everything that was asked of me, no matter how painful, no matter how uneasy it made me feel, no matter how unreasonable the request seemed, knowing that I had no way out of a repeat of the torment again and again for what felt like it would be the rest of my life was traumatizing to such a degree that I still carry emotional scars decades later. It doesn't matter

> whether the perpetrator is a therapist, a teacher, a parent, or an age-peer: bullying is bullying. (Jones 2011, p.54)

As discussed in Step 1, part of autism acceptance is understanding that not all behavior needs to be "fixed." C. L. Lynch (2019a) says there is a difference between trying to stop a child from self-harming and putting them through hours of therapy to stop a harmless stim, such as hand flapping: "You're causing the child emotional discomfort just because the behaviour strikes you as weird." It's important to recognize self-regulation and coping behaviors so they can be understood as a form of communication and thus appropriately responded to. It's unethical to train those behaviors away, says Lynch (2019a).

Yenn Purkis agrees, saying ABA often demonizes Autistic behaviors such as stimming and a lack of eye contact. They say, "I feel that instead of making Autistic children look more neurotypical, and, in the process, giving them the message that their identity is 'wrong,' why don't we make people more understanding and respectful of different?" Purkis suggests that therapy must support the Autistic person while being respectful, supportive, and accepting of differences. "An Autistic child is not a broken neurotypical child, they are a wonderful Autistic person, complete with their own personality, interests, loves and dislikes, strengths and challenges." It follows that any therapy for people on the spectrum should support positive *Autistic* identity development.

Supporting emotional welfare and happiness

Therapy should support the emotional welfare of those who pursue it: "The goal of therapy should be to help the child live a better, happier, more functional life" (Jones 2011, p.54). There are several ways to ensure the relationship between therapist and client is healthy and productive:

1. Families are offered freedom of choice and flexible therapeutic options.
2. Goals are created by the Autistic person whenever possible.
3. Behavior is understood as a communication for therapeutic needs, and supports to manage anxiety and sensory issues are addressed first.
4. Therapeutic programs are centered around respect, empowerment, and validation.

In the following sections, we unpack each of these four key aspects of therapy.

1. Freedom to choose

If a therapy provider pressures families (or individuals) into one particular therapy or passive aggressively communicates that one particular therapy is critical for good parenting or a happy life *and then equates a happy life with NT life*, they aren't putting your child's (or that person's) needs first. Ari Ne'eman (former president of ASAN) says ABA can have a predatory approach towards parents and sends the message that "if you don't work with an ABA provider, your child has no hope" (Devita-Raeburn 2016). Pressure to implement any kind of therapy can have disturbing outcomes, especially when priority is given to end results rather than to the sensitivity and suitability of the approach itself. Whether overtly coercive or passive aggressive, the pressure for therapy implementation feeds off the Autistic person's, parent's, or teacher's fears about a dismal future and might not pay adequate attention to present needs.

2. Autistic-designed goals

Autistic people (like neurotypicals) prefer therapies where they have a choice in the short- and long-term goals of their sessions. Yet, it's common for this simple request to be overlooked or ignored. In Jenna's previous book, *What Your Child on the Autistic Spectrum Really Needs* (Gensic 2019), Australian comedian Jodie Van de Wetering asserts that the more input a person has in choosing any therapy increases its chance for effectiveness. This is all the more true when potentially divergent Autistic priorities are taken into account. "Social skills are actually relatively low on the list of things I'd like addressed in order to have a happier and more productive life," Van de Wetering (quoted in Gensic 2019, p.39) explains, "but they're the first (and usually only) thing therapists want to talk about." Defining her own challenges made an important difference for Jodie, especially once she identified some of her sensory sensitivities. She realized how important it was to address her sensory issues since they were so integrated with how she perceived her world.

When Autistic children are too young to articulate their own desires for therapy goals, parents are still able to follow some best practices for pursuing therapy that will produce happy, successful therapy sessions. Here are the therapy guidelines shared by Professor Anna Nibbs and Unschooling mother Ally Grace, who use these approaches when working with their own ND children:

- **Work at their pace**
  It's vital to adapt to the ND child's timeframe, progression, and sequencing needs, rather than the other way around.

Anna Nibbs was able to find a "brilliant" occupational therapist who worked at her daughter's pace and helped her "take ownership of developing her own skills and having a say in goal-setting." They chose hydrotherapy to address her anxiety around water, and Nibbs said her daughter loved it. Not only did it help her overcome her fear of taking a shower; it was so effective she even had a swimming pool party for her sixth birthday!

- **Follow their interests/make it fun**
  Anna Nibbs explains that therapy does not need to be formal. She plays with her daughter in the ways her daughter wants to play and respects that this is a good way for her to learn. Nibbs says, "It helps that I'm autistic. I'm more stimmy, flappy, and less concerned with standing on ceremony than you might expect many neurotypical parents to be. I really enjoy getting to be a kid sometimes."

  Ally Grace says that if a therapy session isn't fun, there's a problem:

> A child sitting in a therapist's office being told what to do, who may prefer to be outdoors climbing in trees and digging in the dirt, or who may want to be building in Minecraft, or who would rather be making train tracks for their trains to drive on – that is problematic to me.

Grace also asserts that a lack of protest in a particular therapy should not be interpreted as a sign of enjoyment or consent: "When people talk about their children not objecting to certain things; we need to remember this power imbalance. Many kids know they cannot object to all the things that adults choose for them."

> I think we must always remember that not saying no is not the same thing as saying yes. We exist in a power imbalance when we exist alongside our children. As adults and parents, we are more powerful than our children. We must take great care not to take advantage of that and to delicately and deeply consider all of our choices in their lives.

Parents should also consider how much their own ideas for therapy align with their children's interests and needs, says Grace: "I think all our children deserve to have a childhood of play, fun, exploration, and love. Therapy does not always fit in with that, and often will actually get in the way of those things!" While therapy is often a positive choice, there is always an opportunity cost in any activity, because time is limited.

While retaining the ultimate respect for the legitimately varied needs and wants of Autistic people and their families, Jennifer concurs with Grace, recalling her choice to generally forgo formal therapeutic interventions outside of the school setting. While several NT friends questioned her decision, she felt the benefits of her ND son feeling accepted just as he was, recovering from exhausting school days, and having more time to "just be a kid," outweighed the possible gains. Jenna felt similarly when making therapy decisions for her son, who was diagnosed with autism and cerebral palsy. When he was very young, she felt that participating in every recommended therapy meant she was being the best mother possible and doing what was best for him. But as free time grew slimmer and she began doing her own research and engaging with the Autistic community, she learned that being selective with therapy was okay (more than okay—a healthier choice!), and there was plenty of opportunity for development outside of formal therapy sessions.

Of course, every family is unique and must make its own decisions. However, Grace explains that sometimes parents' fears can interfere with therapy considerations:

As an example, if you are wanting to put a 4-year-old into Occupational Therapy that is repetitive and boring, because you see they have atypical fine motor skills and you want to help them learn to write and draw, I would stop there and think more about whether your ideas are more about you and your fears, than them and their needs. It isn't respectful to coerce someone less powerful than you into a situation for your benefit over theirs. If you want to support them to develop their fine motor skills because they wish to do so and because it seems like a helpful thing to do for them, then you can do that in non-coercive ways. You could support them in everyday life. You could ask the advice of a professional but never go to therapy with them. You don't need to make everything into a kind of "therapy" to support your child. So often people equate "force" or "coercion" with "support"—those things are not the same! People may be aiming to support their kids when they coerce them into things; but this is not necessary. It is very possible to support our autistic children to develop skills (just like all kids) while being kind and non-threatening.

- **Celebrate strengths**
  Anna Nibbs helps her daughter recognize her strengths and encourages her to develop them while also supporting her with things she finds challenging: "Supporting her with things she finds difficult is framed in terms of helping her understand that improving some of these things might also make it easier to do some of the things she loves doing." No one wants to constantly be reminded of what they are doing "wrong" or what they need to "work on." A daily habit of celebrating strengths helps build a foundation of self-confidence that is needed for healthy living as well as healthy implementation of therapy.

- **Practice empathy**
  Incorporating Autistic input on therapy is more complicated when parents are making decisions for their children. Ally Grace says that when parents are in doubt about whether or not they should choose a particular therapy, they should consider whether they themselves would enjoy it or not and ask whether their child would choose that therapy for themselves if they were given the option. Grace also asks parents to consider whether their child would value whatever it is the therapy is supposed to be helping with.

  Grace offers some questions for parents to ask before they consider implementing therapy for their ND child:

  - Would you like the same therapy done to you at the same age?
  - Would you like the same therapy done to you at any age?
  - What might your kids be missing out on if they participated in the therapy?
  - Are they going to enjoy the therapy sessions?

> Therapists and others should also carefully consider these ND-formulated questions when proposing and implementing interventions in an Autistic person's life.

3. Management of sensory and anxiety needs with the understanding that behavior is communication

Jones (2011) advises that when considering what kinds of therapy might be a good fit for your child, and especially if your child is unable to articulate what therapy goals they desire, begin by addressing anxiety and sensory needs before anything else; prioritizing sleep for both parents and children is also a good starting point. These goals will help establish comfort and peace in their environments, which is a crucial foundation for any future goals they will desire.

Any parent who is considering whether or not they have made a wise therapy choice, should keep in mind a few cardinal rules. Jones explains that behaviour is communication and that it can also be used as a means of self-regulation. Further, prioritizing communication, human connection, and general comfort and functionality is more important than the neurotypical expectations of speech, eye contact, and "looking normal." Jones also reminds parents that "trust is easy to shatter and painfully difficult to rebuild."

It's vital to find a provider who meets your child where they are, accepts the value of their neurodivergence, and perceives and honors their boundaries. Maxfield Sparrow outlines some salient aspects of what a good fit might look like:

> If your child's therapist is respecting your child, not trying to break down the child's sense of self and body-ownership, treating behavior as communication

> rather than pointless motions that need to be trained away, valuing speech but not at the expense of communication, giving your child breaks to recover and not over-taxing their limited focusing abilities...hold on to that therapist! They are golden! (Jones 2011, p.57)

Again, these guidelines are also relevant for anyone involved in an Autistic person's life in any potentially therapeutic capacity (including procuring said therapy), from teachers to family members to life coaches, and so on.

4. Respect, empowerment, and validation

Autism therapies should also be centered around respect, empowerment, and validation, says Sarah Kathryn, a speech language pathologist (SLP). Kathryn says ableism in the profession is so common that many people don't recognize it. "As clinicians we are taught to see any deviation from 'the norm' as something bad that needs to be fixed, and any deviation that can't be eliminated is seen as tragic or a burden," she explains. Kathryn points out that this ideology is reflected in many places within the therapy provider culture, including books, articles, therapy manuals, clinical education, professional development, and even conversations on social media.

Kathryn suggests that parents engage with the Autistic community to learn what Autistic people have so say about therapy and seek out speech-language pathologist providers who are using approaches that are "person-centered":

> Get to know the needs and wants of the autistic community, and look at how that aligns with the therapist's goals and

objectives. Look at how that aligns with what you know about your child. All therapy should be Person-Centered (meaning each plan is focused on the individual strength, wants, needs, and preferences of the person we're working with), so that's a good term to mention if you feel it isn't happening for your child.

Below are some facets of respectful, empowering, validating approaches.

Taking a whole-person approach

Sarah Kathryn explains that therapeutic modalities that center around empowerment and validation begin by saying, "Your feelings and reactions are valid, and you are a good person worthy of respect and healthy relationships. Here's how you can respect what other people need while making sure other people give you what YOU need." She adds that Autistic people should also be reminded that the things they are good at matter, because many don't hear that often enough. Basically, any truly healthy therapeutic approach must treat each person as a whole person, that is, someone who has their own unique gifts and every right to be treated with respect—and someone who also has every responsibility to do their best to do the same for others.

The Whole Child approach is one philosophy which bases itself on these ideas, says Kathryn. For example, "Boundaries are taught as a two-way street: you need to respect other people's boundaries just like other people need to respect yours," she explains. This can also apply to simple touches or displays of affection: "The [Whole Child] program also teaches people how to ask for consent, how to give/refuse consent, what to do if someone doesn't consent, and what to do if someone ignores a lack of consent."

Communicating with your child's therapist

Sarah Kathryn also reminds parents and others that if they are uncomfortable with an approach being used by a therapist, it's a good idea for them to do their own research to present why a particular approach is unhelpful. For example, Kathryn uses her blog to link to studies about how eye contact is distressing and how stimming does not prevent children from engaging in meaningful play. Such information might be especially useful in communicating with your child's SLP:

> SLPs are bound by evidence-based practice, which means that we base clinical decisions on available resources and clinical experience... The more you have available to demonstrate the negative effects of ableism on the autistic community, the stronger your case will be and the less your SLP will be able to push back.

Kathryn also admits there are gaps in research. She says, for example, "There are a metric ton of articles showing that ABA is effective at increasing and decreasing certain behaviors, but there is abominably little research looking at the long-term social-emotional effects on ABA recipients." However, she suggests a parent can always bring up a lack of research as a concern.

Both concerns and ideas for goals can be addressed collaboratively, says Kathryn. According to her, many therapists are unaware of the ableist assumptions behind their practice. She asserts:

> I do believe very strongly that the majority of us have our students'/clients'/patients' best interests in mind. Plenty of therapists out there have changed their practice after learning about movements like Autism Acceptance and neurodiversity. Logically speaking, there are plenty more who simply haven't had that opportunity yet.

Parents must also remember that they have the right to object to specific approaches and request specific accommodations. "You are not required to agree with anything that makes you uncomfortable," Kathryn states. "If you cannot get a therapist to see where you are coming from, you have the right to give a hard 'no' to anything that you feel is ableist or harmful for your child."

Being aware of the nuances of therapy and masking

Some therapeutic approaches that encourage masking leave Autistic people feeling like there is something fundamentally wrong with them. Sarah Kathryn says that masking is often necessary for success in employment, social interaction, or even physical safety, but how we understand masking and the therapists' approach to masking is fundamental to ensuring a healthy return. She explains:

> The world is not very good at accepting people who are different. So, we aren't necessarily doing autistic people a

favor if we avoid teaching masking altogether. Instead, we can think of masking as a deliberate action that an autistic person can choose to take in order to be more successful in an intolerant world.

According to Kathryn, it's essential that the Autistic person who is working on masking understands that:

1. Their value as a person is not linked to their ability to mask successfully.
2. It is reasonable for them to choose not to mask.
3. Difficulties with NT people who don't understand and/or accept autism are not the Autistic person's fault.

With these #ActuallyAutistic perspectives in mind, parents, therapists, and other advocates will be better able to honor the neurological legitimacy and basic human rights of the Autistic people in their lives.

Advocacy behavior requested by #ActuallyAutistics, No. 2: Honor diverse relationships

Why is this needed?

Autistic people may seek out a variety of different relationships, some of which may seem unusual to neurotypicals. They may also have different socialization needs and preferences that diverge from what the neurotypicals around them have or believe are best. It's important to keep in mind that these differences do not necessarily indicate a problem or area that needs correcting. Honoring the diverse relationships of Autistic people respects unique socialization needs and makes socialization opportunities more comfortable, which, in turn, enables Autistic people to be more engaged in socialization and able to seek out desired relationships with ease.

Respecting the value of a variety of different relationships

Writer Lydia Wayman discussed the importance of valuing a variety of different relationships in an interview for *What Your Child on the Spectrum Really Needs* (Gensic 2019). She says that NT friends can help Autistic people navigate complex social expectations, but she also recommends that parents be open to supporting a variety of relationships for their children. Wayman often hears NT parents and teachers express concern because some Autistic children only want to spend time with "lower-functioning" children, or children who are much older or younger than they are. Conversely, Wayman has had people tell her that her friendships with nondisabled people are not genuine, when she considers these people her closest friends. Wayman contrasts her inclusive experience of friendship with the critical NT view:

> A couple of my closest friends are these kids—we share interests, jokes, and trust. It's really that uncomplicated. I think the world of this kid who's been told it's not really a friendship because I'm an adult and she's a child, and I can't possibly care about her. And the boy she sits with at lunch can't be her friend because she opens his milk. And the boys she plays with after

> school are, well, they're all boys. (Wayman, quoted in Gensic, p.51)

Autistic people may socialize more comfortably with people several years younger or older than they are, or form relationships viewed atypical by neurotypicals in a variety of other ways. However, these differences do not necessarily signify a problem that needs to be corrected. Wayman asks parents not to place unnecessary limits on their children's friendships and suggests all advocates be open to healthy socialization opportunities and relationships from a variety of sources.

Autism specialist and author Lana Grant explains that some Autistic people don't need friendships in the way most neurotypicals do. Additionally, those Autistic people who do want friendships might not know how to initiate and retain relationships. Grant insists, however, that there is no "one-size-fits-all solution" or approach to Autistic people's friendships. The point is, a legitimately autism-friendly approach encompasses any Autistic person's friendship choices, dreams, and needs as worthy of consideration and acceptance, whether or not they mirror NT friendship styles.

Making socialization as comfortable as possible

An important way to support the socialization needs of Autistic people is to follow their lead when setting up socialization opportunities. In addition, avoid forcing unwanted interactions. Ada Hoffmann says it's important not to force or bribe people to be friends with another Autistic person when they aren't interested. Forcing an Autistic person to socialize when they haven't chosen to do so is also harmful. Hoffmann says it's important to "distinguish between social skills based in consideration for other people's boundaries and needs, and social skills based in blind compliance." One problem, Hoffmann notes, is over-teaching the latter while failing to teach the former. Similarly, Marie says that "support doesn't necessarily mean helping Autistic people to be more integrated or like everybody else." They simply want to be accepted for who they are.

Sometimes people encourage socialization in an effort to be inclusive, whether in the classroom or informal social gatherings. For example, Jenna recalls a social media post supporting inclusion where an Autistic woman commented with a warning about being "too inclusive." What she was referring to was forceful inclusion and she gave the example of her mother removing her bedroom door, at her therapist's suggestion, to improve socialization. The woman explained how traumatic this experience was for her and advocated that the Autistic community be the ones to define inclusion and how they want to socialize. Similarly, Tara Campbell, an ND systems analyst, science writer, and mother of ND children says that "birthday parties with every kid in the class invited are miserable."

There are specific conditions that must be met to ensure any opportunity for inclusion is desired, positive, and meaningful. Inclusion doesn't mean that everyone is together doing the same thing. In fact, friends might not even "get together" in the typical way at all, since many Autistic people find online socialization most conducive to the sorts of friendship and connection they seek. Such friendships, like those with people of different ages and abilities, still count.

According to Judy Endow, in her article "Inclusion – how it works best for this Autistic," neurotypicals must realize the extent to which their inclusive opportunities are designed and implemented "NT-style." She explains that to feel true inclusion she needs to feel acceptance in both the larger NT community and the Autistic community:

> While I love being part of the everyday fabric of life in my community, I also need to spend time living my life with other autistics. This is where I find the depth of inclusion my heart and soul searched for my whole life. It feels like home to me. (Endow 2014)

She reflects that she needs a variety of inclusive experiences:

> Given only the opportunity for inclusion only NT style I was left wanting and longing for something I did not understand. It wasn't until I had both that I felt I was no longer an alien, but truly belonged in this world. (Endow 2014)

It's also important to ensure that the underlying conditions for socialization are being met. There's a lot people can do to help support comfortable socialization for the Autistic people in their lives (including themselves). Autistically Alex recommends decompression routines at home for people who are fatigued with the school routine. This also extends to adults, who may need to take the time to decompress after work or other activities. Regular opportunities for rest and time in a safe, quiet space will help with the desire and comfort necessary to socially engage. Assisting in finding and nurturing one mutually desired friendship is also helpful. Dr. Daniel Wendler says that having "one buddy in your corner" will create immense happiness and confidence in your life. He says this is more important than having a lot of friends or being the life of the party:

I think my advice for my younger self would be to look for just one friend—that in the times I felt alone and rejected, don't worry about what the group felt, but just try to find one person who would accept me for me.

Advocacy behavior requested by #ActuallyAutistics, No. 3: Use language carefully—person-first language versus identity-first language

Why is this needed?

It's extremely important for parents—and anyone else involved in the life of a young Autistic person—to carefully consider and discuss the language they will use to talk about that child and practice that language from a very young age. Children are perceptive and part of their self-concept can be based on the language you use about them and autism. Furthermore, we use language to describe how we identify, so, as they grow to become more aware of language, people should be able to choose how they want to be referred to—not have it forced upon them by someone else.

One hot-button topic in the autism community is whether to use person-first or identity-first language. People should consider using language about autism carefully because respectful language use affords the opportunity for Autistic people to find strength and build confidence in who they are. Equally important is that carelessness or insistence on particular identity language removes individual control in Autistic identity development and how the world perceives Autistic people.

Why do some prefer person-first language?

Well-meaning special education teachers, therapists, medical professionals, and parents often feel it is more respectful to use person-first language (PFL) when describing Autistic people ("person *with* autism"). Lydia X. Z. Brown explains that language has a tremendous influence on attitudes, which is why many feel passionately about the topic of autism language. In this article written early in their advocacy career, Brown succinctly expresses why so many choose PFL:

> Many parents of Autistic people and professionals who work with Autistic people prefer terminology such as "person with autism," "people with autism," or "individual with ASD" because they do not consider autism to be part of an individual's identity and do not want their children to be identified or referred to as "Autistic." They want "person-first language" that puts "person" before any identifier such as "autism," in order to emphasize the humanity of their children. (Brown 2011)

Why do some prefer identity-first language?

Many in the Autistic community prefer identity-first language (IFL) because they believe autism to be part of their identity. They believe it's not necessary to assert one's humanity or personhood before autism because it should be assumed that they are human and are treated with dignity accordingly. Hillary writes: "If someone has trouble remembering that I am a person without using a language trick about it, *I don't want them anywhere near me*" (Hillary 2011, p.35).

The choice of the many Autistic people with a strong

preference for IFL should be respected. Daniel Bowman Jr. explains why he prefers IFL: "I am not a 'person with autism' any more than a tall person is a 'person with tallness.' Neither of us can leave behind those identities in any core, comprehensive sense when we walk out the door."

Kat Muir says she prefers IFL and believes neurotypicals can learn to respect individual preferences:

> I personally don't mind whether I'm referred to as Autistic or a person with Autism, but if I were to choose for myself, I prefer to be called Autistic. Autism can't be separated from me. It's like saying I'm blonde. I also don't see Autism as a bad thing that needs to be downplayed. It's not the only or most important thing about me, but neither is being blonde. Many Autistic people, myself included, see it as a cultural identity, similar to being part of the Deaf culture. It's a fine line to walk between being offensive and condescending, and nothing makes everyone happy. Neurotypicals are usually the social awareness experts, and just a little effort goes a long way.

Deferring to the Autistic person

There is no unanimous opinion here. You'll find people from both the NT and Autistic communities prefer both PFL and IFL. But it's important to remember that you can't force an identity classification on another person. "I've seen, too many times to count, an allistic person on a discussion board or in the comment section of an article...actually attempt to correct an autistic person using identity-first language," says Daniel

Bowman. Many Autistic people have been criticized for using IFL, which writer/advocate Paula Sanchez finds bizarre:

> I don't need reminding I'm a person, and my autism really does define me in so many ways, but I don't consider that to be a bad thing. It's ok for people to describe themselves in different ways, but it's not ok for an outsider to challenge that and presume authority.

Katie Oswald agrees:

> How a person identifies should be their personal choice and not forced on them by people in positions of power. The idea that saying "autistic person" is offensive implies that the word autism, and therefore being autistic, is offensive and an insult. That in itself is offensive to people with autism. Please allow each individual to identify themselves in a way that feels comfortable for them.

Even if you disagree with another person's identity language choices, it's not up to you to decide how someone else should identify. Moreover, as Brown (2011) reminds us, we can't dismiss the debate over language:

> The way we use language affects those around us—in our immediate communities and in society at large. Trends of language have the power to transform ideas

and attitudes. To dismiss this as "a silly semantics argument" denies the power of language.

Advocacy behavior requested by #ActuallyAutistics, No. 4: Consider the social model of disability

Why is this needed?

Some Autistic people only consider autism as a disability because of how our culture and environment favors neurotypicals. In other words, having a disability is neutral, not negative; this is often articulated as the social model of disability. The medical model of disability, on the other hand, identifies disability as an abnormality and a clear disadvantage that should be cured or fixed. There's no universal agreement among the Autistic community about which model is more appropriate for autism; however, the social model is gaining public awareness due to the work of many Autistic advocates. Because the medical model is so pervasive in mainstream NT culture, it's beneficial for advocates and allies to learn about the social model and Autistic views of it.

Understanding a mixed model viewpoint

Some Autistic people adopt the social model of disability when it comes to autism, others the medical, and some share a mixed view. In addition, some autism traits might fit better under the social model, whereas others, along with comorbid conditions, might fit better under the medical model. For example, student/advocate Quincy Hansen says that he considers autism to be a central part of who he is—it shapes the way he perceives and understands the world, and it is not something he would want to change. On the other hand, his anxiety is not something he considers to be integral to his neurology, so it is unfair to conflate the two as part of the same thing.

Bix Mediocre warns that autism has a mix of traits that fit under both models, and it makes him uncomfortable and anxious when people make blanket assumptions that assign it a social model label:

> My meltdowns and shutdowns are not the social model. Hyper-focus making me forget to eat or go to the bathroom to the point of bodily distress is not the social model. Certainly, the social model can make things like meltdowns and hyper-focus worse by not responding to or respecting my needs, but that still starts with me suffering an actual physical or psychological problem.

Mediocre says the potential harm is that if we can't accept that some aspects of being Autistic are disabling in and of themselves, we are being dishonest, and "erasing lived autistic experiences." He warns: "It would be bad enough for autistic people to engage in that such erasure amongst themselves, but imagine if NTs picked it up and ran with it."

A social model for public advocacy

Many public advocacy programs use the medical model of disability, according to Sarah Kathryn. These programs can present autism as a tragedy or disorder that places a burden on families and professionals, but stress that it can be overcome through intensive treatment. Kathryn says she sees autism frequently compared to illnesses such as cancer and that "autism 'treatments' focus on outward behavioral change with little to no examination of long-term social-emotional effects." Autism research can also look into causes and cures, sometimes resulting in dangerous ideas, such as connecting autism to vaccines and bleach treatments. "Meanwhile, autistic people are asking for something completely different," says Kathryn.

Kathryn admits there is disagreement within the Autistic community, but she claims a majority of Autistic folk use the social model of disability, which sees a person's struggles as a result of environments and communities that do not meet their needs. She says, "Autistic people generally want autism to be seen as a marginalized identity," and explains:

> We're trying to help non-autistic people understand the ways that they make the world more difficult for autistic people, because everything is seen through a neurotypical lens. Some advocates are asking for more research into the social-emotional effects of ABA, or suicide rates in autistic people, which are disproportionately high among autistic people who mask all the time. These things are largely being ignored, either due to a general lack of awareness or deliberate attempts to ignore autistic people who are saying things non-autistics don't want to hear.

An emphasis on the social model of disability demands systemic changes to current ideologies dominating institutions around the globe. It focuses on meeting the needs of Autistic people at all stages of life and creating equal opportunities for all people, regardless of disability, thus working to make disabilities less disabling. Such an approach does not preclude medical elements, but it does call NT society to task for marginalizing Autistic people.

Advocacy behavior requested by #ActuallyAutistics, No. 5: Practice neurodiversity-friendly school and workplace advocacy

Why is this needed?

A neurodiversity mindset is relatively new to mainstream culture. Autism deficit models still have strongholds in many areas of modern culture, including school systems and many workplaces. For parents, families, and other caregivers, communicating with your local school district leaders, teachers, or employers not only about the specific educational/employment needs of your child, teen, or young adult, but also about the neurodiversity paradigm, will help educators and employers frame the way they speak to and support your child/teen/young adult on an ongoing basis.

At the professional level, educators, administrators, and others working in school settings, including SLPs, OTs, and so on, along with employers, managers, and co-workers in work settings, can also avail themselves of ND perspectives and resources in order to build awareness in their organizations. Finally, NT allies and advocates and adult Autistic people advocating for themselves and/or others in the workplace will likely find an abundance of areas for improvement, above and beyond the preliminary suggestions outlined below. All of these site-specific efforts are worth it. Neurodiversity-friendly school and workplace advocacy will ultimately reduce stress levels for Autistic people in school and work environments and create more positive, healthy atmospheres for learning, working, and life in general.

Whatever role you play in an ND life or lives, perhaps the most important way to use any influence you may have as a parent, colleague, teacher, partner, etc. is to encourage and empower self-advocacy. School and workplace settings vary just like individuals, with some places nurturing autism as a superpower, others stigmatizing it as less-than, and most somewhere in-between. The specific Autistic people who participate in particular environments will know best what they need to succeed. Autistic people who believe in themselves and know their rights are generally more inclined to self-advocate—and they're often the ones who can make the most significant differences! And when a given Autistic person is not comfortable or able to communicate in such a way, there may be others on the spectrum who are willing to collaborate in mutual self-advocacy to share their perspective.

The many influences of the school system

It's a mistake to merely think of school as a place where educational content is delivered. Students spend the majority of their weekdays there, and they not only learn material in a variety of different content areas, they practice other skills such as socialization, friendship, organization, time management, safety, and advocacy. There are numerous interactions that school employees will have with ND children each day, so it makes sense that these other adults should be on board with the neurodiversity principles families follow at home to support healthy child development. For example, when Jenna's son was in elementary school, she had to communicate his discomfort with eye contact and that she didn't want it to be built into a speech goal during the school day. Communicating the stress involved in encouraging this NT behavior was an important part of creating a safe learning space for her son.

In addition, stigma around special education still pervades many schools, especially at the peer level. Typically-abled children and youth do not always exhibit inclusive or respectful behavior, and sometimes they can be quite cruel to those with differences. Thus, cultivating peer awareness, allyship, and advocacy is one extremely important avenue for adult advocates to pursue in whatever way they can, whether via presentations, workshops, clubs, athletic activities, or other creative, effective means. NT siblings and friends in the school system may also be a force for good, working with other allies and advocates to counter the deeply harmful (and erroneous) "shame" mentality surrounding special education in many school communities.

Aligning with progress

School can be a place where a child learns not only certain academic skills but also confidence, social skills, and self-acceptance. Or it can be a place where their self-esteem is destroyed. Until ND inclusion and awareness have become pervasive throughout our schools and society as a whole (since students and adults in schools are influenced by other social environments, too), these institutions remain a site where advocacy can play a huge role in making sure more schools fit primarily into the first category.

Opportunities for growth range from steps that will support a given person, to measures that will have a school-wide impact. Creating a less stressful, more beneficial learning and growing environment for all ND children starts with awareness and sensitivity around the needs of each person. While school advocacy is a subject worthy of another book, Jennifer suggests the following areas as starting points for possible consideration:

- **The classroom:**
  Learning environments that welcome all students tend to foster diverse learning styles as well as actively celebrating and accommodating the differences and needs of each person. Parents and other caregivers can talk with their child's teacher(s) about not only their child's unique needs and learning style, but about their child's preferred language. All advocates, including teachers and aides, can share links and other resources that reflect ND perspectives. Seek opportunities to further neurodiversity awareness and holistic integration in the classroom without singling out any specific child. Reading about ND experiences aloud, or, for older students, assigning educational materials that support neurodiversity, can be a great conversation opener.

- **Therapeutic settings:**
  Therapies that actually help tend to respect the integrity and worth of diverse ways of being, while nonetheless allowing for the possibility of beneficial (e.g., non-coercive, non-discriminatory, non-harmful) growth. Investigate whether neuro-normative testing methods may not be a good fit for a given ND person and may thus not reflect their true capabilities. Bear in mind that most ND students undergo a great deal of testing and observation in order to be diagnosed in the first place; such scenarios may therefore feel loaded for them. Professionals and parents alike can discuss and approach any testing or therapy with sensitivity and respect for the particular student's situation

and encourage others to do the same. When possible, they can check in with the student about their therapeutic goals and their personal experience of therapy sessions.

- **School facilities:**
  Schools can and should look for ways to create a calm environment that's welcoming for all neurologies. Create safe, quiet spaces with sensory and other resources for directed or self-initiated self-care. Share respectful, inclusive stories and images in the hallways, as well as in assemblies and other all-school events. Since peer interactions and influences can have an enormous impact on any child, foster community policies and programs that promote mutual interconnection, such as reading buddies and structured playground activities.

- **School meetings:**
  IEP and 504 meetings, as well as parent–teacher conferences, are excellent settings for advocacy and allyship from all parties present. Such meetings can be fairly brutal under the best of circumstances because they involve investigating and demonstrating the "deficits"/"weaknesses" of the child in question in order to get them the necessary services. Advocates are advised to do their research in advance and come to any school meeting prepared both with knowledge (legal aspects, school policies, ND perspectives) and specific goals for the student for whom the meeting is being held. In Jennifer's experience, this can be particularly important for ND parents and advocates who may find themselves sensorially or emotionally overwhelmed by such meetings and might benefit from written or visual aids.

In fact, almost anybody—teachers included—can get

nervous in this context, especially when advocating for someone in the face of limited school resources and, sometimes, a lack of awareness on the part of some participants. Jennifer has personally seen teachers risk their jobs to fight for her son, and, on the opposite end of the awareness spectrum, one teacher who openly discriminated against him. In her advocacy experience, she's encountered parents who were able to immerse themselves in autism awareness and brought that wisdom to the table at these meetings to educate staff, and parents who learned everything they knew about autism from the caring professionals at these meetings. Jenna has also experienced professionals who wanted to offer support, but their ideas were misplaced (recommending goals for increased eye contact or contrived social role playing). It is hoped that the educational professionals you are working with are willing to both offer ideas for adapting the learning environment and listen to the voices of parent and student advocates. The bottom line? Breathe deeply—and bring everything you've got. Be open to learning, too. And, whenever age-appropriate/desired by the student, include them in any discussions or decisions.

Since institutions and bureaucracies move at a snail's pace, advocates and allies will also frequently need to balance patience with sincere and ongoing efforts to obtain the necessary accommodation(s), modification(s), technology (technologies), treatment(s), inclusion, etc.

The authority of Autistic experience

While Autistic students must clearly abide by certain school rules that protect all members of the community, they must never be forced to participate in therapies or other activities that diminish their humanity and self-worth; nor should they be subjected to bullying from fellow students or school employees who believe they know better what Autistic people need than Autistic people themselves (or their families). Truly inclusive schools enable all students to feel accepted, understood, and safe enough to learn and thrive.

Sadly, Autistic students, along with their advocates and allies, may still find that they face stereotyped thinking and outdated ideas about autism. This is a key area where #ActuallyAutistic voices have so much to contribute. Extrapolating from the previous chapters to the specifics of schools, we can clearly see that Autistic students have certain generally shared fundamental rights and desires. These include the following:

- the right to an inclusive school environment
- the right to communicate and be heard via whatever communication mode works best for them
- the right to have a voice in their own education and potential interventions
- the right to be seen and accepted as ND people who may or may not experience other disabilities and/or medical conditions (and may or may not desire accommodations, modifications, and/or therapies for same)
- the right to be presumed competent
- the right to enjoy the same basic respect as any other student.

Workplace advocacy

Many of these school advocacy/allyship ideas carry over into the workplace. This is not because of developmental differences on the part of Autistic people, but because built environments and established cultures tend to favor NT preferences and strengths. Therefore, in any instance of institutional advocacy and allyship—be it at school or at work—space and support must be created for inclusion and acceptance to foster success on all fronts.

Some organizations are using universal design principles to transform the work setting. Universal design refers to the development of physical environments that are inclusive (functional and aesthetically pleasing) to people of all ages and abilities. Universal inclusivity asks organizations to make procedural and structural decisions that meet the needs of everyone at once rather than spending time and money on individual worker accommodations. Inclusion thereby becomes part of the company culture. Many inclusion policies are low-cost compared to potential accommodations for individuals:

> Adaptations can simply build upon internal processes and company norms that already exist, such as offering different ways for team members to participate in virtual meetings: texting instead of speaking aloud, the option of turning one's camera on only at the start of a meeting or not at all, etc. (Ciampi 2021)

Marcelle Ciampi (a.k.a. author Samantha Craft) is the diversity, equity, and inclusion officer for Ultranauts, a software and data quality engineering firm that is reimagining how companies hire talent. Ultranauts uses universal design principles to create what they call "universal workplaces." These spaces engender what Ciampi refers to as "core inclusion."

Ciampi is an ambassador for, and consultant on, this practice in the workplace, and her company serves as a model for companies looking to improve the inclusivity of their hiring processes. At Ultranauts, 75 percent of employees are on the autism spectrum and 45 percent identify as non-male. Ciampi explains that Autistic employees do not have a separate onboarding process. Every potential employee is treated the same and is not required to disclose disability, allowing for a private and dignified application and hiring process.

> We create best practices for engagement and learning all around the paradigm of neurodiversity that everyone's brains vary, and they all are of value. None are lesser than or better. So everyone deserves equity and equality in the workplace because they have a brain and a mind and they're a human being. And not to choose one subset of a marginalized group over a general population and give them special treatment because that creates othering, "less-than" labels, and inferior/superior constructs.

Ciampi advocates for being open-minded with recruitment and not relying on resumés alone for decision-making, because "you never know what types of skills people can learn or what skill sets are hidden." Ciampi explains that an inclusive hiring process avoids separate but equal segregation that unfortunately occurs in many companies due to an autism-deficit mindset: "Autistic people being siphoned into hiring practices in one separate building through one separate program—that's segregation, and it can be grounds for litigation for any other race, for any other 'minority'."

However, where universal design has yet to be implemented, advocacy for individual needs remains paramount to workplace success. Gavin Bollard, an Australian blogger and IT specialist (interviewed in Gensic 2019) says he used to think he was to blame for his struggles at work. He wasn't able to finish his work as quickly as his colleagues, despite the fact that he would arrive earlier and work later than they did. He had a work-related hand injury due to overuse with an increased job workload. His low muscle tone and hyperflexibility, coupled with his hyperfocus and computer-centered job, resulted in continued stress on his hand. Because of his focus and heavy workload, he didn't even realize he was in pain.

> It didn't occur to me that I needed to talk to my boss about the problem. I simply felt that I wasn't putting enough time into it. It was only when a colleague saw my swollen arms and hands and realized how much pain they were in that they told management and got an intervention sorted out for me. (Bollard, quoted in Gensic 2019, p.73)

Bollard's boss found a typing partner for him while his hand healed, and installed dictation software and a program that helped remind him to take breaks from the keyboard. His company also helped him find an acupuncture therapist and personal trainer to help him manage pain and rebuild muscles needed for the job to regain productivity (Gensic 2019). Bollard knows he needs to self-advocate at his job, and when his boss asks him to take on more work, Bollard asks him what activity he should stop doing in order to accomplish this new task. This helps his boss prioritize work for Bollard and reallocate lesser priority tasks to other employees.

Would-be workplace advocates (including self-advocates) face barriers from decades, if not centuries, of entrenched NT customs and unstated rules, many of which are outdated, discriminatory, and/or incomprehensible/invisible to ND workers. As autism awareness and acceptance grow, so do the legally and socially sanctioned remedies to such unacceptable conditions. As with school advocacy, a good grasp of the available protections is a basic necessity. In some scenarios, forward-thinking companies that value diversity and/or want to reap the benefits of a neurodiverse workforce will ally with ND people and others to actively promote a truly inclusive work culture and office space. Others will need more pressure, including those protections offered under the law.

ND employees have certain generally shared fundamental rights and desires, some of which are both legal and ethical (others, while not necessarily a legal right, are called for in ethical work environments). These include the following:

- the right to an inclusive, functional, aesthetically supportive work environment
- the right to communicate and be heard via whatever communication mode works best for them
- the right to have a reasonable voice in their own work goals and trajectory, in line with that offered NT employees
- the right to be seen and accepted as ND people who may or may not experience other disabilities and/or medical conditions (and may or may not desire accommodations, modifications, and/or therapies for same)

- the right to be presumed competent according to their job-related skill sets and beyond
- the right to enjoy the same basic respect as any other employee.

Of course, workplace advocacy happens after getting past the interview process, which can be difficult for NT interviewers and Autistic applicants. Interviews can be more challenging for Autistic applicants because they may not give standard or expected responses, they may miss nonverbal communication, they may struggle to think quickly and respond eloquently in fluid conversation, and they may be uncomfortable disclosing they are Autistic for fear of discrimination (Boon 2020). In Step 6, Temple Grandin recommends finding a way to display your talent or capabilities in the interview ahead of time to circumvent some of these obstacles.

The advocacy behaviors in this chapter share the same root motivation: the intention to pursue only those activities, therapies, etc. that Autistic people themselves support and want. This is relevant to NT and Autistic advocates and allies, and it applies to both people of all ages and the broader community, but it most often comes into play with children. Adults who have Autistic children in their care will do well to remember that most NT cultures, evaluations, and approaches have historically marginalized and underestimated Autistic people. If therapy is indeed appropriate, Autistic people, advocates, and/or allies should look for Autistic-aware modalities that take the whole person into consideration. In addition, respecting Autistic people's therapeutic goals and choices, language preferences, friendship proclivities, and so on will go a long way towards righting longtime discrimination on both the personal and societal levels. Similarly, working for neurodiversity-friendly classrooms, schools and workplaces will enable more and more Autistic people to gain the confidence and tools necessary for a full and rewarding life.

SUMMARY GUIDANCE

- Avoid therapy that emphasizes looking "normal" or "indistinguishability from peers."
- Ensure your child's therapist identifies and understands behavior as communication and not a strange problem to fix.
- Allow Autistic people to create therapeutic goals whenever possible.
- As a part of any therapy plan, consider addressing ways to manage anxiety and sensory issues first.
- Ensure any therapeutic program is centered around empowerment and validation.
- Allow Autistic people to work at their own pace to achieve short- and long-term therapy goals.
- Advocate for therapy that is fun, engaging, and motivating.
- Practice empathy when making decisions about therapy for someone else (see reflection questions below).
- Keep therapy priorities straight. For example: communication is more important than speech; human connection is more important than forced eye contact; comfort and functionality are more important than looking normal.
- Be careful about teaching masking. Essential understandings of personal value and freedom of

choice must be integrated in any potential masking practice.

- It's okay for Autistic people to have a variety of friendships, regardless of whether or not they look typical.
- Avoid forcing socialization or friendships. Offer opportunities and give Autistic people freedom to socialize in the ways they feel comfortable.
- Defer to the language preferences of the Autistic person you are communicating with.
- Communicate with your child's, student's, or client's school about neurodiversity and how they can create a neurodiversity-friendly educational environment.
- Actively foster peer allyship whenever possible.
- Consider #ActuallyAutistic voices—including the student's—in any school advocacy efforts.
- Consider ways in which the workplace environment might be manipulated to increase Autistic worker comfort and productivity.

REFLECTION QUESTIONS

- ? Would I like my child's/loved one's/client's/student's same therapy done to me at the same age? At any age?
- ? What might that child be missing out on by participating in therapy?
- ? Is that child going to enjoy their therapy sessions?
- ? Are they playing an active role in therapy goal creation?
- ? How can I create more safe, comfortable, and desirable social opportunities for myself, my child/loved one/client/student?
- ? What is my identity language preference? Why?
- ? What is the most stressful part of my child's/client's/student's school day (for adults: work day)? What needs to change in order for this to be better managed?
- ? What individual and larger-scale aspects of the school environment could be more neurodiversity-friendly?
- ? What individual and larger-scale aspects of the work environment could be more neurodiversity-friendly?
- ? For employers, what aspects of my interview process could be improved to be more inclusive or neurodiversity-friendly?

Step 6

Stay Centered on the Autistic Person's Needs and Dreams

> *They assume that we want to "be normal." But really what most autistic people seem to want is just...happiness. And happiness for us may not look the same as it does for a neurotypical person.*
>
> —C. L. LYNCH

Autistic people are asking autism advocates to remember to stay focused on the community they are serving. It sounds so simple. But this desire is still discussed so frequently because we tend to identify with the work we do. Once advocacy becomes a part of our identity, it's tempting to claim expertise, share our own stories, and lose sight of the nuanced needs of those we serve. Autistic people also remind neurotypicals to be careful not only to avoid claiming expertise on autism, but also to understand what it takes to lead a happy, successful life. Different people have different needs and dreams, and it's likely that your child, student, or client's vision and life path will be different from yours. The advice below asks people to ensure their constructive advocacy efforts remain centered on the Autistic person's needs and to avoid pushing NT life expectations. Autistic advocates, especially parents (who may identify strongly with their children), must also bear in mind the specific dreams and needs of the person they are advocating for.

Person-centered advocacy behavior, No. 1: Remember that many Autistic people don't want to look or act NT

Why is this needed?

We may need to reflect on our basic assumptions that Autistic people want to look or act NT. If we are beginning our support efforts from an assumption that Autistic people do want to behave like neurotypicals in order to fit in with society, this misguidance will likely create more stress, encourage masking, and be ineffective. It's important that we avoid upholding NT behaviors as the gold standard for happy living, because this expectation can distract from more helpful ways to offer opportunities for healthy growth as Autistic people.

Preventing unhealthy masking

Emphasis on behavioral differences between Autistic people and neurotypicals, and favoring NT behaviors over Autistic behaviors, aren't necessarily the best ways to foster emotional health in children and they can encourage masking. Author/counselor A. J. Mahari understands that parents love their children and want them to have the best lives possible but says they "sometimes make the mistake of trying to turn them into something they can't be." C. L. Lynch says that assuming Autistic people want the same things non-Autistic people want can cause friction in families. Lynch says that she sees parents who sometimes assume differences between themselves and their children are always negative, but this isn't necessarily how Autistic people view differences:

> I see them break their heart over the inability to talk as if it is the worst possible fate. I see them point to flapping hands as a distressing indicator of difference. Neurotypical people seem very distressed by difference...at least in people. Meanwhile, autistic folk tend to be much more distressed by difference of routine, difference of location, difference of food availability. Difference between one human and another? Well that seems pretty natural to us and not necessarily horrifying or worthy of outcry.

Pressure to mask can even lead to dangerous behaviors, such as drug experimentation. David Gray-Hammond attributes his addiction to "an unmet support need." Gray-Hammond's unmet support need was his mental health after years of masking without an autism diagnosis.

> I grew up trying to hide fundamental parts of myself from society. This took on a new form at age 18 when I started hearing voices and suffering psychotic symptoms. If I had received appropriate support for being autistic, I perhaps would not

> have masked so much. Perhaps if I had known it was okay to show that I was struggling, I would not have turned to drugs and alcohol to self-medicate my psychotic symptoms and the more uncomfortable traits of being autistic. I was lucky to have a very supportive mother, but there was only so much she could do for me when specialists were refusing to diagnose me. Outside of my home, I felt strongly that I had to hide who I was.

Gray-Hammond asks parents, teachers, doctors, and therapists to recognize that addiction is a symptom of a greater underlying issue. He says that "the rituals involved in drug use become repetitive behaviours, almost like stimming but darker" and that people need to be aware that drug and alcohol use can become all-consuming, like a "special interest" for people on the spectrum.

Advocating for autism neutrality

Constantly being treated as if the Autistic "way" is inferior than the NT one is a dismissal of Autistic voice and expertise, and can lead to a poor self-concept for people on the spectrum. Morgan Giosa says people shouldn't be forced to do things the NT way, as if it's the only correct way. He offers an example from his work:

> I think completing tasks should be able to be done in any way, as long as the task gets completed. For example, at the last company I worked for, they wanted me to cut back on the verbosity in my day-to-day communication, but I was still

getting all of the work done, and I was doing it well. I don't see how a bit of verbosity hurt anyone.

According to Alyssa Hillary (interviewed in Gensic 2019), autism shouldn't have to disappear in order for someone on the spectrum to be accepted. In their view, maybe self-actualization or fulfilling human potential should be the goal of life—rather than fitting in, being the same, or passing as NT. Social integration incorporates a process for preventing social marginalization and achieves a state of social harmony, if certain conditions are met (United Nations 2007). Social integration requires everyone—both on and off the spectrum—to work together to live in mutual respect.

Many Autistic people are often implicitly or explicitly told to hide their autism in order to "fit in." But masking causes Autistic people to internalize the belief that autism is bad and that the safest thing to do is to hide their Autistic behaviors, even if doing so is not supportive of their life goals. Hillary says, "I definitely had teachers tell me that I couldn't get away with flapping or rocking 'in the real world.' And I'm a teacher and a writer and a graduate student. I can definitely get away with flapping and rocking" (quoted in Gensic 2019, p.21).

In *The Reason I Jump*, when the nonspeaking author Naoki Higashida is asked if he would like to be "normal," he responds:

> I used to think it'd be the best thing if I could just live my life like a normal person. But now, even if somebody developed a medicine to cure autism, I might well choose to stay as I am. Why have I come around to thinking this way? To give the short version, I've learned that every human being, with or without

> disabilities, needs to strive to do their best, and by striving for happiness you will arrive at happiness. For us, you see, having autism is normal—so we can't know for sure what your "normal" is even like. But so long as we can learn to love ourselves, I'm not sure how much it matters whether we're normal or autistic. (Higashida, Yoshida & Mitchell 2017, p.45)

The assumption that every Autistic person wants to act NT so they can be happy simply isn't true in all cases. And this assumption can be profoundly damaging for children who receive subtle or not-so-subtle, intentional, or unintentional messages from their families about how they "should" act or feel. Shannon Hughes explains:

> Children with autism, diagnosed and undiagnosed, often get their first experiences with invalidation at home, sometimes from loving parents with the best possible intentions, who just don't recognize that a kid who seems robotic and disinterested in the world around them, nevertheless is very sensitive and vulnerable.

Approaching autism, in all its myriad manifestations, as neither good nor bad but neutral, is one way to align with inclusive social integration and self-actualization. From this perspective, particular actions and ways of being may feel "right" for a given person, even as they diverge from the "typical." This stance also recognizes that "acting NT" is, like "acting Autistic," something of inherently neutral value. For some Autistic people, masking or "passing" might feel rewarding or positive; for others, it might feel overly exhausting, negative, or simply not worthwhile.

Respecting different approaches and behaviors

Beyond being grounded in a fundamentally neutral vision of behavior and neurology, Autistic allies and advocates, including self-advocates, best serve the autism community by actively promoting personal and societal awareness of—and respect for—natural human diversity. Perhaps surprisingly for some, many Autistic people already practice this skill regularly. Lynch says that while Autistic people learn very early that the people around them think and behave differently and have different needs, neurotypicals aren't as perceptive: "Neurotypicals take certain base assumptions for granted, and it never occurs to them to think that maybe we don't feel the same way." Writer and advocate Savannah Logsdon-Breakstone says it's a mistake to assume "that autistics should want to present more like neurotypicals, and that we shouldn't want to be associated with our fellow autistics who can't present that way." Similarly, Autistic people shouldn't be forced to "do things the neurotypical way," says Morgan Giosa, "as if it's the 'right' way." Giosa, for example, was able to complete his work in a satisfactory manner, despite being more verbose than his supervisor preferred (see above).

Shaping your support to better meet autistic people's needs

The assumption that NT behavior is always desirable can often shape therapy plans. C. L. Lynch explains:

> Most autism "therapies" are based on NT goals—getting the child to hit neurotypical milestones or learn to do neurotypical things. The idea is that normalcy must be happiness, and it never seems to occur to anyone that this may not be the case.

Lynch explains that oftentimes it is the reactions of NT people that really cause the most suffering for people on the spectrum. She says that autism can be troubling when it interferes with "comfort, love, predictability, stability, acceptance, the ability to express themselves, and the freedom to pursue their own interests." However, NT reactions to (or lack of support) in these situations can compound stress. For example:

> An inability to speak aloud is inconvenient, but if we are given free and easy access to AAC, we can still get our thoughts across. But deny us AAC, and autistic people spend years unable to express themselves, listening to conversations that exclude them, listening to people talk about them as if they aren't even in the room. That is suffering, but is it really autism's fault at that point? Or the fault of the neurotypical reaction to it?

When we (whether we are Autistic or NT) avoid assuming that Autistic people want to look or act NT, we create social and personal space for how each Autistic person actually wants to look and act. As autism advocates and allies, this is one significant step we can take towards opening the door to genuine communication, awareness, and acceptance.

Person-centered advocacy behavior, No. 2: Recognize that a neurotypical's vision of a happy life might not be the same as an Autistic person's vision

Why is this needed?

Neurotypical parents, family members, friends, therapists, and teachers often use themselves as a standard for happiness because that is the standard they intimately understand. They assume that what they need in life to be happy is what their children/clients/students/loved ones also want and need. Perhaps they also have seen how those who have not met this standard have been disappointed in life. Autistic parents, too, may worry that their own struggles will be visited upon their ND children, and so may attempt to steer them towards NT ideals of what constitutes a good, happy life. Projecting NT definitions of happiness occurs when these ideals are upheld as an expectation and Autistic people are pressured to meet them regardless of whether or not they believe in them.

Therapy recommendations, treatment plans, and individual goals often revolve around the assumption that Autistic people want to act NT. In some cases, neurotypicals assume that encouraging Autistic people to act less Autistic is what's best for them, even though an Autistic person might not say this is what they desire for themselves. If neurotypicals build a foundation of support on a vision of a successful future that the Autistic people in their life do not share, all their efforts will be fruitless and no one will end up happy. As we have discussed, the assumption that Autistic people want to act NT can become problematic because it simply isn't true in all cases all the time, and thus it can encourage unhealthy masking that doesn't lead to real happiness and make Autistic people feel like their opinions and desires are not heard or are inferior to those of the neurotypicals in their lives.

But it's not just external pressure to act NT that may weigh upon Autistic people. It's also external pressure to have the same goals and dreams as neurotypicals—in effect, to share in an NT vision of success. These external influences in turn lead to internal challenges and pressures that can become unduly influential at best, and unbearable at worst.

Getting on the same page

Author and life coach Brian King notes that parents often uphold themselves as the standard of how their child should look and behave. "A lot of parents make the mistake of looking at themselves as the standard for what the real world looks like," he explains, "and they try and steer their kids along that path, and their kid is likely nothing like them, and they're taking a very unique path" (quoted in Gensic 2019, p.66). Some skills and behaviors are necessary for independent living, but there are a lot of ways to be independently successful. King encourages parents to help their Autistic children discover their talents and then offer them an eclectic sample of successful living so they can see interesting and manageable paths to their goals. He explains that there are a lot of different tasks Autistic people might need help with, and there's nothing wrong with your success coming as a result of interdependence (Gensic 2019).

Likewise, would-be advocates and allies who play any role in an Autistic person's life would do well to remember the inherent value of every person's vision of success and happiness, as well as the fact that no one accomplishes their goals entirely on their own. Just as a given NT person may benefit from certain supports, such as higher education, business loans, and so on, in their personal journey to their version of success, Autistic people may need supports tailored to their life goals. When it comes down to it, interdependence is part of any successful life.

It's often the independence piece that may be a challenge for some Autistic people. This is why it's even more important to recognize and get on board with the fact that each and every human being has their own dreams and needs, which will require unique supports. These supports do not diminish the worth of the endeavor. Advocates and allies can deepen their listening skills when it comes to aligning with independence-related goals and dreams that may require tailored and/or innovative scaffolding.

Autism consultant and trainer Sarah Hendrickx explains that one mistake parents, teachers, providers, and others (particularly if they are NT) might make is to assume that their view of a happy life is the same as an Autistic's view, because it's highly possible they are different. Hendrickx says:

> My idea of happiness is solitude and silence or rewriting my schedule for the next month over and over again. If an advocate thinks that happiness is lots of social interaction and reducing my repetitive behaviours, then we do not have the same goal.

According to Hendrickx, advocates must respect the Autistic person's right to choose a suitable life, not necessarily a societal norm.

Tom Iland says that sometimes when advocates ask people on the autism spectrum what they want out of life, or where they see themselves in five years, ten years, etc., a common answer is "I don't know." Parents or other would-be advocates/allies often then begin guessing what that person wants and may well start setting them up on a path that they might not be on board with. "When that happens, the young person's future becomes compromised because they're living a life that is essentially not theirs," Iland (2019) warns, "and that is causing the anxiety, depression, hopelessness, crashing and burning, etc. that so many with autism, particularly adults, are experiencing on a daily basis." Iland recommends that all efforts be made to help people on the spectrum live the life *they* want, rather than trying to change the person to live the life that others want for them:

> Rather than hold young people with autism to the same standards or definition of "success" as their peers or as allies see fit, allies of young people with autism need to make more effort to find out what their young person with autism deems "success" and acknowledge and celebrate the little wins. After all, bringing up one small victory (such as showing up and finishing the race) can help overcome a lifetime of defeat (feelings of rejection, depression, hopelessness, etc. that people with autism know all too well).

Others underscore this point. Marie explains that support shouldn't be directed towards "helping" Autistic people act more NT or fit into NT culture (unless that's what the Autistic person wants, of course). "Sometimes we just want to be helped to be accepted for what we are," Bix Mediocre adds. "Advocates need to be careful not to assume their own experiences are reflective of or representative of anyone else's, and should always seek to have not just their own voices heard but those of others."

Redefining happiness

One reason parents, therapists, and others push Autistic people to be more typical is because they equate happiness with acting more NT, according to Lynch. But happiness doesn't always look the same for Autistic people and neurotypicals. Lynch says: "Sure, someone with neuromotor problems will want to improve their ability to move their body, and someone with anxiety will want to decrease their anxiety. But not everything about autism needs to be changed to be happy." Lynch even points out that some aspects of autism cause happiness:

> I'm sad for my husband, who can't experience the bliss of rubbing my stim blanket. It does nothing for him. I pity neurotypicals when I read articles on how to achieve the elusive "flow state" which is so very Zen, because that is a routine part of autistic existence. Why do you think we get so annoyed when you interrupt us from a stim or a special interest?

Lynch explains that neurotypicals take certain base assumptions for granted, never realizing that the Autistic people in their lives might not think about things in the same way they do. Lynch says that therapists, parents, and other would-be advocates and allies sometimes make the mistake of assuming that normalcy equals happiness, which is why therapy goals are often based on NT milestones and behaviors.

Furthermore, Autistic people who attempt to speak out against the inextricable link between happiness and normalcy are often criticized for a lack of empathy. Lynch explains:

> If we try to explain that normalcy and happiness are not always the same thing, we get accused of not caring about other autistic people who are suffering. We don't want anyone to suffer. We just don't want you to assume that being different is the same as being unhappy.

Not only does respecting the possibility that every Autistic person may frame happiness in their own way make much-needed space for those unique visions, but it may also go a long way towards enabling Autistic people to be happier from the start. This is in part because advocates and allies operating from this basic assumption will participate in developing supports and expressing encouragement that will actually be based on Autistic people's real wants, goals, dreams, and needs. But it will also preclude the imposition of external, "normal" NT ideals of happiness on vulnerable children, youth, young adults, and even adults.

Person-centered advocacy behavior, No. 3: Listen to Autistic people (and your child) over NT parents and other "experts"

Why is this needed?

Many Autistic people report that a particularly frustrating and emotionally draining side of autism advocacy is the disparaging remarks they receive from neurotypicals, especially NT parents. Online commentary is easy to dish out, and Autistic advocates are often on the receiving end of both direct attacks and constant written criticism of their advocacy efforts. Many Autistic advocates say that some NT parents and other would-be NT advocates spend too much time either arguing with Autistic advocates or battling each other, and should instead be listening to the Autistic community.

Spending time at war with parents (or other presumptive NT advocates) or Autistic people whose advocacy views don't match your own can distract from the primary goal of trying to ally with people on the spectrum.

A distracting divide

Nic Laughter, a developer and podcast host who was personally attacked online for expressing his opinion, says that vilifying or discrediting Autistic people simply for having a difference of opinion is a serious problem among advocates:

> I was in an autistic support group on Facebook where I responded to an article that I felt was pretty aggressive and unhelpful. I voiced my opinion (what I felt was very respectfully) and was immediately bombarded by people calling me names, accusing me of victim-blaming, sea-lioning, and more. I was banned from the group, and when I contacted the admin to ask about it, she said, "I will sleep well knowing I removed you and that all of the marginalized autistic people in my group don't have to feel bad for the poor privileged oppressor." Sadly,

> this kind of silencing of any sort of difference of opinion seems to be commonplace in many autistic communities.

Costumer and cookbook author Marie Porter says that Autistic people are often attacked when parents try to discredit their expertise as not being applicable to their life of their child (see Step 7). But sometimes parents can get caught up in fighting for their own advocacy worldview and seeking out and challenging others who differ from it. Porter says:

> This is something I—and many autistic self-advocates I know—encounter on a regular basis, especially on Twitter. "Autism parents" frequently take issue with autistics speaking up for ourselves—especially with regards to ABA—and go on the attack. I've been harassed, "shame tweeted," doxxed, and more...and I haven't even had it as bad as many others have. There have been death threats, in-person confrontations, people calling the employers of autistic people, and more.

Porter says it's impossible to fight for a better life or future for Autistic people if you are attacking them for speaking up, and attempting to silence them because their views don't match your own.

Some NT parents or other putative NT advocates not only criticize people on the spectrum, but also each other. Author Jesse Saperstein points out:

> Autism advocates with different viewpoints may waste energy battling each other or proving they are right instead of working together for accommodations to help those who are struggling in a world that is not always equipped to handle our challenges.

Speaker Kerry Magro suggests that this kind of battling among advocates is a distraction from a mission that will really help Autistic people:

> One of the mistakes autism advocates often make is spending too much time worrying about what other autism organizations are doing versus what they can do to help their mission. There is such a huge divide out there. As we ask for autism acceptance, we need to be more accepting of each other while trying to shape our missions to help one another.

Don't assume all parents (or teachers, or carers, and so on) are NT

Neurodivergence is often an invisible difference. Making assumptions about someone's neurological status is a form of discrimination that diminishes that person's unique personhood. Advocates who are themselves Autistic often encounter this form of discrimination. Writer Ada Hoffmann says that she often sees people "[assume] that caregivers and parents are NT, even though autism has a strong genetic component."

Anyone who wants to advocate and/or ally with an Autistic

person and/or the Autistic community would do well to remember that neurodivergence isn't always obvious from the outside, especially when so many Autistic people have learned (often at great personal cost, as discussed above) to mask. Teachers and therapists, particularly, should avoid adopting an "us versus them" mentality when discussing the needs of an Autistic person with others, including family members and/or other professionals.

Although it might be self-evident that professional best practices would mandate using inclusive and respectful language around both individual "cases" and the differences they represent, Jennifer has repeatedly found herself in settings where autism was discussed in terms she found both personally and ethically demeaning. Would those attitudes have been the same had the professionals in question known she herself was ND? Probably not. That said, the intent of this book is largely to eradicate such attitudes overall. The knowledge that ND people are all around us is a crucial aspect of this growing inclusivity and awareness.

With Autistic people making up a significant portion of the population, there are naturally many #ActuallyAutistic parent and professional voices available to the would-be advocates and allies who make the very worthwhile effort to find them. While Autistic parents, teachers, and other advocates certainly have differing perspectives, their particular personal expertise and life experience should, at the very least, be given added weight as compared to NT opinions about autism.

In the end, the only expert viewpoints that should trump those of #ActuallyAutistic advocates are those of the Autistic people themselves. Of course, both Autistic and NT children and youth go through developmental stages where it would be inappropriate to give them free rein, but it's never too early to encourage them to speak up in whatever way they find most comfortable—nor is it ever too early to listen. And if you've been privileging the perspectives of NT parents or other NT "experts" over those of the people who actually experience neurodivergence in their daily lives, it's also not too late to start listening to Autistic people. As Jennifer notes, you may already know more of us than you think.

Person-centered advocacy behavior, No. 4: Be sensitive to using intent as an excuse

Why is this needed?

Sometimes when advocates, especially parents, are faced with the realization they may have made an advocacy mistake, they either attempt to justify their particular behavior within what they deem an exceptional situation, assert that their intentions were always good, or both.

While good intentions are a necessary basis for any advocacy effort, clinging to intent as an excuse for not changing behavior can diminish our accountability to #ActuallyAutistic viewpoints and limit the effectiveness of advocacy by distracting from the real goal of supporting people on the spectrum.

Staying focused on the ultimate goal

It's very natural to be defensive of your efforts to help other people. Your intentions are good. You likely consulted with several autism experts and conducted your own research online before arriving at the best course of action for the loved one(s) in your life. But the Autistic community reminds us that a defensive mindset is the complete opposite of what is needed to truly make a difference for them. It's important to be open to self-improvement, and being a good parent, teacher, therapist, community advocate, etc. sometimes means you have to step outside of your comfort zone, according to Alix Generous. This is all the more true when children are involved:

> It's always a tragedy to see that the child has to do all the work to change and then the parents feel like they don't have to, when, in actuality, the child's success depends on their ability to be a good parent.

Ally Grace says that advocates clinging to intent and good will is a "major problem." Offering insights that certainly hold true for all would-be advocates, Grace tells parents:

> I understand that it can be upsetting to realise you have been perpetuating harm while thinking you were helping, but to throw this back onto disabled people and to have a self-centred response is really problematic. Intent does not negate harm. The way to fix it, after you realise you have been causing harm, is to learn how to not cause harm anymore. The way to approach this is not to claim that your intentions were good and so you therefore have every right to keep on causing harm. This is not at all helpful.

Tracey Cohen reminds advocates to give themselves leeway to acknowledge their own challenges and then adapt their efforts to newfound knowledge:

> It seems as though many people struggle with one thing or another, whether it is apparent or not. Patience, kindness, and understanding are essential for one and all, as is admitting, learning, and growing from our mistakes.

Acknowledging you have room for improvement or that you have made mistakes opens the possibility for forgiveness and growth, both from the Autistic person and the adult advocate, according to Tom Iland. "For a long time, I thought I had to be perfect because I thought my mother was perfect," he explains. "When she explained that she wasn't, I began to see that I could make mistakes and still be all right and still learn from them." Tom also says that his relationship with his mother eventually began to stunt his personal growth because he started to notice areas where her ideas or actions didn't align with what he wanted. Because she had told him she was his ally, he trusted that her word was "gold." When he realized he had a mind of his own, with his own wants, and needs, it was much easier to live his version of success. He says:

> I have...forgiven my mother for the years of denial and for masking my areas of need. I understand that she was doing the best she could and that those efforts have helped make me into the man that I am today. You'd be amazed how much the words "I'm sorry" and "I love you no matter what" can mean to someone with autism.

Only by acknowledging our missteps and misperceptions can we grow to do better. If you have engaged in counterproductive, even harmful, advocacy attempts, it's important to be forthright about where you went awry, however good your intentions may have been, and to own your mistakes. When possible, start by having an open conversation with any Autistic person(s) involved. Next, mobilize the energy behind your good intentions to ensure your efforts going forward align with the needs and wants of the Autistic people in your life and/or the Autistic community.

Person-centered advocacy behavior, No. 5: Distinguish between meltdowns and tantrums

Why is this needed?

Mainstream culture sees tantrums as a behavior resulting from a person—usually a "spoiled" child—not getting what they want. In addition, tantrums may be perceived as in large part the "fault" of the parent or caregiver, or as immaturity or poor judgment on the part of the person "throwing" the tantrum. Setting aside the question of whether or not these characterizations are true, it's quite clear that a tantrum is something that is looked down upon and judged negatively by most people. So when a person cries, yells, shakes, moves erratically, seems to lose control, or just gets very upset in a public space, those around that person will tend to think they are "acting out." Therefore, those observers will blame the person and/or the responsible adult(s) concerned.

Because of their neurological sensitivities, Autistic children and adults often present external behaviors that may be perceived, incorrectly, as tantrums. They are thus frequently judged as being emotionally weak or unstable, when in fact they are experiencing a physiological reaction to overstimulation. These phenomena are more properly known as meltdowns, and essentially consist of neurological overload manifesting in physical and/or mental consequences. So, being clear on the difference between tantrums and meltdowns is one important distinction to deploy when aiming towards person-centered advocacy and allyship.

It's important to note that not all meltdowns look like tantrums. Some Autistic people express and experience meltdowns that closely resemble panic attacks, with such facets as a racing heart, stomach pain, and rapid breathing. Others, like Jennifer (who learned to mask and hide her "wrong" reactions and ideas about the world from a very young age), experience meltdowns internally, manifesting in negative internal mental cycles that may include absolute hopelessness, disorientation, and/or dissociation. Many other Autistic people will "shut down" when in meltdown mode, becoming paralyzed or inert, unable to act, feel, communicate, and/or think.

A "sensory bucket" metaphor, similar to the spoons concept discussed earlier, has worked well for Jennifer in trying to prevent and manage meltdowns in her family. In this model, we all have a certain amount of sensory input (whether positive, such as interacting with a loved one, or negative, such as a loud noise or strong smell) that our neurological "buckets" can hold. When that bucket is full, any more input may well land us in meltdown territory. Once Jennifer became aware of the underlying causes that contribute to meltdowns, she was able to sometimes stave off these devastating reactions by taking a sensory break.

However, she also felt empowered to inform people—on her blog and elsewhere—about the important distinction between getting/acting upset because you don't get something you want and getting/acting upset because your brain is overloaded. While most Autistic people would prefer to avoid meltdowns when possible (for some, almost any sensory environment or interaction can be overwhelming), public awareness around why meltdowns happen contributes to creating safe space for neurodiversity in general.

Trying a gentle approach

Russell Lehmann recalls that it meant the world to him when a complete stranger helped him recover from a very public meltdown. The nerves of flying combined with the stress of a flight delay that ultimately caused him to miss his keynote speaking event sent Lehmann into a panic attack that left him crying for hours in the airport, while no one approached him. People nearby only stared or gave him strange looks. Lehmann remembers how he felt:

> I stumbled to a quiet corner of the (Salt Lake City) airport and sat down—sobbing, shaking, and rocking back and forth. I ended up staying in that same exact spot for the next seven hours—half of that time still crying, disassociating and losing touch with my physical body. All the while, feeling like I was trapped in a living hell—which I was. (Lehmann, quoted in Litz 2017)

The next day, Lehmann returned to the airport to learn his flight had been delayed yet again. He found an empty ticket counter, sat behind it and began sweating and hyperventilating. An airline employee eventually walked up to him, but Lehmann says he doesn't remember the specifics of the encounter.

> I don't remember a whole lot, 'cause for me, in the midst of a meltdown, my brain literally feels like it's on fire, with a vise grip around it, just getting tighter and tighter. I have a hard time comprehending the simplest sentences. I just feel like I'm on a planet all by myself. (Lehmann, quoted in Glenn 2017)

The airline employee simply crouched down next to him and asked him what was wrong. The employee spoke to Lehmann's mother on the phone and helped to comfort Lehmann by assisting with finding an alternative flight. He then told the crew of Lehmann's plane that Lehmann was nervous about the flight, and he invited the captain to come speak to him before boarding. Lehmann was also allowed to board before the rest of the passengers. Lehmann says that the airline worker may not have known anything about autism, but he was compassionate and connected with him at a human level.

Autistic advocates and allies who seek to foster neurodiversity-friendly schools, homes, practices, and other spaces can set the tone for acceptance by clearly and publicly acknowledging both the causes and manifestations of neurological overload. This sets the tone in our environment for responding proactively and compassionately to any meltdowns, including our own, while also increasing awareness around potential triggers.

Person-centered advocacy behavior, No. 6: Practice appropriate aspects of independent living at every age

Why is this needed?

You can't start too early in providing opportunities to practice independent living, according to Michael John Carley. There are various different levels of skills people can work on at different ages. We need not get caught up in the pacing or timing of these skills but we can nevertheless prioritize progress and continual development that aligns with the desires of the Autistic people we are serving. Practicing appropriate aspects of independent living early and often demonstrates faith in Autistic potential and is necessary to support independence throughout their lives. However, "this all has to be taught within the (borderline simplistic) context of learning another language," Carley cautions. "Otherwise it becomes 'our way of doing things is bad, and the neurotypicals' ways of doing things are right,' which is a death sentence for our self-esteem (it's also often not true)."

Creating step-by-step opportunities

Kat Muir says that it's possible Autistic people may need help and be unable to ask for it, but it is nevertheless important to give them a chance to try things for themselves before assuming they need something done for them: "If we aren't given chances to try, we aren't given chances to learn." Muir says she often needs more practice, not less, to be able to learn something new.

> Maybe brushing teeth solo has too many steps right now. That doesn't mean it's impossible to participate. Focus on putting the toothpaste on the brush without help. After lots of practice and making a new routine, more steps can be added. I know it's easier said than done; so does my dad after trying his best for years to teach me to ride a bike. Dad stresses the

importance of encouraging children to strive for just beyond their current skills. A realistic goal that isn't frustrating, but still keeps the motivation going strong. I completely agree!

Presuming competence (Step 3) means you believe independent living is a possibility and are willing to set up the necessary steps to discover if it can be a reality. Once you've discovered it can be a reality, you can gradually execute a plan to teach independent living skills at an appropriate pace, step by step. In the classroom or a therapeutic setting, this might entail granular discussion and practice of career and life skills linked to independent living goals; in the home, hygiene, cooking, cleaning, self-care, laundry, and other such routine elements of the domestic sphere can be explored in manageable chunks over time.

Finding autism-friendly resources

Often parents and other adults will be able teach independent living skills on their own at a child's own pace. But sometimes (especially in the case of an NT parent with an Autistic child), differences in learning needs might create a stumbling block to teaching these skills, and outside resources tailored to people on the spectrum might come in handy. At such times, remember that #ActuallyAutistics perspectives (Step 6, No. 3) will likely be the most relevant to supporting growth and building pro-independence life skills in other Autistic people.

Author Robyn Steward, for example, interviewed, surveyed, and collected existing research from the Autistic community about their experiences with menstruation in order to create a more autism-friendly guide for people on the spectrum.

She recognized a gap in literature on this topic and wanted to create a resource to help assist with independent living skills:

> I didn't want to write a book about menstruation in the same ways other people had, as I didn't think they were very autism-friendly, so I wanted to try and address the issues that I saw within the current books on the topic. For example, there were no step-by-step photos (with the person in the book photographed in such a way the reader could follow without needing to flip their image in their head), to provide information on menstrual cups, cloth pads, and period underwear, something very much lacking in the current books out there, but vital to the autism community.

ASAN in the U.S.A. (https://autisticadvocacy.org) has also made an effort to create autism-friendly resources on independent living (written for and by Autistic people). Some examples are *Roadmap to Transition: A Handbook for Autistic Youth Transitioning to Adulthood*, *Navigating College: A Handbook on Self Advocacy*, and *Accessing Home and Community-Based Services: A Guide for Self Advocates*. As Autistic self-advocacy gains momentum, there are more and more such resources available online and in print form.

Offering practical experiences and hands-on job opportunities

According to world-renowned author, speaker, and animal expert Dr. Temple Grandin, practical and hands-on job experiences are critical for people on the spectrum. Grandin says she wants to emphasize the practical: "Kids have got to get jobs before they graduate high school. They've got to do volunteer jobs when they're 12, and chores when they're eight, and learn how to work." Grandin advocates for skilled trade experiences while kids are still in school. When she worked in heavy construction, Grandin worked alongside two machinery designers who are Autistic and "have a pile of patents each." Grandin says, "One of the worst things our schools have done is taking out the skilled trade classes—mechanics, welding, drafting. Because these people that I worked with were saved by those classes."

Grandin says that no matter what the career path, it's important for families to expose their Autistic children to the available options. Sometimes kids aren't getting exposed to enough activities and job opportunities to figure out what they might be interested in. "How is a kid going to get into computer programming if he isn't getting exposed? And it's all free, online. Let's expose him to programming... Let's find out if that bug bites."

Grandin was using tools such as hammers, screwdrivers, and pliers in second grade. By fifth grade she was in a shop class and began using a small hand saw. She says she was taught how to use it safely, but this kind of instruction at young ages is uncommon now. Exposure to some of these classes, especially in older grades, is sometimes sacrificed to prioritize other classes.

> I'm seeing a kid flunking three algebra classes, and he should be in shop. And you don't need algebra for the kind of stuff that people I worked with did. What you do need is your old-fashioned elementary school math, the way it used to be

taught. That's unique. How do you find the volume of a tank? How do you find the area of a circle? How do you do the cubic yards of concrete you'd need to pour a job? That's what you have to know.

Grandin was 15 when she was taken to her aunt's ranch to work for a summer. She says if she hadn't been exposed to livestock, she wouldn't have chosen that line of work: "If I hadn't gone to my aunt's ranch when I was 15, I would not have gotten involved in the cattle industry. It is that simple."

Preparing for a job interview

Temple Grandin was able to navigate around the social difficulties of job interviews by developing a portfolio to share. "I showed off the drawings. My interview was simply to show the work—show the portfolio." Grandin says that a portfolio can be created for a variety of different jobs, and recommends parents help their children create one for an interview. Educators and other adults can also do the same. Having that tool in hand will serve as a way to interact more comfortably while highlighting one's unique skills. For example, someone's portfolio might be an app that they programmed, and they could demonstrate how it works. They could then show the code behind the app to demonstrate their coding skill.

Grandin adds that some life routines, such as hygiene, are especially "non-negotiable" when preparing for job interviews. Grandin says she learned to use deodorant when it was slammed down on the table in front of her and she was told, "You stink. Use it." She says it's also important to be on time for the interview and to have a clean look. "Eccentric is fine.

I'm eccentric... If you want purple hair, fine. But it better be neat and clean purple hair."

Interviews and other relatively formal job-related events are one area where an evolving checklist that details the various aspects of the task at hand may be useful. Sometimes it is only through experience that certain key components of interactions become obvious. This is true for people of all neurologies but can be especially so for Autistic people for whom many aspects of NT social and professional life are not self-evident. Jennifer recalls assiduously following one such list for an important meeting, only to look down afterwards and see that her black "professional" clothing was completely covered in white cat hair. Clearly, such lists can and should be amended as necessary, as in the case of "Check clothes for cat hair before leaving for an important meeting." Interview practice with a trusted Autistic person or autism-aware adult, ideally but not necessarily in their field of interest, can also be helpful.

Driving as independence

Another independent living skill Temple Grandin advocates for is teaching Autistic children to drive, if possible, even if it takes them longer than their peers. She describes how she developed motor memory after plenty of practice and well before she ever saw traffic. She offers advice for other adults teaching Autistic youth (or adults) to drive:

> Thank goodness my aunt's mailbox was three miles away, so that gave me six miles of practice every day [when retrieving the mail]. When I had racked up 200 miles, that's when we

started doing traffic. But it's going to take longer because of the multi-tasking issues. Driver's ed just chucks them in the deep end of the pool. You need to be spending more time in a very safe space like a dry field, or a great big parking lot.

Grandin recommends parents consider signing their child up for the classroom portion of driver's ed. In fact, any adult ally/advocate can encourage and support the teen, young adult, and/or adult Autistic person(s) in their life to attend driving classes. But Grandin also advises waiting until that Autistic person has had plenty of practice in safe spaces with people who know them well before they try taking the driving test. "Find a parking lot with no light poles. Nothing to hit. That's where you start. If I hadn't learned to drive, there would have been no career in the cattle industry," she explains. "So there's two things that made that possible: Driving and exposure. Those two things were critical."

As Grandin demonstrates, centering your advocacy and allyship on specifically enabling approaches tailored to the interests and needs of Autistic people can foster genuine life satisfaction. So Step 6 basically invites would-be activists and allies to serve a positive role in Autistic lives by allowing their presence and efforts to be fundamentally shaped by two key realizations: that every Autistic person has their own legitimate and valuable hopes, goals, and dreams; and that, chances are, other Autistic people will inherently and naturally understand more about those hopes, goals, and dreams than the average neurotypical.

SUMMARY GUIDANCE

- Ensure your advocacy message is centered on how a given Autistic person or group is struggling (if applicable) rather than on how difficult it is to advocate for Autistic people and/or raise an Autistic child.
- Search for #ActuallyAutistic expertise to augment your understanding of autism.
- Understand that your life path is likely to be very different from that of the Autistic person or people in your life (yes, even if you are Autistic yourself), so make an effort to support their agenda, not your own, for them.
- Understand that the NT way is not superior, and that the Autistic people in your life may not strive to act NT.
- Parents, avoid arguments with other parents or spending time with parents who habitually discredit the authority of Autistic people because they have a disability, are speaking (or nonspeaking), have a high (or low) IQ, know nothing about their child, or for any other reason.
- Even though your advocacy intentions have been good, understand that good intentions are not enough, and take the next right step to determining effective and respectful ways to support people on the spectrum.
- Recognize the difference between tantrums and meltdowns.

- Explore options for building independent living skills, such as practice interviews.
- Offer plenty of driving experience in safe places prior to trying driver's ed.
- Consider skills trade classes if your Autistic student expresses an interest.

REFLECTION QUESTIONS

? How do I react to my own or my child's (student's/client's/loved one's) differences? Are my reactions in any way contributing to my or an(other) Autistic person's difficulties?

? How can I better seek out and rely upon Autistic expertise?

? What is my vision of true happiness? Success? How is this influenced by NT ideals?

? In what ways have I created opportunities for Autistic independence?

Step 7

Include All Autistic People

> *There's a belief that anyone, or any family, who says they experience both autism and happiness must not really be disabled, and that's just demonstrably not true.*
>
> —JULIA BASCOM

There tend to be varying levels of accepting Autistic input. Some people acknowledge that Autistic input is important but fail to actively access it. Others search for Autistic input that suits the beliefs and agenda they have already decided are important. Some are humble and open to a wide variety of input and willing to consider and learn from opinions that question their current worldview. Within the Autistic community, there are advocates with a variety of different challenges and skill sets (just like advocates within the NT community!); yet, some #ActuallyAutistic expertise gets ignored or dismissed because of how neurotypicals classify and categorize people on the spectrum (high-functioning, low-functioning, verbal, nonverbal, self-diagnosed, etc.). This step asks people to treat ALL Autistic input as valid.

It naturally follows that there will be contradicting opinions and advice, but we can still welcome a lifetime of learning with an open mind and avoid dismissing certain voices as inauthentic without careful consideration. Including all Autistic people in your quest for autism understanding respects the dignity of the Autistic person and is an essential practice for advocates and allies alike who seek to gain holistic, practical advice.

Autism-inclusive behavior, No. 1: Defer to Autistic people as the experts in autism

Why is this needed?

We've discussed this topic more broadly in earlier steps. Here, we take a more in-depth view of the subject, in light of the awareness gained in prior steps and with reference to specific approaches and situations. Despite the fact that people on the spectrum have an intimate and uniquely significant understanding of the Autistic condition, parents and other advocates sometimes overestimate the importance of the advice of NT therapists or books they've read by NT authors. Some families, upon receiving a diagnosis, will pour their energy into researching autism. They might read books their doctors or therapists have recommended (or written). They might have regular meetings with therapists, conduct research online, and attend support groups. But this type of narrow immersion can give families a false sense of confidence in doing what's best for their children. Likewise, autism "experts" who rely too heavily on NT research and opinions, perhaps viewing Autistic people as "study subjects" all the while, do a great disservice to their Autistic clients and the Autistic community by essentially ignoring the very real human beings they intend to serve.

Overconfidence in personal or professional expertise from neurotypicals can be problematic because it can lead to advocacy efforts that might not be aligned with actual Autistic desires. Misguided advocacy efforts can also perpetuate stigmas about autism and hinder progress for Autistic people both personally and as a (very diverse) community. We've compiled several actionable tips from #ActuallyAutistic perspectives, which are intended to build pro-neurodiversity connections from which to nourish advocacy and allyship efforts.

Finding an #ActuallyAutistic expert base for personal growth

"I think one of the hardest things to deal with is when non-autistic people assume that because they've read one book or attended one workshop, or know one autistic person, that they're suddenly experts," says Paula Sanchez. Author Anlor Davin recommends:

> If anyone is going to claim that they are an "autism advocate" (or a doctor for that matter), it might be helpful to require that this person lives constantly with one autistic young person for at least six months: autism is often so perplexing, it is hard to fathom. Sometimes neurotypical autism advocates adopt a know-it-all attitude about things they don't really comprehend, much to the dismay of autistic people themselves (and possible harm to younger autistics).

Many other Autistic people agree, and even suggest that overconfidence is a problem not only with those who have done little research or have limited experience, but also with those who spend many hours trying to understand autism, but little, if any, time accessing Autistic expertise. Special education and disability rights attorney Michael Gilberg says that sometimes people assume they know how Autistic people are thinking, which has personally caused him challenges with others:

> I think one common mistake many people make is thinking they understand how autistic people see the world or think. I had experiences where friends or others would do things they thought were funny, but to me were upsetting, and not funny. Neurotypical individuals need to understand our reactions are not going to be the same as theirs.

As these perspectives demonstrate, the importance of actively searching for ways to connect with, and learn from, #ActuallyAutistic people and advocates cannot be overstated. The many Autistic advocates mentioned in this book should provide a great launchpad for this necessary process

Combating stigma

Listening to and uplifting marginalized voices helps reduce stigma surrounding the Autistic community. While this book amplifies more than a hundred such perspectives and provides ample information to seek out a range of additional sources (including interviewees), there are still many, many more Autistic perspectives available to anyone who seeks them out. For example, in *Trauma, Stigma, and Autism: Developing Resilience and Loosening the Grip of Shame,* Gord Gates (2019) wanted to advocate for Autistic people who often have their own voices marginalized. So he reached out to members of this community, and constantly sought their input and advice throughout his project.

Taking her cue from many activist communities, from civil rights to feminism, Jennifer has long felt that one of the most effective ways to combat stigma around autism was through speaking up publicly (in whatever medium one is comfortable with) about one's own neurodivergence. While she is in no way comfortable as a public speaker and realizes that a public role is certainly not for everyone, her writing became over time a personally uplifting outlet for spreading autism awareness and fighting stigma.

Would-be NT autism advocates and allies can help to combat negative myths and stereotypes about autism by seeking out, deferring to, and sharing neurodiversity-friendly, Autistic-driven voices (again, such voices may be expressed in a variety of mediums) and information. Of course, Autistic people can do the same, but they might also consider adding creative or other types of publicly accessible (be they local or more widely disseminated) efforts of their own to the mix.

Acknowledging NT filters

Even though some neurotypicals might think they understand autism, they must remember that the way they process the world is fundamentally different than that of the Autistic person. In some ways, neurotypicals miss out on experiencing the world in truly remarkable ways, according to *The Reason I Jump* author Naoki Higashida:

> So how do people with autism see the world, exactly? We, and only we, can ever know the answer to that one! Sometimes I actually pity you for not being able to see the beauty of the world in the same way we do. Really, our vision of the world can be incredible, just incredible... (Higashida *et al.* 2017, p.59)

Unfortunately, not only can neurotypicals miss some elements of the unique beauty of the world, as Higashida points out, but their NT filters become problematic when they assert their perceptions on others. There is always the risk they will subconsciously misinterpret Autistic behavior and impose their NT views and values through a "neurotypical lens," warns psychotherapist Dr. Natalie Engelbrecht:

> One example is the idea that we are like introverts. Introverts have a system that is very sensitive to dopamine so they do not need much social interaction to feel rewarded. We have a dopamine system that functions differently so we do not get dopamine for social interactions. Think of it this way: an introvert is holding a cup and a couple of drops fill it; the autistic is also holding a cup, but nothing goes into it, and we are wondering what the neurotypical is getting from the social interaction. Neurotypicals think we just need alone time. But unlike the introvert who, despite needing a lot of alone time, still gets rewarded from social interaction, we tend to get rewarded from pursuing our special interests instead. It's not like autistic people lack a social world necessarily, but in our experience social interaction is a means to exchange information and learn—we would rather not have social interaction for the sake of it, and especially not small talk.

But some Autistic people report that even though someone can have a good grasp of the Autistic condition, they still shouldn't be speaking for them. Austin Shinn says, "I've seen very well-meaning people speak out as experts when we could do so as well." This is especially common when neurotypicals are perceiving Autistic people through an NT filter that makes assumptions about verbal ability or mandates a certain type or speed of response. Terra Vance says that some NT advocates learn about autism but then assume Autistic people aren't capable of speaking for themselves or that they need people to speak for them. Vance asserts:

> We don't. We need neurotypical people to use their positions of privilege to bring us to the table and allow us to speak for ourselves. We need them to share their platform with us so that we can be advocates for ourselves.

Not only do Autistic people take issue with neurotypicals who try to speak for them without giving their own voices a platform, they also explain that this usurping of expertise can lead to misalignment with the real desires of the people neurotypicals are advocating for. Writer/artist Austin Jones says:

> Sometimes I feel like what advocates do is very forced. I understand it's for a good cause, but I've met a lot of people on the spectrum who don't want people to know they are on the spectrum and so people who promote autism awareness don't get that.

Savannah Logsdone-Breakstone says she also has well-intentioned friends who misunderstand the nuances of personal advocacy:

> I've also had friends who were really well intentioned get outraged and stand up on my behalf even when it's a battle that I've chosen not to fight that day. Sometimes I have to choose what battles to fight for really complicated reasons, and when someone assumes that they know these things, it actually does more harm than good. Sometimes something is a minor inconvenience to me, but worth being able to access an environment so I can fight for something else. Maybe I'll get to that inconvenience later but know dealing with it now will make it harder to do another thing that is already difficult to get changed!

There's a seemingly simple solution to the problem of NT filters. Start by observing, thereby enabling Autistic people to speak and act for themselves if they choose to do so. And if you are moved to take some sort of action, ask questions before doing so—and listen carefully and respectfully to the response. And by the way, Autistic people can be prone to similar biases, since NT filters can be ingrained by neuro-normative life experience.

Autism-inclusive behavior, No. 2: Acknowledge and respect the authority of all Autistic people of varying skills sets

Why is this needed?

A common criticism of the Autistic community is that the loudest voices are those on the "high-functioning end" of the spectrum. As noted in the Introduction, many in the Autistic community reject this label. Not only is it inaccurate and misleading, but people often use it as a compliment, when the impact can be the opposite. Amazon driver and parent Ben Kartje explains:

> When a doctor or another person refers to me as being on the "high-functioning" end of the spectrum, that doesn't really make sense to me. Does that mean that I'm almost "normal"? What pops into my head is "There's Ben; he's that dot right there!" Like they're graphing the whole thing. I don't really understand what they are basing their decision on. What is normal? Do people think it is a compliment to be considered "high-functioning"? To be considered "almost normal"? (Kartje quoted in Gensic 2019, p.15)

For this reason and others detailed below, neurodiversity advocates and allies, including those on the spectrum, would do well to replace functioning labels and hierarchical characterizations of Autistic ways of being with both a willingness to consider a wide range of Autistic perspectives and the active intent to see every Autistic as a person entitled to their own opinions.

Avoiding inaccurate labeling

In Step 4, C. L. Lynch was quoted on the importance of avoiding autism severity labels and how it made more sense to talk about each Autistic person's specific struggles rather than comparing them as "being better or worse off than someone else who also has autism." Even though autism is often referred to as a "spectrum," many people discuss it as if it were a "gradient" (Lynch 2019b). As an example, another spectrum, the visible spectrum, contains several different colors. But people typically don't discuss colors the same way they discuss people on the autism spectrum. "When people discuss colours, they don't talk about how 'far along' the spectrum a colour is" (Lynch 2019b). Autism is currently defined as a variety of different conditions, but you need not present with all conditions to be considered Autistic (and you also can't only have one—or that condition is called something else!). It's complicated! Yet society tries to simplify this highly varied way of being with severity labels.

While some mistakenly use functioning labels as praise, others erroneously deploy them as an excuse to dismiss Autistic expertise. For example, "That person doesn't have real autism. She's high-functioning. She doesn't know what it's like to have real autism," or, conversely, "That person is low-functioning, how can I trust what they say?" Including ALL Autistic people in your quest for autism understanding respects the dignity of Autistic personhood and helps you gain the best insight to support those you love and/or work with. The labels and categorizations neurotypicals prefer to assign to Autistic people that prevent them from accepting and integrating Autistic expertise aren't always accurate or respectful, and thus neurotypicals (and even some Autistic people) end up missing out on crucial advice to support their advocacy efforts.

Author/illustrator Georgia Lyon says she sees NT allies often try to neatly label people within the Autistic community as high- or low-functioning. But autism is not a linear spectrum. As an example, Lyon explains that an Autistic person might not diverge too much from a neurotypical's ability to communicate, but they may have extreme sensory processing issues (which sounds a lot like Jennifer):

> The labels of high and low-functioning create a dichotomy between autistic people that are likely to be successful and those that are less likely. However, this system misses that many autistic people simultaneously possess incredible strengths and face daunting challenges, preventing us from seeing the unique needs of each autistic person. From my life experience, I can say that success originates from parents' and educators' ability to meet autistic people where they are at rather than the exact diagnosis a doctor gives them.

Honoring all experiences as authentic

Validating the experiences of those on the spectrum is foundational to learning anything about autism. Ada Hoffmann says she would like to see more people understand that autism can look like a lot of different things and that many people mask. Hoffmann says autism goes beyond the stereotypes visible on TV. "I still see a lot of invalidation of autistic self-advocates, either because we don't look stereotypical enough, or because it's assumed that if we can type about our problems, we've never had really bad ones," she says.

Author/speaker Liane Holliday Willey explains that there needs to be a fine balance between understanding people on the spectrum to have challenges and recognizing the unlimited potential they have in a variety of areas: "My biggest complaint is when advocates dismiss my challenges as not challenging enough, because, apparently, I, like others, can make autism look too easy to navigate." She says that just because people on the spectrum often learn how to mask in some situations, it "doesn't mean we can think along the same lines as current social standards would have us." She continues:

> At the same time, I don't like it when advocates think we are affected in ways that automatically mean we couldn't possibly fend for ourselves, get a decent job to our liking, understand social dialogue, engage in relationships, etc. If advocates engage in honest and open and regular dialogue with us, they will get to know how autism affects us as individuals and, from there, we can all learn how to relate to one another.

Regardless of how Autistic people present and how those around them perceive their capabilities in a variety of life areas, we can nevertheless appreciate each person's expertise and potential for teaching us something new. And we don't need to label the "functional" viability of that Autistic human being—or the perspectives they impart.

Autism-inclusive behavior, No. 3: Remember that while one particular Autistic person may have unique autism characteristics, they may nonetheless have broadly useful insights

Why is this needed?

Not only should advocates respect Autistic expertise as authentic, we can take one step further and acknowledge how their insights may be useful to our lives, even if the Autistic expert presents in different ways than our children, siblings, students, clients, partners, colleagues, or we ourselves do. Each person on the spectrum is an expert on how autism impacts them. However specific, their unique insights may nonetheless bear wisdom, understanding, or connection for another person.

Some Autistic people study autism more generally as well, and work to advocate for and with many different people on the spectrum. Just like neurotypicals who work as allies with the Autistic community to learn about and advocate for the awareness, understanding, and needs of Autistic people, other Autistic people also do this work for the good of the Autistic community. Yet, sometimes an Autistic person's expertise is dismissed by neurotypicals because that particular Autistic person's life experience is different from that of the neurotypical's child or the Autistic people they live or work with.

If, however, you are able to recognize that even though one particular Autistic person may have unique autism, they still may have broadly useful insights, you'll be opening up your family (practice, classroom, home, etc.) to a trove of potentially useful advice and insights. This open-mindedness also demonstrates to your family (and/or Autistic loved one(s)/student(s)/client(s)) that you respect and value Autistic expertise.

Welcoming a variety of different autism representations

Sometimes people get too caught up in advocating for the needs of a very specific type of autism at the expense of helping others on the spectrum or being open to making connections between different manifestations of autism. This narrow-mindedness can overlook practical insights to be found in a variety of different places and people. Chris Bonnello recalls how when Julia was unveiled as an Autistic *Sesame Street* character, some parents objected to her because her autism was "not severe enough" and wasn't an "accurate" depiction of autism: "What they actually meant was it wasn't a depiction of their own child's autism, therefore it did not serve their advocacy purposes."

Anna Nibbs explains that she has been made to feel that because she can "speak" for herself, she can't make a contribution to advocating for other nonspeaking Autistic people. She is frustrated with this assumption and asks people to recognize the authority of all Autistic people and the potential for them to help serve all types of people on the spectrum.

> This is insulting to autistics of all types or levels of support need. I can't, of course, speak for all autistics—I can only speak for myself. But I do share some common experiences with many other autistics, speaking or nonspeaking, high or low support need, with or without comorbid intellectual disabilities. The more a neurotypical carer or parent can learn from the experiences of all the different autistic people "speaking" out there, the more likely it is that they might stumble upon that one piece of information or nugget of wisdom that really helps them and the autistic person or people they love and care for.

Savannah Logsdon-Breakstone says that assuming that Autistic people are unable to advocate for other Autistic people's needs (that don't match their own) or don't care about others' differing needs is "absolutely wrong." She says, "This is related to assuming that an NT parent of a non-speaking autistic knows more about autism than an autistic who speaks all or part of the time, which happens a lot."

Marie Porter says she has regularly seen Autistic people attacked online for their advocacy (and experienced it herself). She says, "I have been harassed, 'shame tweeted,' doxxed, and more...and I haven't even had it as bad as many others have." She asserts that you can't advocate for a better future for Autistic people by attacking them for speaking up or attempting to silence them.

> A lot of the attacks I see online are about trying to discredit autistics, to render their views somehow less applicable. Many times, this comes as some variation of "You're not like my kid!" (said to an adult!) or "You must be really high-functioning if you can tweet." There are even attacks on nonverbal autistics, claiming that they're faking being nonverbal, because they can type! (I'll never understand that.)

Porter explains that listening to the people who were Autistic kids at one time will help you learn and prepare a better future for your Autistic kid. She cites parent defense of ABA as one example and says, "If you're feeling the need to shut autistics up when it comes to autistic issues, you should take a long, hard look at what you're actually advocating for."

Marcelle Ciampi suggests re-examining the *DSM-5* (APA

2013) and the responsibility the authors have in categorizing different conditions, rather than blaming a cultural movement for any distraction from those with higher support needs. The neurodiversity movement is based on individuals' right to equity and equality. "I don't think we should blame people for uprising to be heard, and they shouldn't be shamed, ostracized, isolated, and shunned," she explains. To that end, Ciampi advocates for creating "a safe space for mature and comfortable conversations, and then working toward unity, and not separating and segregating a culture of people that are already segregated and separated."

Seeking out and truly listening to an inclusive range of #ActuallyAutistic viewpoints will nourish the efforts of anyone who hopes to ally and advocate with Autistic people. And it will genuinely contribute to progress in awareness and acceptance on several levels. On a larger scale, when we welcome all people in the autism community, that community is enriched immeasurably. At the same time, on a more personal level, the diverse members who comprise the larger group will likely benefit, too, not least because they'll be spared the historically prevalent dismissal and painful stereotyping borne of ignorance.

SUMMARY GUIDANCE

- Avoid using functioning labels to describe autism, whether as a "compliment" (see "good intentions" above) or justification for dismissal.
- Avoid dismissing "high-functioning" expertise. Keep an open mind and look for similarities

between Autistic advocate experiences and the Autistic people in your life.

- Respect that speaking Autistic advocates may have the knowledge and expertise to be allies for people who don't present like they do.
- Recognize that autism can be an invisible disability and that "high-functioning" people can still experience daily struggles.
- When faced with differences in opinion about Autistic advocacy and allyship, try to hold space for ideas you don't yet understand and privilege #ActuallyAutistic expertise over NT-filtered points of view as you move towards resolution.
- Look for a variety of different autism representations to gain a better insight into the Autistic condition.

REFLECTION QUESTIONS

? Have I read or listened to Autistic people who present in a variety of different ways? What research or engagement goals do I have to improve my understanding and acceptance of autism?

? How might I develop a more welcoming attitude towards diverse perspectives and Autistic ways of being?

? What can I personally do to combat stigma in my

social environments (classroom, practice, workplace, neighborhood) and/or private life (home, family, friendships, etc.)?

? What are my motivations for engaging with Autistic people?

? How have I engaged with Autistic people online? How open am I to advice?

? Could any of my comments or questions be interpreted as critical or aiming to discredit someone on the spectrum?

STAGE THREE

Public Advocacy for Autism Understanding and Acceptance

You will likely adopt a variety of different advocacy and allyship roles in your lifetime. Some of you will find yourselves inadvertently becoming an advocate outside of your home or workspace. This could be as simple as politely correcting a misunderstanding about autism among friends. It also could occur in an IEP meeting, as you offer educators some background about autism that might help them better serve your child. Or perhaps you work in the education or medical field and you might be asked to deliver training about autism to your colleagues. Others will choose this role for themselves and seek out opportunities to ally with the Autistic community at local, regional, or national events. Still others will want to focus their efforts at the policy and/or political level, working for more opportunities, inclusion, and civil rights as desired and defined by the Autistic community.

We come to autism advocacy and allyship in as many ways as there are human beings touched by neurodiversity. In addition, our efforts can be very private and personal (for ourselves or our child, in our family or marriage), hyperlocal to our community, national, international, somewhere in-between—or all of the above! They can be occasional, frequent, constant, spontaneous, intentional and/or highly planned. They may be grounded in being Autistic, or knowing an Autistic person or many Autistic people, and/or even entirely abstract and based on principle. What we have attempted to convey in this book, however, is that whatever your style and methods of advocacy/allyship, they should fundamentally be directed by #ActuallyAutistic voices. This becomes, arguably, even more important in the shift to a more public role, in which we may be looking to change not only minds, but laws, policies, and more. The key to allying with the Autistic community on a larger platform is to maintain constant, respectful engagement with

Autistic people. This section illustrates what that respectful connection looks like and identifies ways to maintain forward progress in preserving and furthering Autistic rights.

Step 8

Connect Respectfully with Actually Autistic People

If you have a platform, elevate autistic voices.

— MARIE PORTER

While we have long been unrepresented and underrepresented in mainstream culture and organizations, Jennifer has been heartened to see a proliferation of ND perspectives become increasingly available and influential online and elsewhere. While these perspectives are by no means univocal or unanimous, the growing ND presence alone is a leap in the right direction. Still, there is plenty of room for improvement.

Moved by the preponderance of autism in her immediate family, about six years ago, Jenna began regularly interviewing Autistic people and publishing interviews on her website as a way to connect parents and caregivers with Autistic voices and expertise. The most common request she hears from

Autistic people is a resounding desire for advocates and allies to connect with the Autistic community. Again and again, the Autistic people she interviewed reiterated the same basic requests: They ask others to listen to what Autistic people are saying, to read Autistic-authored literature, and follow Autistic advocates on social media. They want researchers to include all Autistic people in their research and prioritize Autistic expertise at conferences and other educational events. They want their presence valued and not tokenized and to be treated like people and not study subjects. They also want their allies to support organizations that prioritize all of the above. This chapter explores in detail what a respectful connection with the Autistic community looks like and how you can engage with the Autistic community in this way.

Respectful connection strategy, No. 1: Reach out to the Autistic community (take the first step)

Why is this needed?

Autistic advocates are telling us it is not enough to agree that Autistic input is important. We need to actively seek it out and integrate it into our advocacy and allyship strategies. Sarah Kathryn says, "The root of the problem with public autism advocacy programs is that they ignore and exclude autistic people." The Autistic community should be at least as valued a resource as any experts, such as doctors, educators, or therapists. Depending on the knowledge and experience of the Autistic people and autism-focused groups you may be involved with (and/or the knowledge and experience of the care team(s) you may have assembled or taken part in), you may well find that #ActuallyAutistic expertise informs/

elevates your current approach or calls it into question. We need to actively engage with the Autistic community because the more you reach out to the Autistic community, the more familiar you will actually be with autism. With that greater, deeper knowledge, you will not only be better equipped to meet the needs of the Autistic people you love and/or work with, you'll be able to further the public presence, representation, awareness, acceptance, and inclusion of neurodiversity in ways that those people will actually support and benefit from. Many Autistic people have lived experiences of autism they want to share with the world. They intimately understand the Autistic condition better than any NT doctor, therapist, teacher, or parent will ever be able to. Any and all genuine autism allyship and advocacy must align with and amplify that understanding.

Finding Autistic voices

Kieran Rose says that the person best equipped to talk about autism is the Autistic person:

> Someone who has experienced the emotions, the sensory overwhelm, the anxiety and fear and confusion, the trauma and invalidation; someone who has, by taking the difficult route, established a way of communicating those things. Things that, unless you have expressed them to the depths that we have, you cannot have any ability to understand what they mean, how they feel, or how exhausting they are.

Rose is adamant that while non-Autistic views are important, current culture views Autistic viewpoints as the least important and so they are the most drowned out, which is an "enormous problem."

When we attempt to amplify #ActuallyAutistic perspectives, we are making inroads to addressing this unjust disparity. But we are also acknowledging the worth and unique aspects of the Autistic experience, which entails the objective recognition that only Autistic people can give neurotypicals a glimpse into autism. For example, professionals working with Autistic people will find their practices much improved by incorporating feedback from Autistic people themselves, rather than basing their work merely on neuro-normative, autism-objectifying research findings. Likewise, Autistic parents are the only ones able to come close to truly understanding their Autistic child's life experiences. Neurotypicals can guess or imagine what it's like to be Autistic, and NT parents most certainly know their Autistic children well, but NT parents don't know what it's like to *be* their child.

Programmer/student Avery Rowe says that it might be upsetting for parents if they are told they don't know what it's like to be their child, but they shouldn't take this as an insult: "Take it as an opportunity: there is a rich resource of people who can understand some of your child's experiences even better than you can – use them!" Similar opportunities abound for those who work with Autistic people. Kmarie adds that even though Autistic people have diverse opinions (for example, some believe in the social model of disability, while others prefer the medical model), "our divergence on topics should not stop people from listening to us and gleaning information on how to parent or care give to those with autism."

RoAnna Sylver says that finding Autistic voices and then *listening* to them is also important. She brings up how she's seen some neurotypicals who insist on using person-first language despite the objections of the Autistic community. "I understand wanting to protect your child/relative/friend from an ableist world, but a good way to start is with yourself, and actually listening to them and their individual needs."

Tara Campbell points out that personal stories from Autistic people are often more helpful than parents' perspectives, which tend to focus on martyr stories rather than helpful supports. "I don't want to dismiss the agony of having to parent disabled children in a society that offers little to no supports," she explains. "I know how isolating and hopeless it feels when the world is telling you that you've got to fix your kid so they'll somewhat conform to the norms, and you're on your own emotionally, socially, and financially." But Campbell adds that reading about autism through the lens of the non-Autistic person "will only feed your misery." NT support groups can have this effect as well. Instead, she recommends engaging with the Autistic community and tells family advocates to "surround yourself with people who accept your child as they are, that's it." Autistic people and anyone else who cares about them may also find the Autistic community a good source of such acceptance.

Increasing Autistic representation

Many Autistic advocates believe that better Autistic representation is needed in the media, in the professional world, and in positions of power in autism organizations. Improved Autistic representation can shatter stereotypes, normalize autism, cross the cultural divide, and communicate to the Autistic community that there are other people like them in the world.

Kieran Rose says that the views of NT advocates are the ones often showcased in articles, on social media, and in the news:

> Charities with no Autistic voices on their boards or hierarchy (aside from the odd token member who only speaks the company line) are given preference publicly over Autistic-led organisations such as ASAN, or Autistic UK, for example. We are treated like children who are shushed while the adults speak about them. When you look at other marginalised and stigmatised groups, very few are so poorly represented in their own narrative, let alone the wider societal one, or spoken for and over by others, the way Autistic people are.

As another example, writer/speaker Courtney Johnson mentions that the first season of the Netflix series *Atypical* was criticized for not including Autistic voices in its creative process.

Poet/teacher Daniel Bowman Jr. says one of the reasons he first started writing about his experience with autism was because he wanted to increase the representation of creative Autistic people.

> I wanted to add another image to what R. P. Blackmur called "the stock of available reality" [see Wolfe n.d.]. I had only seen autism associated with computer hackers, *Rain Man*, and scientists like Temple Grandin. I wanted to show people that you can be autistic and be a creative writer, an artist, too. The popular imagination has made little or no room for that yet. It's the old idea of representation: "If you can see it, you can be it." I want autistic kids who wish to paint or make movies

> or write novels or do anything, to see that it's possible. The ways we do it will be different, but it is possible.

Roy Dias is a science fiction writer of the *Aspeans* series and was inspired to create characters that helped the world understand the experience of people on the spectrum. Dias says that society labels different people as strange and not worth their time, and he wanted to create stories that illustrated the hurt this treatment brings to Autistic people. "Through science fiction, I tried to show the readers that we sometimes feel like aliens and that we are sometimes treated like aliens too."

RoAnna Sylver and Ada Hoffmann are both fiction writers who are also working to increase Autistic representation in literature. Hoffmann says that Autistic representation in fiction is improving, but there is plenty of work to do in terms of educating readers beyond superficial awareness. She adds:

> We shouldn't underestimate the power of representation. Even a flawed portrayal can be intensely helpful for readers who are not used to seeing representation at all. But that doesn't mean we as authors should settle for something with obvious flaws.

Hoffmann says her favorite portrayals are not only accurate, but they "involve autistic characters who have agency and get to do cool things." The stories that feature these characters take seriously the need for others to respect and accept them and show understanding of what that actually entails, explains Hoffmann. On the other hand, Hoffmann says her least favorite books are the ones that portray the Autistic character as a burden, "someone that it's okay to use, talk down to, violate the boundaries of, or forcibly 'fix,' because they are too weird or difficult to be taken seriously."

Token and casual use of autism in fiction and other media can also feel painful to Autistic people and contribute to ongoing discrimination. One of Jennifer's least favorite occurrences is when she is enjoying a book and suddenly comes upon a random "autistic" character, usually slotted in to represent some stereotype developed in NT culture. Hoffmann recommends the article "Autistic representation and real-life consequences" by Elizabeth Bartmess (2015) for a more detailed discussion of the tropes in fiction that can be hurtful to Autistic people.

Sylver describes some of the humanization necessary in an Autistic fiction character that she created and loves:

> Anh Minh "Annie" Le—she's gloriously autistic and doesn't give a single shit. She has a badass motorcycle, a helmet specially designed to shut out painful light and noise stimuli, and a cool black leather jacket with studs that spell out different words on the back when she goes nonverbal. (All things I wish I had!) She also has EDS, a connective tissue disorder that leads to joints dislocating really easily (which I do have), and wears cool metal braces that end up looking like dystopian armor and...I just really love her.
>
> Mostly because she cares so hard. (Which also ties into her being aromantic and asexual; everybody thinks aro/ace people are emotionless robots too.) Annie loves her friends and found family with every cell in her body, and she's a direct combat-book face-kick to the idea that autistic people are cold or uncaring, "lack of empathy" aside.
>
> She's so important to me to write, and I've heard the same

> from many readers, because what little autistic representation we do get tends to be the same: young white men who do display unfeeling/robotic tendencies, clearly written by people who don't understand autistic people at all. I want to show that we're not all the same, and there's as much variety among us as the rest of the population.
>
> Also...damn, it's just fun to write her kicking ass and rocking out and being herself, unapologetically. We need that too.

NT authors can develop stereotypical portrayals in their writing that can be humiliating and frame the definition of what disability looks like and how it is discussed in society, says writer Lyn Miller-Lachman. Miller-Lachman recommends NT authors use sensitivity readers to check their work. She adds:

> I suggest consulting more than one because we autistic authors are very different in terms of personalities, strengths, and experiences. A lot of sensitivity readers are writers themselves, but for a wider range of experiences, you should work with people who aren't writers as well.

Miller-Lachman says that it's also best practice to buy, read, and help promote books written by Autistic authors and create opportunities for Autistic authors by mentoring and advocating on their behalf. "None of us want to hear that there's no slot for our books because the publisher(s) just bought them from an NT author."

Inviting Autistic people to be public autism experts

Another way to respectfully connect with the Autistic community is to use your privilege to offer Autistic people the public opportunity to share their autism expertise. This behavior combats tokenism and is another way to increase Autistic representation. Actor Mickey Rowe says that he sees autism advocacy organizations talk to parents of Autistic children, but they often leave Autistic people out of the public conversations. Rowe says this is an advocacy misstep: "After all, each of those autistic children whose parents are being talked to will one day be an autistic adult."

Speaker/writer Nera Birch says that neurotypicals sometimes don't even consider Autistic input, simply because it never crosses their mind.

> I think the biggest mistake people make is to not remember that autistics are our own best experts. One of my favorite presentations I ever wrote is about sensory issues. I was sitting in a conference proposal meeting, listening to NTs bemoaning the fact that there are no sensory experts, such as a doctor or psychologist out there. I raised my hand and said I could whip up a little something, considering I live the sensory experiences every day. It just never occurred to them that I was somewhat of an expert.

Similarly, Georgia Lyon says it's "troubling" that there can be entire conferences devoted to autism and not one Autistic person is invited to speak:

> Why is it that doctors who have studied autism are always invited and those that have lived with autism are not? Does 15, 20, or 40 years of personal experience living with autism not count as expertise? Until neurotypical allies include autistic people in conversations about our wants and needs, we will not live in a society that treats autistic people justly and equitably.

Sometimes events will include one or two token Autistic people, says attorney Sam Crane, but avoid offering them the title of expert: "I've seen events in which there was one token self-advocate on the panel, but they were only asked to 'share their story,' while everyone else was invited to share their expertise or express opinions on policy issues." Attorney Larkin Taylor-Parker agrees: "If the extent of inclusion is letting an Autistic person speak about personal experience as a volunteer on a panel, there is probably tokenization going on." It is a mistake to assume there's a distinction between "self-advocates" and "experts," Crane adds. "Autistic advocates are also often experts! I've seen a lot of advocacy events in which there was an entire panel of speakers, and not a single self-advocate." Crane invites neurotypicals to take ownership of their privilege and active roles in correcting this: "If you're being invited to an event that isn't accessible to autistic people, or in which there isn't meaningful autistic participation and leadership, refuse to participate until that changes."

Similarly, Marie Porter says there are ways people can actively correct the imbalance of power in autism expertise. If you are being interviewed about autism, Porter recommends asking the reporter how many Autistic people will be interviewed and offering contact information if this is something they haven't considered. Porter says, "It's absolutely mind blowing how often articles will be written about autism—or even specific autistics—that don't quote any autistics, or even the person the article is supposed to be about!" She says the same principle should apply if you are invited to speak at a public event:

> I was once on a panel about how to thrive on the spectrum, and only two of the five speakers were autistic. The moderator was an "autism mom" that was a fan of Autism Speaks. The two of us autistics on the panel were constantly being spoken over and "corrected." It was a horrific experience.
>
> One panelist—whose only credential is that she "tended to date autistic men"—responded to an autistic audience member who spoke about being slapped by her parents for "saying the wrong thing" by telling that girl to "just remember that your parents were doing the best they could, with what they had."

Porter says that these kinds of situations can be prevented by centering autism events on Autistic voices.

After recognizing the lack of representation Autistic people have in autism training and events, Irish speaker/consultant Evaleen Whelton began designing her own training courses to deliver. She designed a social skills/"non-autistic culture and language" course for Autistic kids. Whelton also delivers courses all over Ireland to parents and professionals so they can learn the skills to help the Autistic people in their lives. Upon receiving her diagnosis, Whelton immediately reached out to the Autistic community for a two-way relationship of support and allyship. She organized two Walk in Red events (a virtual and social media campaign intended to spread positive awareness of neurodiversity) and several talks featuring Autistic voices within months of receiving her diagnosis, and has also organized Ireland's first-ever all-Autistic conference.

Whelton's strategies exemplify some of the many ways we can actively take (the first) steps to reach out and find Autistic voices. Public advocacy and allyship may then entail efforts towards building #ActuallyAutistic representation in the arts and media and beyond, using NT privilege to amplify and disseminate ND perspectives, and/or increasing the public and professional presence of Autistic expertise.

Respectful connection strategy, No. 2: Conduct inclusive research

Why is this needed?

There's a lot to consider when it comes to autism research. Our own perspectives impact how we internalize what we read, see, and hear. And many, many elements, including inevitable biases, shape the research itself. For these reasons and more, it's always important to approach autism research with certain factors in mind, whether you are Autistic or NT, and whether your role involves designing, doing, and/or participating in research or simply learning from it. Important questions include:

1. Who is conducting the research?
2. Is the research conducted in as unbiased a fashion as possible?

3. What is the sample size?
4. Who is funding the research?

Including Autistic people in the planning and development of professional, academic, and/or scientific research methods is likely to improve the validity and usefulness of the conclusions drawn. Additionally, advocates who conduct both qualitative (non-numerical) and quantitative (numerical) research will gain a wide perspective of the Autistic experience. Lay people relying on research for their own learning and advocacy purposes can also deploy this strategy to vet any findings around autism they come across.

Utilizing both quantitative and qualitative research

Keeping the Autistic community at the foundation of all research creation and implementation efforts is a great guide for advocates. Dr. Natalie Engelbrecht says that by talking with other Autistic people, you are able to understand what kind of research is actually helpful to them in better understanding themselves in order to make the improvements they desire; to access this information, it's valuable to stay up to date with the latest research, question your understanding and assumptions, and conduct both quantitative and qualitative research.

Engelbrecht adds that it's important to compare different types of research for consistency or search quantitative studies to see if they complement each other in some way. Sometimes it happens that we receive new insights after reading different studies or considering our own personal experiences. Engelbrecht offers this example, connecting autism to findings about alexithymia (the inability to identify or describe emotions; Serani 2014):

> We have come to understand alexithymia (of which certain aspects have been confused with autism itself) and psychosomatization as protection mechanisms of the mind; alexithymia renders negative emotions less accessible, and through psychosomatization negative emotions are dumped in the body so that the mind doesn't have to deal with it. So even though alexithymia and psychosomatization can cause a lot of challenges, they are really double-edged swords. They are imperfect, but in a way successful adaptations. Autism might be perceived to be the same way, especially if you have trouble controlling the deficits and utilizing the advantages.

Engelbrecht believes it is wonderful when research highlights strengths such as this, because she knows it will empower and enrich the lives of those on the spectrum.

While autism research based on large sample sizes can be "tremendously illuminating," Engelbrecht asserts it's also important to access qualitative research (the lived experience) and engage with Autistic people directly "to better understand individual proclivities, interests, opinions, experiences, etc." Engelbrecht explains as an example that hearing a statistic about a high suicide rate among Autistic females is horrifying, but it is speaking with Autistic females about their life experience that truly enriches our understanding of what it is to be Autistic. The statistics alone tend to overlook these nuances.

Writer Joey Murphy also values the benefits of story-sharing as research. She says that sharing stories is important for any people, especially "marginalized or erased people." Murphy says that Autistic women are marginalized and have a history muted by research, diagnostic profiles, and treatment protocols that haven't included them. She says:

> Sharing our stories is a way of offering support to other women who are struggling; it's a way of building up anecdotal evidence to point researchers towards; it's a way of normalizing ourselves to ourselves. It's a way of creating a community and a space in the world for ourselves.

Studies that actively solicit Autistic input at every stage will result in research with real relevance to Autistic people, autism advocates and professionals (both Autistic and NT), and NT allies.

Being wary of biased research

Dr. Engelbrecht warns that as parents, educators, or anyone else interested in autism conducts informal and formal quantitative or qualitative research, they should be aware that research can be negatively biased, which can result in stigmatization and the perpetuation of false stereotypes: "For example, there are some studies and books that could be classified as being part of the Cassandra movement, where personal traumas in neurotypical–autistic relationships are generalized and extrapolated." Engelbrecht says that this is an example where qualitative work, when driven by personal biases, can lead to very damaging research.

We can also be biased in the research we choose to accept as fact. "Our cognitive biases make us really prone to, well, cognitive errors," says Engelbrecht. For example, the confirmation bias makes it simple to see what we want to see, but less likely for us to see a result that doesn't confirm our current beliefs. Research both keeps people accountable and reveals where gaps of knowledge exist. It's useful to take an inventory of any existing beliefs and biases you have (either through personal reflection or implicit bias testing, which can be found online from various reputable sources) so you are aware of how they may interfere with the research you are conducting or how you interpret the research you come across.

Respectful connection strategy, No. 3: Treat Autistic people as people, not study subjects

Why is this needed?

Many people are willing to share their stories and personal expertise for the good of others in the Autistic community; however, no one wants to be treated as a study subject or useful only for their specialized knowledge of the Autistic condition. Lydia X. Z. Brown warns that Autistic people don't exist as props or perpetual resources for other people. "We have our own lives and goals," they explain. "It's rather objectifying and dehumanizing to think about autistic adults as existing only for the benefit of non-autistic parents, but not being able to exist in our own right" (quoted in Gensic 2019, p.51). It's critical for neurotypicals to engage with the Autistic community, but that engagement must be based on a foundation of respect for human dignity as well as the authority of Autistic personal experience.

Objectifying treatment

Jennifer, who has done human-subject research herself, says

she has unfortunately seen Autistic people treated more like study objects than humans in some contexts, including graduate programs that train people to work with people on the spectrum. One such situation arose when her son participated in a social group for youth on the autism spectrum at a local university. While there may indeed have been questionable elements of the program mentioned in very fine print in one of the enrollment documents she signed, she didn't read very closely because she trusted the institution had her son's best interests in mind. However, neither she nor her son was explicitly made aware that many adults would also be at the sessions, watching the kids from behind a one-way mirror.

For reasons unknown, it was only in the third or fourth session that she was invited to join the group of observers, having spent the earlier ones in a waiting room, unaware of the other space. As the children played with some graduate students in a classroom, a group of adults composed of graduate students, faculty, and parents was assembled in an adjacent room, on the other side of a window that looked like a mirror to those in the classroom. Some of the observers had clipboards and were taking notes, and people were casually commenting on the activity in the classroom in a way that felt to Jennifer as if they saw the Autistic kids as specimens. She immediately began asking whether the children had consented to being monitored in prior meetings, and how those present felt about watching Autistic people in this way.

The reactions of the adult observers led Jennifer to believe they—including the parents—were all not only NT, but perfectly at ease with seeing those children as unwitting research subjects. She wondered if her own neurodivergence was the only thing that made her feel they deserved better, and whether that lack of empathy on the part of the NT adults involved could be clinically measured. When she talked with her son afterward (carefully avoiding disclosing what she had seen in fear of making him feel like a laboratory specimen), she learned that the kids didn't even know they were being watched, and she immediately withdrew him from the group. Furthermore, when she attempted to discuss her concerns with the organizers of the social group-cum-research study, "professional to professional," no one would respond to her queries.

Jenna observed a similar objectifying session where her son's therapist was being trained by another therapist while they were working with him. Jenna was observing a "school prep" therapy session where her son (who was five at the time) was supposed to be learning and practicing the kindergarten routine (circle time, calendar, reading time, art, snack, etc.) to prepare him for a typical school day outside of the house. But what she witnessed was extremely contrived, with the therapists talking about her son and his behaviors in front of him. They would also have him repeat sentences and behaviors so that the new therapist could practice the ways she was supposed to prompt him. This bothered Jenna, who thought her son was being used as a prop for the training. This is not to mention her indignation when she realized the session was more focused on compliance-based behaviors, such as "quiet hands and bodies" and eye contact with the teacher, than on education routines and communication in a new environment. Needless to say, after a meeting with the therapy center revealed their unwillingness to adjust program goals, Jenna removed her son from the therapy program.

While Autistic people want their voices and stories to be represented in public through research and other forums, they typically prefer to share on their own terms and on a reasonable (e.g., not unlimited, not without permission) basis.

Self-advocates are particularly vulnerable to objectifying treatment from curious neurotypicals. Julia Bascom says she sees neurotypicals get excited to encounter self-advocates and begin bombarding them with questions about their lives and children. Bascom acknowledges that it's understandable to seek insight, and often self-advocates will try to answer what they can because they want an improved life for the next generation; "but it's important to remember that we aren't walking autism dictionaries, that we get to have our own personal boundaries, and that every autistic person is different."

Engagement guidelines to remember

Larkin Taylor-Parker offers some guidelines for anyone interested in engaging with the autism community. Taylor-Parker says that NT advocates can't control or take responsibility for the feelings of Autistic people around them, but they can nevertheless keep certain best practices at the forefront of their minds. For one thing, avoid treating Autistic people in over-familiar ways, as you might a child: "As you get to know an Autistic adult, err on the side of formality."

In addition, Taylor-Parker says don't assume that person has all the time in the world to interact: "Don't ever act entitled to someone's time unless you genuinely are because of some kind of commitment, probably a paid one." Additionally, Taylor-Parker notes that any respectful hiring of an Autistic adult obviously abides by general employment norms and any applicable laws or employment contracts.

Respectful connection strategy, No. 4: Learn about the intersection of race and disability

Why is this needed?

If you are not a member of a racial minority, it's likely you are actively or passively participating in systems that perpetuate racism and stigmatization of disabilities. Racial minorities experience disability in different ways than their white counterparts. All disabled people will share similar experiences, but there are unique ways that race plays a role in their daily lives, and understanding the intersection of race and disability will help expose the burden of the environment so positive change can happen. Writer Teona Studemire says, "It's really important that the way race and disability intersect does not go ignored or brushed over anymore..." She continues:

> My experiences as a Black disabled woman are not going to be the same as a White disabled woman's... The way I'm treated while navigating the world of disability, medical treatment, etc. is impacted both by my disabilities and the color of my skin.

Lydia X. Z. Brown (2020) writes that the histories of ableism and racism "are co-dependent and intertwined". They note that an understanding of those linked histories is necessary to fully comprehend the inequities and injustices disabled people of color (POC) face:

> Both disabledness and abledness are defined based on proximity to and approximation of whiteness as an idea. What that means is that to be defined as

> fully nondisabled requires being white—white disabled people's disabilities detract from their whiteness, and disabled people of color's disabilities accentuate our supposed inferiority and in-humanity due to race. (Brown 2020)

Honest and complete discussions about disability must include race.

Weighing daily microaggressions

Racial minorities carry the burden of overt racism as well as daily microaggressions which continually add stress and deplete their spoon count. For example, Eric Evans says people regularly act fearful in his presence and use defensive body language. He has also been tailed and "eye-stalked" in stores. Evans explains that he constantly deals with microaggressions because he can't mask his Blackness:

> The one microaggression that seems to always trigger my emotions are the stares and looks of white people being inconvenienced by my presence. I'm not sure I could accurately put in words how that actually makes me feel. I'm used to my presence not being wanted or desired based on me being on the spectrum and operating differently, but I can hide that in public places.

Evans explains how a typical dinner out might play out for him:

> [It can't be put into words.] The thought that someone's night out with their family was going so well, reliving memories through storytelling, and exchanging light-hearted jokes and then would all be ruined by the sight of my skin color walking through the door. Me sitting down and feeling the stares all around me, triggering my anxiety, now making it extremely hard to blend in with proper societal social cues and manners; it's just an awful feeling.

Evans says he is sometimes unfairly categorized as a hermit when it comes to "going out." "But it's not because it does not sound like fun, " he says. "I'm just black and on the spectrum. I wish I could, but some days I truly can't."

Evans also regularly experiences microaggressions as a result of being Autistic, encountering people who are surprised at his intelligence or communication skills or tell him they couldn't even notice, so his autism must not be "that bad." But Evans explains that this is due to his masking efforts, which are compounded because he is Black and on the spectrum.

> One of the effects of my diagnosis is being a "fixer." One of my "fixes" is combating unwanted and negative attention to myself. Because I'm black, I have to be very creative. In short, I purposely try to dress nice, consciously speak as clearly as possible, be polite as possible, walk as "normal" as possible, pretty much anything that combats black male stereotypes. It's a defense mechanism to avoid conflict and fit in, but the irony of it is that it brings more attention to me (as mentioned by the "compliments"). I can't win, but it's all I know right now.

Writer/musician Khali Raymond says people also act surprised that he can talk intelligently and tell him that he speaks like he is "white." Similarly, he was written-off after he received an Asperger's diagnosis. Autistic POC are often doubly marginalized, as Raymond demonstrates in describing people's complex reactions to him:

> How is acting civilized and polite tied to a certain group of people?... When people found out I had Asperger's, they constantly called me retarded and wrote me off as a loon. They thought I was mentally incapable of doing anything.

Understanding how obstacles are compounded

Given the unique challenges of disabled POC, their voices are especially important ones for would-be advocates and allies, especially those with white and/or NT privilege, to hear. Yet, as advocate Kayla Smith points out, representation of Autistic POC is also poor. As a result, Smith feels like she lives in a world that doesn't see her as a human being. She says, "Autistic POC don't get the recognition like their white peers do." She explains that the intersectionality of race and autism is important, but it's not discussed enough in the public conversations about autism, and that "society thinks I am either a threat, tragedy, or both." Not enough people are willing to be an ally to Autistic POC, so Smith focuses on bringing more awareness and recognition of Autistic POC, especially Black Autistic people.

A lack of representation perpetuates stereotypes about race and disability that carry over to a variety of life areas, including the medical realm, says Teona Studemire. Studemire says that one stereotype she encounters is that Black people don't experience pain the same way white people do, an idea dating back to the slavery era and later promoted by the eugenics movement. Studemire says this stereotype is still alive in the healthcare system today, influencing the "medication seeking" label that targets Black chronically ill and disabled people. The multiple, pervasive stereotypes around being Black, Autistic, ADHD (attention deficit hyperactivity disorder) with myalgic encephalomyelitis and hyper-mobile Ehlers-Danlos syndrome make going to seek treatment "an exhausting and even impossible task," says Studemire.

> The constant medical gaslighting, doctors who barely take a glance at you long enough to see past your skin color telling you that nothing is wrong with you and putting in your charts that you're just "overreacting" and seeking medication to abuse. Black pregnant people dying before, during, or after birth because doctors aren't listening when they tell them that something is wrong or the pain is too much to bear. It's so hard. So many Black disabled lives lost because of doctors and their stereotypes... I try to find other Black doctors and specialists, but this is more difficult to do and also doesn't mean that those same doctors won't put me through the medical gaslighting I'm accustomed to.

Eric Evans says being both Black and on the spectrum complicated his likelihood of having a negative encounter with police. He says that every Black person gets a "talk" from their parents when they are younger about racism and how they have to be extra careful around authority figures, especially the police. But he said his race "talks" with his mother were also related to autism:

> A good example of them seemingly meshing was my mother's no toy gun rule. I liked toy guns like most boys in America, all types of guns. Water, Nerf, BB, Pellet, Cap, all kinds really. But my mother wouldn't ever buy me one. She told me that she did not want me to emulate what I saw in the streets and media, and that guns are not meant to be toys at all. She also told me that I would be looked at as a threat by police, and that black boys that play with toy guns get shot. The correlation that has with having Asperger's is that my form of approach to understanding requests comes from a place of questioning. Direct and hard "Why?", "What for?", "Why should I?" All of which are perceived by society as being combative, resisting, or rebellious. That combined with society's fascination with authority figures is a recipe for disaster for anyone looked at as a potential threat by law enforcement, let alone someone black.

Evans remembers arguing with his mom about buying him a "super-ridiculous and oddly shaped/colored toy gun which resembled a real gun in no way shape or form," but she still told him he couldn't buy it. He says, "In a lot of ways, I felt trapped and isolated from being an honest and expressive person as a child, because I had this burden of being black and thinking differently."

Lydia X. Z. Brown contends that the combination of a thorough understanding of race and disability with a desire for equity necessitates that society acknowledge racist systems and reinvent the therapy profession. "We do not want or need to be the extra diversity spice in overwhelmingly white, nondisabled spaces. We do not want or need to be included into oppressive systems" (Brown 2020). The therapy profession can't exist merely to support Autistic or otherwise disabled people. Brown insists that it's dangerous to act as if assisting disabled people can take place in a vacuum: "everything that therapists, teachers, and other professionals do takes place in context." They say that the therapy profession must "align with our work to end the violent conditions that we contend with and make a better world possible and real."

Autistic people of color bear the perpetual burden of living in a world that favors both NT and white people and groups. They regularly experience microaggressions, stereotyping, and more as a result of their dual marginalization. Actively making public space for, and truly listening to, Autistic POC is an absolutely essential facet of autism advocacy and allyship. For those who engage in more political- and/or policy-oriented advocacy/allyship activities, the intersection of race and autism is, when informed by Black Autistic perspectives, a front-line civil rights concern that is ripe for enormous change and progress. Ashkenazy states:

> When we slow down and think about what we're assuming, saying, and doing, we just might offend a lot less people and become empowered to nurture enlightened respectful conversation and to embrace the future of a truly mixed nation that truly includes autistic people of color. (Ashkenazy 2017, xxxix).

Respectful connection strategy, No. 5: Support and/or work with/for organizations that are disability-friendly

Why is this needed?

Several Autistic people Jenna interviewed emphasized that advocacy mistakes are compounded when large, influential organizations have incorrect assumptions about Autistic people and goals that don't match the agenda of much of the Autistic community. Organizations that spend time and money on advertising negative autism portrayals, prioritize research into cures over money spent on supporting Autistic people throughout their lifetimes, and do not access Autistic input and expertise at all levels of decision-making were the most commonly cited issues Autistic people had witnessed. Conducting preliminary research with special consideration for which autism organizations are disability-friendly and endorsed by the Autistic community will help ensure your work, contributions, advocacy and/or allyship are aligned with a movement focused on helping Autistic people now and throughout their lives and not contributing to any further marginalization.

Finding autism organizations that are not cure-focused and that utilize positive autism portrayals

It's important for autism organizations to keep their goals aligned with the needs and desires of the Autistic community, says Nic Laughter. According to Laughter, organizations that suggest there is a cure for autism or use language about making Autistic people "better" tend to prey on scared, vulnerable parents. Sometimes organizations can make "wonderful children out to be the impending bane of any semblance of happiness they [the parents] once had." Laughter says organizations should stop using fear as motivation for support and instead provide resources that actually help Autistic people live the lives they want, whether through enabling parents to help their Autistic children do so or otherwise.

Elizabeth Crawford has also seen negative messaging among autism organizations, including an ad in which autism was represented as a demon coming to take away children. In another, parents were complaining in an interview about their struggles as parents, when their Autistic children were standing right next to them. "I really don't like this portrayal of autism because it takes away agency from the individuals themselves," she explains.

A. J. Mahari says that autism organizations should support and advocate for ways to push Autistic people to grow and develop, but not force them to present as more NT. "I've found ways to push myself to grow and develop. You can grow children but don't advocate this way, thinking you will make your child neurotypical."

Organizations that regularly welcome and recruit Autistic people as board members, CEOs, or in other leadership positions, are also more likely to be aligned with the needs of the communities they advocate for. This is quite different from organizations that bring Autistic people on board as token "after the fact" consultants for initiatives already in motion. Tom Iland says he was treated this way while working with a leading autism organization in the U.S.A: "Yes, they wanted to consult with me about how to issue a statement and/or what to say well after the fact; however, it was too little, too late, and I felt I was getting the runaround.

Intentionally seeking out and then supporting and/or aligning with organizations that avoid spreading the message that autism needs to be "cured" is one way to further autism awareness that honors the personal worth and integrity of Autistic human beings just as they are. Such organizations will generally be more likely to promote inclusive, positive, respectful ideas, visions, and stories of autism, whether at the local, national, or international level.

Granting grace

Tom Iland says that it's important for allies and advocates to remember that everyone makes mistakes, and as long as a person is willing to acknowledge their mistakes and keep growing, we should grant them grace. "It's never too late to seek redemption, and the best way to foster change is from within rather than from the outside." Iland says that holding grudges against people is toxic to the person holding the grudge:

> I have gotten to where I am today because I have a team of people with me as opposed to going it alone AND I have kept an open mind rather than being closed off to those I do not necessarily agree with... At the end of the day, a unified front, rather than a divided front, is more critical than ever.

Paul Isaacs agrees that autism politics can be distressing and that militant stances on the part of people both on and off the autism spectrum can be uncomfortable to deal with. "My personal opinion is that everybody has a story and that their realities are just as valid as anyone else's—there should not be a single representation," he suggests, "but a more egalitarian outlook where all personhoods and realities are taken into account." If we are open to a variety of different opinions and realities, we can continually evolve our own understanding and acceptance of the Autistic community.

This may mean focusing our public-facing work, financial and other support, advocacy, and/or allyship on groups that uphold #ActuallyAutistic values and amplify Autistic voices. Or, occasionally, it may entail being open to working for change in those organizations that have yet to align with the Autistic community or have a mixed record as far as meaningful, respectful engagement is concerned. Either way, guidance from Autistic people themselves must take center stage if our efforts are to genuinely improve their lives.

Autism organizations endorsed by the #ActuallyAutistic community

This list certainly isn't exhaustive, but below you'll find some of the larger and more popular organizations with an emphasis on autism acceptance and celebrating Autistic voices and expertise.

- Autistic Self Advocacy Network (ASAN): https://autisticadvocacy.org
- Autism Women & Nonbinary Network (AWN): https://awnnetwork.org
- Thinking Person's Guide to Autism (TPGA): www.thinkingautismguide.com
- NeuroClastic: https://neuroclastic.com
- Ollibean: https://ollibean.com
- Autpress: http://autpress.com
- The Association for Persons with Severe Handicaps (TASH): https://tash.org
- The Arc: https://thearc.org

SUMMARY GUIDANCE

- Read Autistic authors, seek out Autistic speakers, and actively pursue Autistic voices.
- Read and share literature with normalized and human Autistic characters.
- Seek out representations and voices of Autistic POC.
- Invite Autistic people to be public autism experts at autism events.
- Include Autistic people in the planning of autism-related events.
- If you are invited to an event that isn't accessible to Autistic people or in which there isn't meaningful Autistic participation and leadership, request a change or refuse to participate.
- Take an implicit bias test to inform your research bias.
- Seek out both quantitative and qualitative autism research.
- Remember that Autistic people are human and not study subjects.
- When getting to know an Autistic adult, err on the side of formality.
- Search for autism organizations that prioritize centering and amplifying Autistic voices and expertise, rather than eradicating autism.
- Grant grace to advocates and organizations willing to acknowledge mistakes and make changes.

REFLECTION QUESTIONS

- ? Take an inventory of the number of Autistic people involved in the planning and execution of your autism event. How can I recruit or welcome more Autistic participation and make the event more inclusive?
- ? Similarly, take an inventory of the number of Autistic people involved in the planning and execution of your research. How can I recruit or welcome more Autistic participation and make my research more inclusive?
- ? Where do I obtain my information about autism? How can I access a wide variety of Autistic sources and expertise on a regular basis?
- ? Do I have any Autistic friends? How can I improve my interactions with Autistic people [for Autistic people, read: my fellow Autistics] to treat them with the dignity and respect they deserve?
- ? How can I reach out to those I've held grudges against or who think differently than I do? How can I join with others to make peaceful progress to help the Autistic community?
- ? What role would I like to play vis-à-vis autism-focused organizations? Do my contributions, choices, and efforts so far reflect #ActuallyAutistic priorities?

Step 9

Put Theory into Practice

> *Don't be sucked into thinking that you need to be doing loads of therapy and interventions, or that if you don't, you'll miss some magic window of development. Our children's developmental paths will be unique and our role as parents is to help smooth their paths, not force them onto a different route.*
>
> — PAULA SANCHEZ

The previous chapters offer some of the best advocacy advice you will ever receive, because it comes directly from the Autistic community. But it's not enough to understand what support path is best. It will take time to not only learn about these best practices, but to integrate a deep and active belief that they work, shift your focus to esteeming the Autistic community as the foremost experts on autism, and implement the resulting ideas and actions. There is a fair amount of effort necessary to actually implement this advocacy/allyship path! But this is nothing we can't do. After all, you already have likely devoted countless hours to supporting the Autistic person or people in your life, whether they be your child(ren), student(s), client(s), friend(s), partner, and/or self. You are primed and ready to change the world, and thereby help many others for years to come. This final chapter inspires advocates to avoid stagnation or the temptation to put this book on a shelf and go about life as usual. Autistic advocates want people to acknowledge past flaws, share their new insights, act on what they've learned, and continue to grow their wisdom and efforts based on #ActuallyAutistic input.

Ensuring execution tip, No. 1: Be a continual student and implement your own advice

Why is this needed?

Neurotypicals tend to do an awful lot of teaching to Autistic people. It's difficult for neurotypicals to understand the exact perspective of Autistic people, and they can project their advice through an NT filter, without proper empathy for the Autistic person. "Because neurotypicals process things through their view of the world...there is always the risk they will subconsciously impose their views and values on us, and interpret autistic behavior through a neurotypical lens," says Dr. Natalie Englebrecht. But the Autistic community is asking parents and others to listen and be students.

Only by listening with humility can we really begin the process of supporting, advocating, and/or allying with people on the spectrum. Autistic people not only want us to practice what they advise, but also to implement their own advice more literally as well. Marie explains this in more detail below.

Practicing what you preach

"The most common mistake I have noticed is sometimes the inability to put theory into practice," says Marie. She says that the Autistic community has clearly articulated that they have difficulty with nonverbal cues and prefer literal speech, but simply explaining this isn't enough. She says:

> They seem to forget in practical life. For example, if they say something will happen "next week," we really expect it to happen next week. Sometimes I think they don't quite understand us when we are blunt either, even if they "know" many of us can be blunt in our honesty.

Marie says that sometimes Autistic people are treated as typical people with no need for accommodations, when they in fact have very specific needs that are overlooked.

Elizabeth Crawford suggests that people on the spectrum may have better listening skills than neurotypicals and that neurotypicals tend to violate their own social rules regarding listening. When they do so, Crawford suggests, they see an NT breach as more socially acceptable than an Autistic breach. Crawford explains that this is due to a difference between what people see and perceive and what they are conscious of conveying to others:

> I tend to be listening at all times and on a deep level, but my behavior doesn't really broadcast that at all unless I'm putting considerable effort into showing that I'm listening, which doesn't become fully activated until someone is talking

> to me directly. When this happens, I know I need to make some eye contact and react in some way throughout their time speaking. These gestures include nods and smiles. I also giggle a whole lot in reaction to just about anything during social interaction (unless I can tell it's inappropriate). This is because I've learned that people are receptive to smiles, and it also helps one not to stick out. If I don't smile and giggle like (my) normal, I inevitably get comments like "Are you okay?" and "What are you thinking about?"

Based on Crawford's experience, neurotypicals tend to not exert nearly the same level of effort into demonstrating active listening. Despite this apparent lack of effort, "there seems to be this unstated understanding that everyone is listening to each other, and it is mind boggling," says Crawford. She gives the examples of people texting or using their phones during conversations:

> I've watched people have entire conversations with each other in person while both spend the entire time with their noses in their phones. Yet, I get called out for looking displeased or inattentive when I'm giving everything I got to look interested (even when I'm not, which is often!).

Jennifer has noticed a similar phenomenon. She has often needed to make what feels like an extraordinary and exhausting effort to "seem normal" and "act like she is listening" and "respond 'appropriately" when interacting, because of her innately divergent natural self-presentation and responses, while observing that neurotypicals (for whom interaction is so much less draining in the first place!) can often be rude, inattentive, or distracted without consequences because of their overall "acceptable" demeanor.

The takeaway for advocates and allies? Once you've learned about autism, find ways to put that knowledge into action. This might include any number of possible processes, from learning how interaction (eye contact, etc.) may impact the Autistic people in your life and shifting to a more comfortable conversational approach, to discovering an #ActuallyAutistic linguistic preference and speaking up about that in a meeting.

Avoiding stagnation

Eric Evans says sometimes advocates have mild interests in helping but they easily slip into stagnation. "A retweet, or a profile picture change, or whatever is trendy to do that takes zero sacrifice is the same as doing nothing to me," says Evans. Some well-meaning advocates and allies may also get stuck in a particular mode of "help" that isn't necessarily all that helpful. Others may find their niche and stay in it beyond the point of proactive advocacy.

What we think and know about neurodiversity also changes over time, so advocates and allies who consider one bout of research and/or outreach enough may find themselves far behind the times rather quickly. Like other civil rights movements, autism awareness naturally evolves over time, with deepening and shifting perspectives around language, status, access, and more. So staying on top of developments in the #ActuallyAutistic world is also an important part of any truly autism-friendly advocacy/allyship effort.

Ensuring execution tip, No. 2: Stay on top of technology trends

Why is this needed?

Autistic people have the right to access technology to assist with communication. Unfortunately, they are often denied this opportunity due to varying insurance policy coverages, varying therapeutic philosophies for speech, or a simple lack of exposure. As discussed above, the disabled community is no stranger to sluggish access to accommodations. The Autistic community asks advocates and allies to embrace technology trends, especially those that would improve access to communication and general independence. In addition, tech-savvy advocates and allies, along with those with a strong social media presence, can use their skills and/or platforms to further these same goals on the public stage.

Embracing/encouraging progress

Laura Nadine says that some of the biggest issues in autism advocacy are "the limitations of rigid structures and bureaucracies that suffocate progress." Nadine explains that it takes too many committees too long to make decisions and act. Sometimes these actions even come after they are no longer needed. Nadine offers this example:

> Despite the first lightweight, folding wheelchair being around since 1933, and curb-smashing protests in the 1960s, it was not until 1990 that the Americans with Disabilities Act was passed into law requiring public space modifications for them. That means at least two generations of people in wheelchairs

lived without accommodations. Today this sluggish cadence of change is even more absurd when you consider the pace of innovation in the new millennium.

Additionally, while access to AAC devices has improved in recent years, many families and individuals still struggle to gain insurance approval and implement a communication method in a timely manner (Senner 2018). Paperwork required for insurance funding for these devices can take months to process, and families can be denied coverage for a variety of reasons. When Jenna's son's speech therapist first recommended trying an AAC device, the therapist immediately suggested Jenna buy an iPad and speech app on her own if she could afford it. The SLP knew how long it would take to receive a device through insurance channels, and she thought Jenna's son would benefit from having the device immediately.

As new technologies and learning tools become available, opportunities for Autistic communication, education, independence, and connection increase. Knowing the significance of such advances for the Autistic community, advocates and allies can follow #ActuallyAutistic advice by standing up for progress whenever possible.

Ensuring execution tip, No. 3: Recognize and acknowledge past flaws, and move forward

Why is this needed?

Real change won't happen unless we acknowledge that it is necessary. In order to acknowledge the need, we must acknowledge the mistakes and imperfections of the present. But that's what drives positive, powerful transformations anyway—a passion to do better. To be better. This book is about inspiring us to grow in these ways. Leanne Libas says a common mistake among advocates is "not acknowledging their mistakes and flaws as an advocate." We hope that this book has helped you discover specific areas to grow as an advocate and/or ally, as well as how to align your efforts with what the Autistic community is advocating for.

It's not enough to have good intentions

While we have covered this topic in some depth above, we want to remind readers that it's always possible to grow in your advocacy and allyship. Autistic people remind us again and again that actions—not intentions—have real consequences, highlighting the importance of obtaining autism-friendly information to shape actions that have a positive impact.

In addition, those who wish to be of service must center the person(s) and/or group they wish to serve. Ally Grace reminds us that defensive statements about good intentions can be viewed as self-centered to the disability community: "Intent does not negate harm. The way to fix it after you realise you have been causing harm, is to learn how to not cause harm anymore."

Tom Iland says he believes it is critical that adult advocates without autism acknowledge that "they didn't always get it right." In his view, "this opens the possibility for forgiveness both from the person with autism and for the adult advocate him/herself."

Whether you are Autistic or NT, a parent, family member, professional, friend, partner, or play any other role in the Autistic community, moving forward as an autism advocate/ally means continuing to reflect on your actions and intentions so as to better serve Autistic interests. It entails engaging with, and learning from, the Autistic people in your life, as well as other available Autistic sources. We wish you the best in this revelatory and worthwhile journey!

SUMMARY GUIDANCE

- Ask the Autistic people in your life if they notice any areas where you don't exactly "practice what you preach."
- Support any new technology improvements or accommodations that aim to boost inclusivity and independence for the disabled community.
- Admit your mistakes and begin addressing ways you can become a better advocate for the Autistic people in your life.
- Seek to turn listening and abstract learning into concrete action.
- Keep asking questions and soliciting new information about neurodiversity.

REFLECTION QUESTIONS

? What expectations do I have for my Autistic child(ren) (students/clients/loved ones) that I don't have for my NT child(ren) (students/clients/loved ones) or myself?

- ? In what ways has my own neurological status, whether Autistic or NT, shaped my impressions of #ActuallyAutistic voices?
- ? What mistakes have I made as an advocate and/or ally according to the advice given by the contributors in this book?
- ? What changes can I make in my life now to better align my behaviors with the desires of the Autistic community?

Advocacy Goals Checklist for Easy Self-Improvement

Use this list to align your advocacy behaviors with the #ActuallyAutistic community.

- ☐ When I first learn about someone's autism diagnosis and am asked for guidance, I direct families to resources authored by Autistic people.
- ☐ I avoid language that reflects a mission to fight, cure, or eliminate autism, and I avoid identifying as an autism warrior.
- ☐ I research neurodiversity and encourage others to do so.
- ☐ I read about the medical and social models of disability.
- ☐ Before sharing stories on social media, I consider whether they could be viewed as inspiration porn.
- ☐ I focus on what barriers might be causing negative behaviors.

- ☐ I learn about the different reasons for the stims of the Autistic people in my life (and/or my own stims) and embrace them as communication rather than discouraging them.

- ☐ If NT, when I see a need for new accommodations or supports in my school, community, or workplace, I do what is in my power to initiate and implement the change. I don't wait for someone else (typically an Autistic person) to take on this responsibility.

- ☐ If Autistic, I understand that the entire onus for positive, inclusive change does not fall on me. Nonetheless, I know that I have the right to express my needs and preferences and to work towards improved conditions.

- ☐ I learn about and practice the language preferences of the Autistic people in my life.

- ☐ I study diverse portrayals of Autistic characters so I don't develop stereotypical thinking about Autistic strengths and weaknesses.

- ☐ I consider the ways the world is not so accommodating for Autistic adults, and the role I can play in improving this, however small.

- ☐ I recognize the advantages or benefits autism offers those around me (and/or me).

- ☐ I celebrate the strengths of the Autistic people in my life (including my own strengths, where applicable).

- ☐ I teach others that autism has positive, negative, and neutral traits so that it can be celebrated, supported, and accepted without minimizing anyone's life experiences.

- ☐ I presume competence. If this does not come naturally to me, I will make it my mantra until it does.
- ☐ I learn about the specific symptoms of common comorbid conditions.
- ☐ I have a healthy skepticism of NT-developed competency tests.
- ☐ I am patient when speaking with Autistic people, especially if they are speaking more slowly than I am accustomed to.
- ☐ I don't interrupt or attempt to speak for an Autistic person without their permission.
- ☐ I offer the Autistic people in my life regular opportunities to develop independence. If Autistic, I also practice and assert my personal right to independence according to my own life goals.
- ☐ I practice respectful story-sharing that is framed on celebrating strengths or identifying supports and areas needing change.
- ☐ I ask for permission before sharing personal stories about other people.
- ☐ I get to know people on the spectrum as people, not as a collection of symptoms.
- ☐ I maintain a positive outlook. I look for positive Autistic adult role models.
- ☐ If NT, I avoid trivializing the Autistic experience by saying Autistic people are just like me or that I sometimes have the same problems.

- ☐ I ask the Autistic people in my life, whenever possible, about their specific goals and, when appropriate, help them seek out therapy that addresses those.
- ☐ For professionals and parents/guardians: I check in with my child/client/student, etc. before, during, and after each therapy session to evaluate whether or not it is a good fit for them.
- ☐ I honor the diverse relationships Autistic people have, even if they seem atypical to my personal experiences (whether I am Autistic or NT).
- ☐ For professionals, parents/guardians, and family members: I ask my child/client/student often what they want out of life—I don't assume I know what they want to do or how they want to present themselves.
- ☐ I try to set up a home, school, or work environment that relieves the pressure to mask.
- ☐ I am humble and open to change.
- ☐ I distinguish between meltdowns and tantrums.
- ☐ If/when I am in a position to do so, I invite Autistic people to speak, teach, lead workshops, and offer expertise in a variety of ways.
- ☐ I acknowledge Autistic people as experts on the Autistic condition (and at the very least, on how autism personally affects them) and, in my advocacy efforts, I recognize and seek out Autistic people who have developed a professional platform.
- ☐ For neurotypicals: As a neurotypical, I recognize I have an NT filter through which I perceive everything about the

world. This will have to be navigated when I communicate with Autistic people, as well as (where applicable) when I work with them to identify supports.

- ☐ I read fiction and/or nonfiction authored by Autistic people.
- ☐ I seek out both qualitative and quantitative research.
- ☐ I make an effort to learn about the intersection of race and disability.
- ☐ I seek out a range of expertise from Autistic people who present in many different ways. This may include people with varied modes of communication, abilities, opinions, symptoms, comorbid conditions, and so on.

Interviewee Bios

This bio section includes those Autistic people with whom Jenna has personally corresponded who are quoted in this book. It does not include additional Autistic advocates cited in this book whom she has not interviewed. Details on these may be found in the references. Capitalization, identity language, and other terms in this section are aligned with the requests of each contributor and may not be consistent throughout.

Megan Amodeo

Megan Amodeo is a writer, Autistic self-advocate, and stay-at-home mother to three, two of whom are on the spectrum. Prior to staying at home with her children, she worked in special education. She currently writes for geekclubbooks (https://geekclubbooks.com/megan-autism-insider) as an "Autism Insider."

Angela Andrews

Angela Andrews is a mother of five (four of whom are on the autism spectrum) and avid musician. She is a data scientist at Johnson & Johnson, experienced at working with multiple forms of data and database systems.

Julia Bascom

Julia Bascom serves as Executive Director at the Autistic Self Advocacy Network. Previously, she did state-level work in her home state of New Hampshire, where she served on the Developmental Disabilities council and co-led an inter-agency team to revitalize self-advocacy within the state. Julia edited *Loud Hands: Autistic People, Speaking* (2012), an anthology of writings by Autistic people, and currently serves on the advisory board of Felicity House, and the boards of the Consortium for Citizens with Disabilities, the Institute for Exceptional Care, and Allies For Independence.

Nera Birch

Nera Birch is a self-advocate from Cleveland, Ohio, with a passion for speaking and writing on topics related to autism advocacy. Birch blogs at "I'm Not Drunk, I'm Autistic." You can visit Nera's website at https://theautisticpinup.home.blog.

Chris Bonnello

Chris Bonnello is an Autistic public speaker and writer from the U.K. He formerly taught in primary education and is now a special needs tutor for Autistic students. Bonnello blogs at www.autisticnotweird.com, where he writes to raise awareness about the needs of people on the spectrum and offer guidance to other Autistic people. He is also the author of the *Underdogs* novels, a dystopian series featuring neurodiverse heroes from a special school.

Elizabeth Boresow

Elizabeth Boresow is a board-certified music therapist, writer, direct support provider, and Autistic advocate. She regularly uses her experience as a person on the autism spectrum to both serve and educate others about autism acceptance.

Daniel Bowman Jr.

Daniel Bowman Jr. is an Autistic writer, poet, and associate professor of English at Taylor University. He's the author of a collection of poems titled *A Plum Tree in Leatherstocking Country*, a blog contributor for "Ruminate," and has written articles and poems featured in a variety of other publications. You can visit Daniel's website at www.danielbowmanjr.com.

Lydia X. Z. Brown

Lydia X. Z. Brown is an advocate, educator, and attorney addressing state and interpersonal violence targeting disabled people living at the intersections of race, class, gender, sexuality, faith, language, and nation. Lydia is Policy Counsel for Privacy & Data at the Center for Democracy & Technology, focused on algorithmic discrimination and disability, as well as Director of Policy, Advocacy & External Affairs at the Autistic Women & Nonbinary Network. They are founding director of the Fund for Community Reparations for Autistic People of Color's Interdependence, Survival & Empowerment, and co-editor of *All the Weight of Our Dreams: On Living Racialized Autism* (published by DragonBee Press, 2017). Lydia is an adjunct lecturer/core faculty in Georgetown University's Disability Studies Program, and adjunct professorial lecturer in American Studies at American University's Department of Critical Race, Gender & Culture Studies. They serve as a commissioner on the American Bar Association's Commission on Disability Rights. In addition, they are chairperson of the ABA Civil Rights & Social Justice Section's Disability Rights Committee, and the Disability Justice Committee's representative to the National Lawyers Guild, National Executive Committee.

Jennifer Brozek

Jennifer Brozek is an award-winning author, editor, and tie-in writer. *Never Let Me Sleep*, (Permuted Press, 2016), *The Last Days of Salton Academy* (Ragnarok Publications, 2016) and *A Secret Guide to Fighting Elder Gods* (Pulse Publishing, 2019) were finalists for the Bram Stoker Award. She was awarded the Scribe Award for best tie-in Young Adult novel for *BattleTech: The Nellus Academy Incident* (Catalyst Game Labs, 2018). *Grants Pass* (Morrigan Books, 2009) won an Australian Shadows Award for best edited publication. A Hugo finalist for Short Form Editor, Jennifer is an active member of the professional writing organizations SFWA, HWA, and IAMTW. She keeps a tight writing and editing schedule and credits her husband Jeff with being the best sounding board ever. Visit Jennifer's worlds at www.jenniferbrozek.com.

Tara L. Campbell

Tara L. Campbell is a speculative fiction and creative nonfiction science writer with a professional background in technology. She enjoys writing at the intersection of science, technology, and disability. Stories about overlooked or misunderstood people and concepts are key aspects in her work.

Michael John Carley

Michael John Carley is the Consultant for Diversity Inclusive Culture at New York University. Additionally, he is a consultant for other schools and businesses who remotely sees individual clients. He is the author of three books, dozens of columns, and he was the founding Executive Director for two non-profits in New York City, including the largest membership organization in the world for adults on the spectrum. Covered by every major media outlet, his speaking spans almost 20 years and 250 engagements—his 2018 schedule alone included keynoting autism conferences in Malaysia, Australia, Canada, and Argentina. For more information, please visit www.michaeljohncarley.com.

Bob Christian

Bob Christian, of Bob Christian Poetry, is a father, husband, writer, and poet on the autism spectrum. He blogs about his life on his website "The Ramblings of Bob Christian" (https://bob-christian.com). He is also the author of a number of poetry books, which are available on Amazon.

Marcelle Ciampi

Marcelle Ciampi M.Ed. (a.k.a. Samantha Craft), a respected Autistic author and worldwide advocate, is best known for her writings found in the well-received book *Everyday Aspergers* (https://everydayaspergers.com). She is also the author of *Autism in a Briefcase* (published by Your Stories Matter, 2021) and a contributing author of *Spectrum Women: Walking to the Beat of Autism* (Jessica Kingsley Publishers, 2018). She serves as the Ambassador and Senior Manager of Diversity, Equity, and Inclusion at Ultranauts Inc., an engineering firm with a neurodiversity-hiring initiative, where Ciampi is credited for developing an innovative universal design approach for inclusion. She also provides keynotes, workshops, corporate training, consulting, and life coaching for Spectrum Suite (www.myspectrumsuite.com).

Tracey Cohen

Tracey Cohen is an experienced ultrarunner, author, speaker, and educator, and has competed in thousands of races around the world. She was diagnosed with Asperger's Syndrome at the age of 39 and speaks regularly about autism at conferences and to a variety of organizations, including libraries, autism societies, and school groups. Tracey is the author of *Six-Word Lessons on Female Asperger Syndrome* (Pacelli Publishing, 2017), *Six-Word Lessons on the Sport of Running* (Pacelli Publishing, 2017), and *My Life on the Autism Spectrum: Misunderstandings, Insight & Growth* (Pacelli Publishing, 2020).

Sam Crane

Sam Crane is the legal director at the Autistic Self Advocacy Network's national office. Sam graduated from Harvard Law School and previously served as a staff attorney at the Judge David L. Bazelon Center for Mental Health Law, focusing on enforcing the right to community integration as established by the Supreme Court in Olmstead v. L.C.

Elizabeth Crawford

Elizabeth Crawford is an Autistic freelance book editor and writer who blogs at "Return to Innocence" (https://midwestaspie.com). She is on a mission to support other women with Asperger's Syndrome by writing about her life experiences. Elizabeth is also the author of *Chameleon: An Asperger's Memoir* (published 2019).

Emma Dalmayne

Emma Dalmayne is Autistic and an autism advocate and activist from the U.K. who speaks out against all mistreatments of Autistic people. She has published several articles and has written two books (available from STASS Publications) aimed at helping Autistic individuals and parents of Autistic children. Her advocacy work has been featured in *The Guardian*, *The Times* and the BBC. Emma is also a home educator to her children, who are Autistic, and CEO of the Autistic-led organization Autistic Inclusive Meets.

Anlor Davin

Anlor Davin is a French-born American for whom meditation has been a central part of life over the past 20 years. Currently, she offers free meditation online via Zoom three times a month (visit www.Autsit.net). Anlor is the author of *Being Seen* (www.AnlorDavin.com), a memoir about an Autistic French woman (herself), and she and her partner have been organizing "autism & meditation" events for the past nine years.

Roy Dias

Roy Dias teaches English as a second language at a school in Portugal, where he lives with his wife and two sons. He and his two sons are diagnosed with Asperger's Syndrome. In addition to teaching and caring for his family, Roy writes fiction to promote autism understanding and acceptance, including the *Aspean* series (visit https://roysdias.com/books).

Gillan Drew

Gillan Drew is a British author and father of two daughters. He was diagnosed with Asperger's Syndrome at 28 and blogs about his life at Aspie Daddy (https://asdaddy.com). Gillan is the author of *An Adult with an Autism Diagnosis: A Guide for the Newly Diagnosed* (Jessica Kingsley Publishers, 2017).

Alex Earhart

Alex Earhart is an Autistic nonbinary blogger with a degree in Intercultural Communication. They were late-diagnosed at the age of 27 and now run the blog "Autistically Alex" (https://autisticallyalex.com) where they write openly and honestly on a vast variety of topics, including sensory overload, meltdowns and shutdowns, depression and anxiety, ableism, eating disorder recovery, chronic illness and disability, LGBTQIA+ matters, and much more. Popular posts include "When You Don't Believe I'm Autistic," "Sick While Autistic," Alex's "Sensory Series," and "Seeking Sara, Finding Alex."

Natalie Engelbrecht

Dr. Natalie Engelbrecht, a late-diagnosed registered psychotherapist practicing for more than 25 years, has a passion for helping individuals with autism reach their potential. She blogs on a variety of autism topics, including the latest autism research, at her research-based website, "Embrace ASD" (https://embraceasd.com/blog). Dr. Engelbrecht provides autism assessments, both self-referred and for medical professionals (i.e., psychiatrists) who suspect their patients may be on the spectrum. She also provides training for medical professionals on how to work with Autistic people, and lectures on autism. Dr. Engelbrecht hosts a podcast on various current and relevant topics regarding autism and is currently training police in the U.K. on how to prevent suicide in calls they get to assist an Autistic person in distress.

Eric Evans

Eric Evans is a communication specialist from Philadelphia with an interest in developing innovative solutions to communication-based conflicts, as well as curriculum development for educational seminars ranging from mental disabilities to community outreach. He has developed training programs for police to learn to identify Autistic civilians and interact with them in safe and appropriate ways.

Bennett Gaddes

Bennett Gaddes is the former president of Autistic Self Advocacy Atlanta. He is especially interested in creating accessible technology.

Alix Generous

Alix Generous is an activist, writer, entrepreneur, child psychologist, story-teller, and artist. Her TED talk "My Inner Life" has received over 1.9 million views, and she has spoken around the world on her life experiences. She takes on projects that increase awareness and acceptance of those with mental differences and advocates for non-violence, sustainability, and equality.

Michael Gilberg

Michael Gilberg is a special education and disability rights attorney from New York (www.michaelgilbergesq.com). He is passionate about helping others on the spectrum after a childhood without the proper supports or diagnosis. Michael says, "My life experience of having been where your child is drives my desire every day to fight for justice for children with disabilities and their families."

Morgan Giosa

Morgan Giosa is a web developer, blues guitarist, photographer, and visual artist from Connecticut. Morgan says his music and visual art ultimately come to him from his "unique and unconventional intuition and emotions, and his quirky, idiosyncratic view of the world." Morgan has released an album of original music with his band, the Fake News Blues Band, which is available on Spotify, YouTube, and all major streaming services (http://morgangiosa.com).

Ally Grace

Ally Grace is an Autistic mother of five from Australia. Ally strongly believes in challenging the pathology paradigm of autism. She blogs at "Respectfully Connected" (http://respectfullyconnected.com) about her family, rejecting conventional autism assumptions, challenging social norms around raising children, unschooling, and being Autistic.

Temple Grandin

Dr. Temple Grandin is a designer of livestock handling facilities and a Professor of Animal Science at Colorado State University. Facilities she has designed are located in the U.S.A., Canada, Europe, Mexico, Australia, New Zealand, and other countries. Almost half of the cattle in North America are handled in a center track restrainer system that she designed for meat plants. She has appeared on many television shows, including *20/20*, *48 Hours*, CNN, *Larry King Live*, *PrimeTime Live*, *60 Minutes*, and the *Today* show. She has been featured in *People* magazine, The New York Times, Forbes, U.S. News and World Report, *Time Magazine*, *The New York Times* book review, and *Discover* magazine. In 2010, *Time Magazine* named her one of the 100 most influential people. Interviews with Dr. Grandin have been broadcast on National Public Radio and she has a 2010 TED Lecture titled "The World Needs ALL Kinds of Minds." She has also authored more than 400 articles in both scientific journals and livestock periodicals on animal handling, welfare, and facility design. She is the author of *Thinking in Pictures* (published by Penguin, 2006) and her books *Animals in Translation* (published by Harcourt, 20006) and *Animals Make Us Human* (published by Mariner Books, 2010) were both on the *New York Times* bestseller list. Her book, *Calling All Minds* (published by Philomel Books, 2018) was a *New York Times* bestseller for middle school students.

Lana Grant

Lana Grant is a specialist advisor and advocate for Autistic people and their families, and has worked within the field of autism for nearly 20 years. She specializes in autism and females, particularly pregnancy and motherhood. Her book *From Here to Maternity: Pregnancy and Motherhood on the Autism Spectrum* (published by Jessica Kingsley Publishers, 2015) is to date the only book that focuses on this issue. Lana is a trained birth partner (doula) specializing in supporting pregnant women on the autism spectrum and their partners. She has recently contributed to the Scottish Autism Right Click Women and Girls Programme. Lana is a passionate advocate for female empowerment and speaks for the U.K.'s National Autistic

Society and other organizations about female issues. You can visit her website at www.lana-grant.co.uk.

David Gray-Hammond

David Gray-Hammond is an Autistic adult from the U.K. He has helped commission services for addicts in Brighton as an independent consultant. David is in recovery from drug and alcohol addiction (now sober) and blogs at "Emergent Divergence" (www.facebook.com/emergentdivergence).

Quincy Hansen

Quincy Hansen is a college student and Autistic advocate from Denver, Colorado. He has been formally diagnosed with Autism Spectrum Disorder and Generalized Anxiety Disorder and has fine motor skill impairments resulting in Dysgraphia-like traits. Quincy has found that writing offers a good outlet for communicating his ideas that do not easily come through speaking, and he blogs his experiences at "Speaking of Autism..." (https://speakingofautismcom.wordpress.com). He is also a public speaker and is the author of *Shake it Up!: How to Be Young, Autistic, and Make an Impact* (to be published by Jessica Kingsley Publishers in July 2022).

Emmalia Harrington

Emmalia Harrington is a nonfiction writer with a deep love of speculative fiction. Her work has previously appeared in "Disability in Kidlit" (http://disabilityinkidlit.com/?s=emmalia+harrington), *All the Weight of Our Dreams* (DragonBee Press 2017), *FIYAH* magazine, and other venues. She's a member of the Codex and Broad Universe writing guilds.

Sarah Hendrickx

Sarah Hendrickx is an independent specialist (www.asperger-training.com) and former public speaker and trainer in autism spectrum conditions. She is Autistic with a late diagnosis of Asperger's Syndrome in her 40s. Sarah has a lifetime of personal experience of autism, its mental and physical impact and how to live with it, and shares this during training along with her professional expertise. She has travelled internationally, delivering more than 1,000 autism training sessions and speaking at conferences worldwide. A number of these presentations can be found on YouTube. She has also worked with more than 1,000 Autistic individuals as an assessor, coach, and consultant in care, schools, relationships, and employment. Sarah has written six books on autism and related conditions (www.amazon.com/Sarah-Hendrickx/e/B001JP1YAU). She was also featured in a BBC *Horizon* documentary on autism.

Ada Hoffmann

Ada Hoffmann is the author of the space opera novel *The Outside* (published by Angry Robot, 2019) the collection *Monsters in my Mind* (published by NeuroQueer Books, 2017) and dozens of speculative short stories and poems. She was diagnosed with Asperger's Syndrome at the age of 13, and is passionate about Autistic self-advocacy. Her Autistic Book Party review series is devoted to in-depth discussions of autism representation in speculative fiction. Much of her own work also features Autistic characters.

Liane Holliday Willey

Liane Holliday Willey is a professor of education with a specialty in psycholinguistics and learning style differences. Since being diagnosed with Asperger's Syndrome 25 years ago, Liane remains most interested in autism and equine therapy, interpersonal communication, and personal safety. Her most impassioned message is the importance of celebrating individual differences. Liane is a respected advocate, consultant, speaker, and author with a bevy of internationally successful publications. Her life story and insights have been shared in *The New York Times, USA Today, Psychology Today, NPR, BBC 4,* and many other media sources, some of which coverage has been lucky enough to win lovely awards.

Shannon Hughes

Shannon Hughes is a writer, designer, and autism advocate with a special interest in autism research. She believes strongly in promoting autism acceptance by removing the barriers—practical, ideological, legal, and social—that marginalize and isolate those with autism.

Anthony Ianni

Anthony Ianni is a national motivational speaker for the Relentless Tour, an initiative of the Michigan Department of Civil Rights to eradicate bullying. Anthony was diagnosed on the spectrum with pervasive developmental disorder at the age of four, and struggled with bullying throughout childhood. He rose above the low expectations of doctors and specialists to graduate from Michigan State University and play basketball for Tom Izzo during his time there. He was the first Division 1 Basketball player in NCAA history to be diagnosed with autism.

Robbie Ierubino

Robbie Ierubino is an American artist with autism studying Arts and Creative Technologies, and learned Graphic Design at Staffordshire University in Stoke-on-Trent, U.K. He has developed his own style of art, which he calls "shapism" and uses his art to communicate his unique world perspective and advocate for acceptance (http://ierubino.com). He is currently gaining new digital skills for future creativity by investigating motion design, creative coding, and extended reality (XR).

Tom Iland

Thomas ("Tom") Iland was diagnosed with autism at 13 years old. Since accepting his diagnosis, he has been recognized as an author, speaker, and emerging thought leader. Tom left his career as a certified public accountant in 2015 to become a keynote speaker, diversity and inclusion consultant, and certified human potential coach. His mission is to educate and motivate people to reach their full and true potential. He is the author of the award-winning, bestselling book *Come to Life! Your Guide to Self-Discovery* (Porterville Press, 2017), and in 2019 became the only Toastmasters International Accredited Speaker with autism in the world! Tom has spoken at the United Nations TWICE: once on World Autism Awareness Day to share his knowledge and first-hand experience about assistive technology and successful law enforcement interactions for people on the autism spectrum, and once for the International Day of Persons with Disabilities, during which he discussed practicing diversity and inclusion in employment. You can also see him on the TEDx stage in his talk titled "How to Come to Life." Tom currently lives in Santa Clarita, California, with his dog, Bridget, and has just received Junior Chamber International's Ten Outstanding Young Americans (TOYA) Award.

Paul Isaacs

Paul Isaacs is an autism advocate, trainer, and public speaker from the U.K. He says that public speaking about his experiences and the experiences of others has helped him find his voice and develop a true skill. He always emphasizes the positive aspects of how life can be lived with autism. He uses the acronym PEC to describe the qualities people who work with autism should have: positivity, empathy, and compassion. He is also a published author and blogs at "Autism from the Inside" (https://theisaacs22.wordpress.com).

Courtney Johnson

Courtney Johnson is a writer, public speaker, and chemistry Ph.D. candidate on the autism spectrum. She manages the website www.AutismAchiever.com, where her goal is to share information she has learned through her varied life experiences to help individuals on the spectrum reach their full potential.

Rochelle Johnson

Rochelle Johnson is an Autistic parent of three daughters, two of whom are Autistic, and lives in Melbourne, Australia. She is an advocate for neurodiversity and writes about the full acceptance and protection of Autistic people. Rochelle also contributes to the Penfriend Project Autistic writing team on www.geekclubbooks.com.

Austin Jones

Austin Jones is an Autistic artist, art teacher, gamer, storyteller, and advocacy writer. He graduated with an illustration degree from the

Art Center College of Design in Pasadena, California. He loves Magic the Gathering, Spiral Knights, and Mexican food. Austin can be found at: austinjohnjones.com; his etsy shop, www.etsy.com/shop/AustinJohnJonesArt?ref=search_shop_redirect; and https://3-austin-jones.pixels.com.

Sandra Jones

Professor Sandra Jones is an Autistic mother of two Autistic sons and Pro Vice-Chancellor (Engagement) at Australian Catholic University. She has studied Autistic adolescent development, the impact of diagnostic labels, community understanding of autism, and the inclusion and exclusion experiences of Autistic adults.

Sarah Kathryn

Sarah Kathryn is a cisgender Autistic woman, blogger (https://deepcontemplationblog.wordpress.com), and speech-language pathologist (SLP).

Braydon Keddie

Braydon Keddie is a former journalist turned blogger/photographer and currently works as a caretaker. He blogs at "Confidence with ASD" (https://confidencewithasd.wordpress.com). Keddie is also a part-time student in building environmental studies, and a self-identified movie fanatic and comic book geek.

Kmarie

Kmarie is an Autistic wife, mother, and blogger from Canada. She is drawn to music and often uses song lyrics to express her emotions. Her beautifully written blog (https://worldwecreate.blogspot.com) details a variety of different life experiences, including (but not limited to) living with Asperger's, INFJ (introverted, intuitive, feeling, and judging) personality, low ferritin, and chronic illness.

Jamie Knight

Jamie Knight is a developer, writer, public speaker, and mountain biker who lives in London, U.K. By day, he works for the BBC, where he is a senior research engineer and spends his time working to make BBC products usable by the whole audience. Outside of his day job, Jamie develops tools used by banks and foreign exchange providers to detect financial crime. He also co-hosts the BBC podcast *1,800 Seconds on Autism*. Lion is his four-foot plushie who goes everywhere with Jamie and has been working with him for over 15 years! You can reach Jamie at http://spacedoutandsmiling.com.

Nic Laughter

Nic Laughter is a developer and public advocate with a podcast focused on autism in adults called "Autistic AF." He writes and speaks about issues related to autism with a special interest in eliminating the barriers many autistics face to entering the workforce.

Russell Lehmann

Russell Lehmann is an award-winning and internationally recognized motivational speaker and poet with a platform of autism and mental health. A graduate of MIT's Leadership in the Digital Age course, Russell is on the national Board of Directors for The Arc and is a council member for the Autism Society of America. He currently travels the world spreading hope, awareness, and compassion in a raw and dynamic fashion, while also setting his sights on erasing the stigma and stereotypes that come with having a disability. Russell's passion is to be a voice for the unheard, because he knows how difficult and frustrating it is to go unnoticed. For more information about Russell and his work, visit his website at www.theautisticpoet.com.

Leanne Libas

Leanne Libas is a writer, college student, and Autistic advocate. She started her advocacy work after a life-changing experience at the Youth Leadership Forum for Students with Disabilities. Leanne was an Autistic Scholarship Fellowship Recipient from the Autistic Self Advocacy Network and is a regular contributor to the "Art of Autism" blog (https://the-art-of-autism.com).

Kirsten Lindsmith

Kirsten Lindsmith is an author, artist, consultant, and autism advocate from New York City (https://kirstenlindsmith.wordpress.com). After receiving an ASD diagnosis at the age of 19, she began co-hosting the online television show *Autism Talk TV* and speaking at conferences and events about her experience as a young woman on the spectrum. Kirsten has written columns for "Wrong Planet" and "Autism After 16," and was profiled in *The New York Times*. She graduated from the University of Massachusetts, Amherst, with a degree in vertebrate ontogeny and phylogeny. Kirsten currently works as a therapist in partnership with Melody of Autism, and as a consultant for behavioral and sensory needs.

Savannah Logsdon-Breakstone

Savannah Logsdon-Breakstone has led advocacy campaigns at national, state, and local levels. She is an active member of, and social media coordinator for, the Autistic Self Advocacy Network, and board member and current vice president of the Pennsylvania-based SAU1 (Self Advocates United as 1). Savannah blogs at "Cracked Mirror in Shalott" (https://crackedmirrorinshalott.wordpress.com) and writes for many other multi-contributor blogs.

Frank L. Ludwig

Frank L. Ludwig is an Irish author of several short stories, plays, essays, and poems. He writes about autism appreciation, among other topics, and believes "Autism is not only a natural but an indispensable part of human neurological diversity." He was also a speaker at the AUsome Conference in 2020. He can be reached at http://franklludwig.com.

C. L. Lynch

C. L. Lynch is a novelist and Autistic advocate from Vancouver. Her breakout novel *Chemistry* (One Tall Tree Press, 2016) came about from the intention to write a book that was "the exact opposite of *Twilight*." She also writes about her recent autism diagnosis, and advocates for improved autism awareness and understanding, as well as a complete overhaul in autism severity labeling (beyond merely avoiding "high-" and "low-functioning" labels).

Georgia Lyon

Georgia Lyon is an author, illustrator, and autism advocate who was diagnosed with autism at age three. In her book *How to Be Human: Diary of an Autistic Girl* (Creston Book, 2019) she details her journey trying to figure out facial expressions, make friends, and navigate the social world of school. In May of 2019, she graduated *cum laude* with a B.A. in Politics from Whitman College, Walla Walla, and currently works as a political communications professional for the election law non-profit Campaign Legal Center in Washington (https://campaignlegal.org/staff/georgia-lyon). Georgia believes that there cannot be disability justice without a strong democracy.

Kerry Magro

Kerry Magro is an award-winning international motivational speaker who's on the autism spectrum. Kerry's books *Defining Autism from the Heart* (2013) and *Autism and Falling in Love* (2014) reached the Amazon bestsellers list shortly after being released. You can learn more about Kerry on Facebook (www.facebook.com/kerry.magro), Twitter (www.twitter.com/kerrymagro), and Instagram (www.instagram.com/kerrymagro).

A. J. Mahari

A.J. Mahari is a counselor, life coach, mental health and personal development coach, and author on the spectrum. Mahari was diagnosed with Asperger's Syndrome at age 40 and manages the website aspergeradults.ca, which seeks to talk about not only her own experience and insights as an adult with Asperger's Syndrome, but also to call attention to the gender differences in females and males with Asperger's.

Marie

Marie is a published poet, writer, translator, puzzler, and artist who lives on the South Coast of Australia with her handsome cockatiel.

She advocates for people on the spectrum, and believes she owes her creativity to having Asperger's Syndrome (http://marieswondrousworldofaspergers.my-style.in).

Gretchen McIntire

Gretchen McIntire is a poet and author who writes under the pen name "Gretchen Leary with Asperger's Syndrome." She has written a variety of short stories and poetry. Her illustrated children's books *Really, Really Like Me* (2015) and *The Quiet Bear* (2018) help raise awareness and promote acceptance of individuals on the autism spectrum. She was Executive Director of BostonCalm until it was dissolved during the Covid pandemic because of lack of funds. She spoke at TEDxNatick2020 in January 2020 with the goal of inspiring others never to give up hope. She can be reached at https://gretchenleary.wordpress.com.

Bix Mediocre

Bix Mediocre is a writer, late-diagnosed Autistic advocate, and former urban goatherd from Oregon.

Lyn Miller-Lachman

Lyn Miller-Lachman is a married author, teacher, editor, and writing consultant/sensitivity reader on the autism spectrum. She loves traveling and is fluent in Portuguese, Spanish, and English. She writes historical fiction featuring characters who are also on the autism spectrum. She has two novels forthcoming in 2022 with autistic protagonists: one a verse novel for middle grade readers, co-authored with Zetta Elliott; and the other a Young Adult historical novel set in Czechoslovakia in the aftermath of the 1968 Soviet invasion and occupation.

Kat Muir

Kat Muir is a speech-language pathologist employed at Easterseals Crossroads. She has a B.S. in speech and hearing science and an M.A. in bilingual speech-language pathology. She is fluent in English, Spanish, German, French, Farsi, and ASL, speaks some Mandarin, and is currently working on learning Vietnamese. She is also a member of Mensa and a public speaker.

Joey Murphy

Joey Murphy is a freelance writer and writing coach. She teaches at the University of Pittsburgh and hosts a podcast (The Tism) targeting women on the spectrum who were diagnosed later in life.

Laura Nadine

Laura Nadine is a Canadian Autistic self-advocate, parent of a child with autism, and teacher of people with autism. Nadine is an accomplished violinist and runs an online music school called Enlightened Audio, LLC, an innovative music education concept working to make music available to all students, no matter their geographic location or their disability, and teaching students from around the world (https://enlightenedaudio.org). Nadine believes neurodiversity is the key to building a pedagogy that truly embraces the idea that any child can learn to play music. She recently took a break from her autism advocacy work but plans to return to this focus in 2021. She is a public speaker, author, educator, and consultant and blogs at https://thelauranadine.wordpress.com.

Anna Nibbs

Anna Nibbs is an academic developer/educator, blogger, and married mother of two from the U.K. She was recently diagnosed with autism, and both her children are also Autistic. You can find Anna's work at https://mamapineappleblog.wordpress.com.

Old Lady With Autism

"Old Lady With Autism" is on a mission to advocate for late-diagnosed people on the spectrum as well as Autistic elderly who may not have received a diagnosis. She self-diagnosed with autism a year ago and is currently in the process of receiving a formal diagnosis. She says discovering her autism diagnosis (as well as her mother's) has helped her make sense of her life and realize a critical need for autism awareness and understanding among the caregivers of the elderly.

Katie Oswald

Katie Oswald is Executive Director of the non-profit Full Spectrum Agency for Autistic Adults (https://fullspectrumasd.org), which provides programs and services that assist with socialization and other activities to help Autistic adults become less isolated and lead fuller lives. She also manages the Autistic Adults Meetup group (https://www.meetup.com/Ann-Arbor-Autistic-Adults). Katie facilitates virtual peer support groups, social groups, and sexuality education classes for Autistic adults around the world, and provides life coaching for adults with autism.

Marie Porter

Marie Porter is a professional spandex costumer (www.queenofspandex.net) and cookbook author from Canada. She is an award-winning cake artist, and her cakes have even landed her international magazine coverage, including a mention in *Every Day with Rachael Ray*. She blogs about new recipes, celebrations, crafts, and occasionally, autism, and is the author of the *Evil Cake Overlord* cookbook (2013) (https://celebrationgeneration.com/about-this-blog).

Yenn Purkis

Yenn Purkis is an Autistic and nonbinary author, public speaker, and self-advocate. They have worked in the Australian Public Service since 2007 and have a master's degree in Fine Arts. They are the author of eight books on autism (www.jeanettepurkis.com). They have given many presentations including at TEDxCanberra 2013, and presented alongside Professor Temple Grandin and artist Tim Sharp in Melbourne in 2015. Purkis facilitates an autism women's group. They were named the 2016 Australian Capital Territory(ACT) Volunteer of the Year and won the ACT Chief Minister's Achievement in Inclusion Award in 2019.

Khali Raymond

Khali Raymond is a writer and musician from Newark, New Jersey. He could read at the age of two, and his work ethic and love for words has led to a prolific writing career (with 163 books to date).

Khali's love for his city and community is extremely strong and is a primary influence for his work. You can visit his website at www.khaliraymond.com.

J. R. Reed

J. R. Reed is a late-diagnosed Autistic blogger and advocate. He currently runs the blog/website "Not Weird, Just Autistic" (www.notweirdjustautistic.com) where his goal is to promote autism acceptance by removing the barriers—practical, ideological, legal, and social—that marginalize and isolate those with autism. He also writes for "The Mighty" (www.themighty.com/u/notweirdjustautistic).

Kieran Rose

A campaigner for Autistic rights, Kieran Rose is an international public speaker, author and consultant for organizations across the world, whose writing focused on advocacy and acceptance for Autistic and ND people has been read by over a million people at his blog www.theautisticadvocate.com. The freedom for ND people to speak for themselves and be heard is paramount for Kieran, mostly because he has spent his whole life immersed in Autistic life and culture as an actually Autistic person. He and his family all live happily in the North East of England, while Kieran co-produces research on Autistic masking and identity and writes his book on Autistic culture.

Avery Rowe

Avery Rowe is a nonbinary Autistic person from England, currently pursuing a degree in Math and Physics while self-teaching Java programming and wildlife photography.

Mickey Rowe

Mickey Rowe is the first Autistic actor to play Christopher Boone in the Tony Award-winning play *The Curious Incident of the Dog in the Night-Time*, and one of the first Autistic actors to play any Autistic character. He has been featured in *The New York Times*, PBS, *Teen Vogue, Playbill*, NPR, CNN'S *Great Big Story, Huffington Post*, and more. Mickey is also Artistic Director of Arts on the Waterfront, a high-quality free theater and arts program in downtown Seattle where many homeless community members live. You can visit his website at https://mickeyrowe.com.

Paula Sanchez

Paula Sanchez spent 18 years supporting adults in the criminal justice system before leaving her job to pursue a PhD exploring the experiences and needs of Autistic mothers of Autistic children. Both she and her son are Autistic.

Ron Sandison

Ron Sandison works full time in the medical field and is a professor of theology at Destiny School of Ministry, Roseville. He is an advisory board member of the Autism Faith Initiative of the Autism Society of America, the Art of Autism, and the Els Center of Excellence. Ron has a Master of Divinity from Oral Roberts University, Tulsa, and is the author of *A Parent's Guide to Autism: Practical Advice, Biblical Wisdom*, and *Thought, Choice, Action* (published by Siloam, 2016). He has memorized over 15,000 Scriptures including 22 complete books of the New Testament. He speaks at over 70 events a year, including 20-plus education conferences. Ron and his wife, Kristen, reside in Rochester Hills, Michigan, with their daughter, Makayla. His website is www.spectruminclusion.com, and his Facebook fan page is www.facebook.com/SpectrumRonSandison.

Jesse Saperstein

Jesse Saperstein is a bestselling author, autism advocate, and motivational speaker. He currently serves as the activities and media liaison for The College Experience, a program helping students with disabilities to attend adaptive college programs and learn to live independently.

Maxine Share

Canadian Maxine Share is an Autistic writer, advocate, workshop developer/presenter, and co-founder of the popular Facebook page Autism Goggles. She has a keen interest in changing how we educate

Autistic students and sits on the Minister's Advisory Council on Special Education.

Austin Shinn

Austin Shinn is an author, editor, film buff, husband, father, and advocate for people diagnosed with autism. He is diagnosed with Asperger's Syndrome and blogs mostly about his life with perspectives on autism, disability, and advocacy at "A Flickering Life" (https://aflickeringlife.wordpress.com). Austin is also the author of *A Flickering Life: A Memoir of Autism* (2016), which chronicles his struggle to live life no differently than anyone else.

Kayla Smith

Kayla Smith is an Autistic advocate from North Carolina.

Robyn Steward

Robyn Steward is an international public speaker, autism advocate, musician, and author from the U.K. On top of her training and consultancy work, she has been an advocate for inclusivity and raising awareness around sexual abuse. In 2018, Robyn was named as one of the 100 Most Influential Disabled People in the U.K. Steward has written two books: *The Independent Woman's Handbook For Super Safe Living on the Autistic Spectrum* (Jessica Kingsley Publishers, 2013) and *The Autism-Friendly Guide to Periods* (Jessica Kingsley Publishers, 2019). You can visit Robyn's website at www.robynsteward.com.

Teona Studemire

Teona Studemire is a writer and college student majoring in Library Sciences. Teona is Autistic and ADHD, has myalgic encephalomyelitis and hyper-mobile Ehlers-Danlos syndrome and is an advocate for other multiply-disabled people. You can find Teona's blog at https://teespoonie.com.

RoAnna Sylver

RoAnna Sylver is passionate about stories that give hope, healing, and even fun for LGBT, disabled, and other marginalized people, and thinks we need a lot more. Aside from writing oddly optimistic dystopian books, RoAnna is an Autistic blogger, artist, singer, and voice actor. You can find RoAnna at https://sylvernebulae.wordpress.com.

Larkin Taylor-Parker

Larkin Taylor-Parker is an attorney practicing in North Carolina, having graduated from Agnes Scott College, Decatur, and the University of Georgia School of Law. Larkin is a proud member of the Autistic community. Larkin lives in Raleigh and enjoys spending time with friends and family, playing the tuba, and riding and maintaining a pair of vintage English three-speed bicycles. You can find Larkin at http://autisticfuture.com.

Terra Vance

Terra Vance is an industrial and organizational psychology consultant and founder and CEO of NeuroClastic, Inc. (https://neuroclastic.com, formerly known as The Aspergian). Her passions are in the intersections of social justice, equity, literature, Truth, and science.

Daniel Wendler

Dr. Daniel Wendler is a bestselling author, nationally recognized keynote speaker, and proud Autistic self-advocate. Dr. Wendler taught himself social skills as a way of overcoming the social challenges of his Asperger's Syndrome diagnosis, and founded www.improveyoursocialskills.com to help others achieve social success, too. He went on to write two books, *Improve Your Social Skills* (2014) and *Level Up Your Social Life* (2016), speak at TEDx (twice), and complete a doctorate in clinical psychology. Today, he uses his Autistic insight and psychological training to help create a world where everyone can find a place to belong. Dr. Wendler is based in Austin, Texas, where he works as a therapist at Deep Eddy Psychotherapy. You can connect with him and pick up a copy of his books at www.danielwendler.com.

Evaleen Whelton

Evaleen Whelton is a public speaker and trainer advocating for positive change for Autistic people in Ireland. As an advocate, Evaleen concentrates her efforts on raising appreciation for Autistic thinking, delivering educational workshops, writing articles, and organizing conferences relating to autism (including Ireland's only all-Autistic conference). Evaleen has trained professional groups, schools, and businesses on Neurodiversity and Inclusion.

Brent White

Brent White is Autistic, dyslexic, and multiply ND. He designs and directs adult programs for ND young adults for a non-profit in Berkeley, California. Programs include an adult transition program he designed for the Berkeley Unified School District. Brent is a grassroots researcher, scholar, and advocate.

Bob Yamtich

Bob Yamtich is a marriage and family therapist specializing in Nonviolent Communication coaching and neurodiversity. He works as an independent consultant and therapeutic coach, and blogs at https://bobyamtich.org.

References

APA (2013) *Diagnostic and Statistical Manual of Mental Disorders, 5th Edition.* Arlington, VA: American Psychiatric Association Publishing.

Ashkenazy, E. (2017) "Foreword: On Autism and Race." In L. X. Z. Brown, E. Ashkenazy & M. Giwa-Onaiwu (eds) *All the Weight of Our Dreams: On Living Racialized Autism*. Lincoln, NE: DragonBee Press.

Autistic Self Advocacy Network (2018) *Everybody Communicates: Toolkit for Accessing Communication Assessments, Funding, and Accommodations.* Office of Developmental Primary Care. Available at https://odpc.ucsf.edu/communications-paper. Accessed on February 21, 2020.

Autistic Self Advocacy Network (2019, August 5) *ASAN has ended partnership with Sesame Street.* Available at https://autisticadvocacy.org/2019/08/asan-has-ended-partnership-with-sesame-street. Accessed on March 21, 2020.

Bartmess, E. (2015, December 18) Autistic representation and real-life consequences: An in-depth look. Disability in Kidlit. Available at https://disabilityinkidlit.com/2015/12/18/autistic-representation-and-real-life-consequences. Accessed on May 23, 2021.

Bascom, J. (2012a) "Foreword." In J. Bascom (ed.) *Loud Hands: Autistic People, Speaking*. Autistic Self Advocacy Network.

Bascom, J. (2012b) "Quiet Hands." In J. Bascom (ed.) *Loud Hands: Autistic People, Speaking*. Autistic Self Advocacy Network.

Bonnello, C. (2017, October 2) *We need to stop saying "We're all a little autistic."* Available at https://autisticnotweird.com/stop-saying. Accessed on September 29, 2019.

Boon, S. (2020, October 27) *Why can job interviews be so challenging for autistic people?* Available at https://autisticallysarah.com/2020/10/27/why-can-job-interviews-be-so-challenging-for-autistic-people. Accessed on May 28, 2021.

Brown, L. X. Z. (2011, August 4) *The significance of semantics: Person-first language: Why it matters*. Autistic Hoya. Available at www.autistichoya.com/2011/08/significance-of-semantics-person-first.html. Accessed on September 26, 2020.

Brown, L. X. Z. (2012a, February 24) *15 things you should never say to an Autistic*. Autistic Hoya. Available at www.autistichoya.com/2012/02/15-things-you-should-never-say-to.html. Accessed on September 22, 2019.

Brown, L. X. Z. (2012b, May 27) *You are not a burden*. Autistic Hoya. Available at www.autistichoya.com/2012/05/you-are-not-burden.html. Accessed on September 25, 2019.

Brown, L. X. Z. (2016, February 11) *Disabled people are not your feel-good back-pats*. Autistic Hoya. Available at www.autistichoya.com/2016/02/disabled-people-are-not-your-feel-good-back-pats.html. Accessed on September 24, 2019.

Brown, L. X. Z. (2020, June 18) *We can't address disability without addressing race. Here's why*. Learn Play Thrive. Available at www.learnplaythrive.com/single-post/Racism. Accessed on February 12, 2021.

Ciampi, M. (2021, January 13) *Neurodiversity: Paving the way to universal design inclusivity in the workplace*. Available at www.recruiter.com/i/neurodiversity-paving-the-way-to-universal-design-inclusivity-in-the-workplace. Accessed on January 19, 2021.

Des Roches Rosa, S. (2016, September 22) *How "autism warrior parents" harm autistic kids*. Medium. Available at https://medium.com/the-establishment/how-autism-warrior-parents-harm-autistic-kids-6700b8bf6677. Accessed on December 2, 2019.

Devita-Raeburn, E. (2016, August 11) *Is the most common therapy for autism cruel?* The Atlantic. Available at www.theatlantic.com/health/archive/2016/08/aba-autism-controversy/495272. Accessed on October 12, 2019.

Disability Inclusive Messaging: What is inspiration porn? SMG. Available at https://disability-marketing.com/2018/08/23/disability-inclusive-messaging-inspiration-porn. Accessed on November 20, 2019.

Endow, J. (2014, August 02) *Inclusion – how it works best for this autistic*. Available at www.judyendow.com/advocacy/inclusion-how-it-works-best-for-this-autistic. Accessed on December 26, 2020.

Gates, G. (2019) *Trauma, Stigma, and Autism: Developing Resilience and Loosening the Grip of Shame*. London: Jessica Kingsley Publishers.

Geggel, L. (2013, September 10) *Eating aversion*. Spectrum. Available at www.spectrumnews.org/opinion/eating-aversion. Accessed on November 24, 2019.

Gensic, J. (2019) *What Your Child on the Spectrum Really Needs: Advice From 12 Autistic Adults*. Shawnee, KS: AAPC.

Glenn, H. (2017, September 22) *How an air traveler with autism found strength in a stranger's kindness*. NPR. Available at www.npr.org/2017/09/22/552644276/how-an-air-traveler-with-autism-found-strength-in-a-stranger-s-kindness. Accessed on October 12, 2020.

Higashida, N., Yoshida, K. & Mitchell, D. (2017) *The Reason I Jump: The Inner Voice of a Thirteen-Year-Old Boy with Autism*. New York, NY: Random House.

Hillary, A. (2011) "Autism and Language." In M. Sutton (ed.) *The Real Experts: Readings for Parents of Autistic Children*. Fort Worth, TX: Autonomous Press.

Hus Bal, V., Katz, T., Bishop, S. L. & Krasileva, K. (2016, December) "Understanding definitions of minimally verbal across instruments: Evidence for subgroups within minimally verbal children and adolescents with autism spectrum disorder." *Journal of Child Psychology and Psychiatry* 57(12), 1424–1433.

Iland, T. (2019) "Helping or hindering me? Five breakthroughs from a man with autism to his mother." Personal communication, October 18, 2019.

Jones, Sparrow Rose (2011) "ABA – Applied Behavior Analysis." In M. Sutton (ed.) *The Real Experts: Readings for Parents of Autistic Children*. Fort Worth, TX: Autonomous Press.

Kim. C. (2011) "Socially Inappropriate." In M. Sutton (ed.) *The Real Experts: Readings for Parents of Autistic Children*. Fort Worth, TX: Autonomous Press.

Litz, S. (2017, June 15) "Reno airport worker 'a blessing' to autism advocate." *Reno Gazette Journal*. Available at www.rgj.com/story/life/2017/06/15/reno-airport-worker-a-blessing-autism-advocate/399828001. Accessed on October 12, 2020.

Lovaas Institute (2020) *The potential benefits of intensive behavioral intervention*. Lovaas Institute. Available at www.lovaas.com/approach-benefits.php. Accessed on August 6, 2020.

Lynch, C. L. (2019a, March 28) *Invisible Abuse: ABA and the things only autistic people can see*. NeuroClastic. Available at https://neuroclastic.com/2019/03/28/invisible-abuse-aba-and-the-things-only-autistic-people-can-see. Accessed on September 26, 2020.

Lynch, C. L. (2019b, May 04) *Autism is a spectrum doesn't mean what you think*. NeuroClastic. Available at https://neuroclastic.com/2019/05/04/

its-a-spectrum-doesnt-mean-what-you-think. Accessed on January 03, 2021.

Mead, K. (2019, March 12) *Inspiration porn: How the media and society objectify disabled people*. Thinking Person's Guide to Autism. Available at www.thinkingautismguide.com/2019/03/inspiration-porn-how-media-and-society.html. Accessed on September 30, 2019.

Merriam Webster (2020) "Advocate." Available at www.merriam-webster.com/dictionary/advocate. Accessed on February 21, 2020.

Miserandino, C. (2020) *The spoon theory. But you don't look sick*. Available at https://butyoudontlooksick.com/articles/written-by-christine/the-spoon-theory. Accessed on September 22, 2019.

Monje Jr., M. S. (2011) "Not That Autistic." In M. Sutton (ed.) *The Real Experts: Readings for Parents of Autistic Children*. Fort Worth, TX: Autonomous Press.

Moss, H. (2020, January 31) "Parents' online sharing can be particularly problematic for autistic kids. Here's why." *The Washington Post*. Available at www.washingtonpost.com/lifestyle/2020/01/31/parents-online-sharing-can-be-particularly-problematic-autistic-kids-heres-why. Accessed on September 20, 2020.

Murphy, T. (2019, January 10) "Different normal." *Brown Alumni Magazine*. Available at www.brownalumnimagazine.com/articles/2019-01-10/different-normal. Accessed on November 24, 2019.

Muzikar, D. (2018, November 5) *21 tips for presuming competence*. The Art of Autism. Available at https://the-art-of-autism.com/21-tips-for-presuming-competence. Accessed on October 1, 2020.

Perry, D. M. (2015, June 2) *Inspiration porn further disables the disabled*. Aljazeera America. Available at http://america.aljazeera.com/opinions/2015/6/inspiration-porn-further-disables-the-disabled.html. Accessed on September 29, 2019.

Picciuto, E. (2017, April 14) *They don't want an autism cure*. Daily Beast. Available at www.thedailybeast.com/they-dont-want-an-autism-cure. Accessed on September 22, 2020.

Russo, F. (2018, February 21) *The costs of camouflaging autism*. Spectrum. Available at www.spectrumnews.org/features/deep-dive/costs-camouflaging-autism. Accessed on November 24, 2019.

S., C. (2016, July 31) *How to avoid "inspiration porn" when talking about disability*. The Mighty. Available at https://themighty.com/2016/08/how-to-avoid-inspiration-porn-when-talking-about-disability. Accessed on September 22, 2019.

Scutti, S. (2019, August 15) *Taking "miracle" solution as cure for autism or cancer is the "same as drinking bleach," FDA says*. CNN Health. Available at www.cnn.com/2019/08/15/health/bleach-miracle-cure-fda-warning/index.html. Accessed on March 23, 2020.

Senner, J. E. (2018, December 3) *Key AAC issues*. Available at https://ussaac.org/speakup/articles/key-aac-issues. Accessed on January 08, 2021.

Sequenzia. A. (2011) "Attitudes." In M. Sutton (ed.) *The Real Experts: Readings for Parents of Autistic Children*. Fort Worth, TX: Autonomous Press.

Serani, D. (2014, April 03) *The emotional blindness of alexithymia*. Available at https://blogs.scientificamerican.com/mind-guest-blog/the-emotional-blindness-of-alexithymia. Accessed on January 04, 2021.

Sinclair, J. (1993) "Don't mourn for us." *Our Voice 1*(3). Available at www.aane.org/dont-mourn-for-us. Accessed on October 1, 2020.

Sinclair, J. (2019, March 16) *Is everyone on the autism spectrum?* Autistic & Unapologetic. Available at https://autisticandunapologetic.com/2019/03/16/is-everyone-on-the-autism-spectrum. Accessed on September 29, 2019.

Smith, L. (n.d.) *Ableism*. Center for Disability Rights. Available at http://cdrnys.org/blog/uncategorized/ableism. Accessed on September 30, 2019.

Solutions Marketing Group (2021) *Disability inclusive messaging: What is inspiration porn*. SMG. Available at https://disability-marketing.com/2018/08/23/disability-inclusive-messaging-inspiration-porn. Accessed on September 22, 2019.

Stout, A. (2020) *Presuming competence: What is it and why is it important?* The Autism Site. Available at https://blog.theautismsite.greatergood.com/presume-competence/#:~:text=In%20a%20sentence%2C%20presuming%20competence,systems%20to%20help%20them%20succeed. Accessed on September 28, 2020.

Szalavitz, M. (2016, March 1) *Autism—it's different in girls*. Scientific American. Available at www.scientificamerican.com/article/autism-it-s-different-in-girls. Accessed on November 24, 2019.

TV Tropes (n.d.) *Very Special Episode*. Available at https://tvtropes.org/pmwiki/pmwiki.php/Main/VerySpecialEpisode. Accessed on February 12, 2021.

United Nations (2007) Participatory Dialogue: Towards a Stable, Safe and Just Society for All. United Nations Publication. Available at www.un.org/esa/socdev/publications/prtcptry_dlg(full_version).pdf. Accessed on May 23, 2021.

Walker, N. (2011) "Foreword." In M. Sutton (ed.) *The Real Experts: Readings for Parents of Autistic Children*. Fort Worth, TX: Autonomous Press.

#WalkinRed. (2020) *#WalkinRed*. Available at http://walkinred.weebly.com. Accessed on October 1, 2020.

Williams, D. (1992) *Nobody, Nowhere*. New York, NY: Crown.

Wisconsin Medical Society (n.d.) *Savant syndrome*. Wisconsin Medical Society. Available at www.agnesian.com/blog/savant-syndrome-2013-myths-and-realities. Accessed on May 28, 2019.

Wolfe, G. (n.d.) "The stock of available reality." *Image Journal 26*. Available at https://imagejournal.org/article/the-stock-of-available-reality. Accessed on May 28, 2021.

Wright, J. (2015, October 19) *Gender disparities in psychiatric conditions*. Spectrum. Available at www.spectrumnews.org/news/gender-disparities-in-psychiatric-conditions/#:~:text=Many%20psychiatric%20disorders%2C%20such%20as,have%20depression%20or%20bipolar%20disorder. Accessed on November 24, 2019.

Zeliadt, N. (2016, September 5) *Words say little about cognitive abilities in autism*. Spectrum. Available at www.spectrumnews.org/news/words-say-little-cognitive-abilities-autism. Accessed on September 28, 2020.

Subject Index

ableism 22, 252–3
Accessing Home and Community-Based Services: A Guide for Self Advocates (ASAN) 203
adults
  mental health needs of 74–6
  older adult needs 76–7
  support for 73–4
advocacy
  and autism acceptance 61–5
  backing off 30
  checklist for 275–9
  communities 63–5
  mistakes during 28–30, 271–3
  shortcomings of 15–18
  social model for public 159–61
  questions on need for 18–20
advocacy for individuals
  co-occurring conditions 109–11
  getting to know individual 112–15
  honoring diversity of individuals 122–7
  inspiration porn avoidance 118–22
  as learning opportunity 125–7
  one-size-fits-all-solution avoidance 115–17
  reflection questions 127–8
  respectful story sharing 103–7
  respecting privacy 120–1
  stereotype avoidance 107–11
advocacy for wants of Autistic people
  honoring diverse relationships 149–54
  language use in 154–8
  reflection questions on 175
  in schools 161–7
  and social model of disability 158–61
  using Autistic-initiated therapies 132–49
  in workplace 168–73
alienation avoidance 81–2
applied behavioral analysis (ABA) 133, 134, 137, 138
Asperger's Syndrome 22–3
assessments of competence 90–2
Atypical (TV series) 237
autism
  language use 23–6
  neutral position on 179–82
  reframing as way of being 41–51

autism acceptance
advocacy for 61–5
barrier elimination 51–6
bigger picture emphasis 61–5
and negative behaviors 51–6
reflection questions 66–7
reframing as way of being 41–51
replacing grief with 37–40
Autistic community 23
autism-inclusive advocacy
broadening unique insights 22–5
combatting stigma 213–14
deferring to Autistic people 211–17
information processing differences 214–17
reflection questions on 226–7
respecting all skill sets 218–21
Autistic-initiated therapies
anxiety and sensory needs in 144–5
Autistic-designed goals for 139–44
and camouflaging 148–9
communicating with therapist 147–8
emotional welfare support 137–9
empowerment in 145–9
freedom to choose 138–9
need for 132–3
positive/healthy personal development as goal 133–7
respect in 145–9
validation in 145–9
whole-person approach to 146–7
autism neutrality 179–82

backing off 30
barrier elimination
finding solutions to barriers 51–3
societal changes for 56–61
understanding stimming 53–6

bigger picture emphasis 61–5

camouflaging
as gender issue 78–80
and person-centered advocacy 177–9
in therapy 148–9
checklist for advocacy 275–9
co-occurring conditions 109–11
communication needs of Autistic people 92–6
competence, presumption of
assessments of 90–2
communication needs of Autistic people 92–6
description of 86–7
and intellectual disabilities 87–90
over-sheltering 96–100
reflection questions 101
"Costs of Camouflaging Autism, The" (Russo) 79

deferring to Autistic people 211–17
Diagnostic and Statistical Manual of Mental Disorders (APA) 22, 224–5
diagnosis validation 124
disability-friendly organizations 259–62
"Disabled people are not your feel-good backpats" (Brown) 119
diversity
benefits of 61
and diagnosis validation 124
honoring individual 122–7
and person-centered advocacy 182
in relationships 149–54
respect for Autistic experience 122–4

emotional support in therapy 137–9

empowerment in therapy 145–9
Everybody Communicates (Autistic Self Advocacy Network) 19

families
- grief replacement for 38
- and respectful story sharing 103–7
- tone after diagnosis 39–40

gender issues 77–80
grief replacement
- for families 38
- need for 37–8
- tone after diagnosis 39–40

happiness 184–9
high-functioning autism 23–4, 218–21
"How 'Autism Warrior Parents' Harm Autistic Kids" (Des Roches Rosa) 41–2
"How to Avoid 'Inspiration Porn' When Talking About Disability" (S.) 120

identity-first language 24, 154–8
inclusive research 244–8
independent living development 200–7
individuals versus people 24–5
information processing differences 214–17
inspiration porn avoidance 118–22
intellectual disabilities 87–90
intent as an excuse 194–7

language use 22–6, 154–8
lifespan support 72–7
Loud Hands, Autistic People, Speaking (Bascom) 27, 55
low-functioning Autism 23–4, 218–21

masking *see* camouflaging
meltdowns 197–200
mistakes during advocacy 28–30, 271–3

neurotypical/neurodivergent/neurodiverse 25
Nobody, Nowhere (Williams) 14
"Not That Autistic" (Monje Jr.) 74

older adult needs 76–7
100 Day Kit 39–40
one-size-fits-all-solution avoidance 115–17
opportunities for Autistic people 47–8
Our Voice (Autism Network International Newsletter) 38
over-sheltering 96–100

parents *see* families
person-centered advocacy
- and autism neutrality 179–82
- and camouflaging 177–9
- independent living development 200–7
- intent as an excuse 194–7
- listening to Autistic people 189–94
- meeting needs of Autistic person 182–3
- need for 176–7
- reflection questions on 209
- respecting difference in 182
- tantrums and meltdowns 197–200
- visions of happy life 184–9

person-first language 24, 154–8
personal experience, authority of 27–8
perspectives of autism
- gender issues 77–80
- importance of balanced 68–9
- lifespan support 72–7
- reflection questions 85

perspectives of autism *cont.*
savantism assumptions 69–71
strengths and weaknesses acknowledgement 80–4
practice of advocacy
acknowledging mistakes 271–3
becoming students 266–9
practice what is preached 267–9
reflection questions on 273–4
and technology trends 270–1
privacy, respecting 120–1
pronouns 26

race and disability intersections 252–8
Rain Man 69
reaching out
for Autistic voices 234–6
increasing Autistic representation 236–40
inviting Autistic people as public experts 241–4
need for 233–4
Real Experts, The 16, 54
Reason I Jump, The (Higashida) 180–1, 214–15
reflection questions
on advocacy for individuals 127–8
on advocacy for wants of Autistic people 175
on autism acceptance 66–7
on autism-inclusive advocacy 226–7
on person-centered advocacy 209
on perspectives of autism 85
on practice of advocacy 273–4
on presumption of competence 101
on respectful connections 264
reframing autism as way of being
breaking stereotypes 48–51
expanding opportunities 47–8
reasons for 41
and "remedies" for autism 41–5
stress for Autistic people 45–7
relationships, diversity in
need for 149–50
socializing needs 151–4
value of 150–1
"remedies" for Autism 41–5
respect in therapy 145–9
respectful connections
conducting inclusive research 244–8
disability-friendly organizations 259–62
first reaching out to Autistic community 233–44
race and disability intersections 252–8
reflection questions on 264
Roadmap to Transition: A Handbook for Autistic Youth Transitioning to Adulthood, Navigating College: A Handbook on Self Advocacy (ASAN) 203

savantism assumptions 69–71
schools
advocacy for wants of Autistic people 161–7
Autistic experience in 166–7
influences of 162–6
Sesame Street 39, 223
social model of disability 158–61
societal changes
avoiding stress and fatigue 59–61
burden on Autistic people 57–9
diversity in 61
need for 56–7
and social model of disability 158–61
spectrums in autism 26
"Spoon Theory, The" (Miserandino) 59
stereotypes
and advocacy for individuals 107–11

breaking through reframing Autism 48–51
and presumption of competence 89–90
stigma, combatting 213–14
stimming 53–6
story sharing 103–7
strengths and weaknesses acknowledgement 80–4
stress
and reframing autism 45–7
and societal changes 59–61

tantrums 197–200
technology trends 270–1
"They Don't Want an Autism Cure" (Bascom) 44
Trauma, Stigma, and Autism: Developing Resilience and Loosening the Grip of Shame (Gates) 214

validation in therapy 145–9

What Your Child on the Spectrum Really Needs: Advice From 12 Autistic Adults (Gensic) 15, 139, 150
workplace
advocacy in 168–73
and independent living development 203–6

Author Index

Amodeo, M. 44–5, 280
Andrews, A. 48–9, 50, 88–9, 97, 280
APA 22
Ashkenazy, E. 258
Autistic Self Advocacy Network (ASAN) 19, 39–40, 203

Bartmess, E. 239
Bascom, J. 27, 44, 55, 210, 281
Birch, N. 241, 281
Bonnello, C. 104, 123, 223, 281
Boon, S. 172
Boresow, E. 58–9, 73, 92, 281
Bowman Jr., D. 105, 156–7, 237–8, 281–2
Brown, L. X. Z. 71, 106–7, 118–19, 155, 157–8, 248, 252–3, 257–8, 282
Brozek, J. 93, 116, 282–3
Brunton, J. 131

Campbell, T. 152, 236, 283
Carley, M. J. 124, 283
Christian, B. 108, 283
Ciampi, M. 224–5, 283–4
Cohen, T. 116, 195–6, 284
Crane, S. 242, 284
Crawford, E. 260, 267–8, 284

Dalmayne, E. 28–9, 285
Davin, A. 212, 285
Des Roches Rosa, S. 41–2
Devita-Raeburn, E. 138
Dias, R. 238, 285
Disability Marketing 118
Drew, G. 82–3, 98–9, 109, 122–3, 124, 285

Earhart, A. 108, 285–6
Endow, J. 152–3
Engelbrecht, N. 215, 266, 286
Evans, E. 58, 104, 253–4, 256–7, 269, 286

Gaddes, B. 118, 286–7
Gates, G. 214
Geggel, L. 80
Generous, A. 60, 195, 287
Gensic, G. 15, 53, 99, 139, 150–1, 180, 185, 218, 248
Gilberg, M. 213, 287
Giosa, M. 42–4, 99–100, 179–80, 287

Glenn, H. 200
Grace, A. 35, 47–8, 104, 140–1, 142, 195, 272, 287
Grandin, T. 114, 203–7, 287–8
Grant, L. 114, 151, 288
Gray-Hammond, D. 73, 75–6, 178–9, 289

Hansen, Q. 109–10, 158–9, 289
Harrington, E. 68, 289
Hendrickx, S. 186, 289–90
Higashida, N. 180–1, 214–15
Hillary, A. 155, 180
Hoffmann, A. 69–70, 88, 151–2, 220–1, 238–9, 290
Holliday Willey, L. 221, 290
Hughes, S. 181, 290

Ianni, A. 28, 291
Ierubino, R. 49, 291
Iland, T. 186–7, 196, 260, 261, 272, 291–2
Isaacs, P. 63–4, 261, 292

Johnson, C. 98, 237, 292
Johnson, R. 110, 292
Jones, A. 216, 292–3
Jones, S. 54, 55, 62–3, 136–7, 144–5, 293

Kartje, B. 218
Kathryn, S. 145–9, 159–60, 293
Keddie, B. 108–9, 113, 293
Kim, C. 54
King, B. 185
Kmarie 46, 63, 235, 293
Knight, J. 51–2, 293–4

Laughter, N. 190–1, 259–60, 294
Lehmann, R. 123–4, 199–200, 294
Libas, L. 272, 294
Lindsmith, K. 78–9, 81–2, 294–5
Litz, S. 199
Logsdone-Breakstone, S. 93, 217, 224, 295
Lovaas Institute 134
Ludwig, F. L. 49–50, 61, 295
Lynch, C. L. 55–6, 88, 89, 110–11, 137, 176, 178, 182–3, 188–9, 219, 295
Lyon, G. 220, 241–2, 296

Magro, K. 192, 296
Mahari, A. J. 177–8, 260, 296
Marie 107, 152, 187, 266–7, 296
McIntire, G. 28, 297
Mead, K. 120, 121
Mediocre, B. 159, 187–8, 297
Merriam-Webster 21
Miller-Lachman, L. 240, 297
Miserandino, C. 59
Mitchell, D. 181
Monje Jr., M. S. 74
Moss, H. 106
Muir, K. 125–6, 156, 201–2, 297
Murphy, J. 70–1, 298
Murphy, T. 80
Muzikar, D. 95

Nadine, L. 86–7, 270–1, 298
Ne'eman, A. 138
Nibbs, A. 50–1, 90, 95, 140, 142, 223, 298

"Old Lady With Autism" 62, 76–7, 298
Oswald, K. 53–4, 64–5, 95–6, 157, 298–9
O'Toole, J. 80

Pelphrey, K. 79
Perry, D. M. 121
Picciuto, E. 44
Porter, M. 191, 224, 232, 242–3, 299
Purkis, Y. 46, 137, 299

Raymond, K. 255, 299–300
Reed, J. R. 48, 300
Rose, K. 234–5, 236–7, 300
Rowe, A. 235, 300

Rowe, M. 241, 300–1
Russo, F. 78, 79, 80

S., C. 120
Sanchez, P. 157, 212, 265, 301
Sandison, R. 37, 301
Saperstein, J. 191–2, 301
Scutti, S. 44
Senner, J. E. 271
Sequenzia, A. 48
Serani, D. 245
Share, M. 57–8, 86, 301–2
Shinn, A. 108, 113–14, 216, 302
Sinclair, J. 38, 41, 46, 126
Smith, K. 255, 302
Smith, L. 47
Sparrow, M. 54, 135–6, 144–5
Steward, R. 202–3, 302
Stout, A. 86
Studemire, T. 252, 256, 302
Syler, R. 235–6, 238, 239–40, 302–3
Szalavitz, M. 80

Taylor-Parker, L. 242, 251, 303
TV Tropes 119

United Nations 180

Van de Wetering, J. 52–3, 139
Vance, T. 94, 108, 117, 303
Walker, N. 16
Wayman, L. 150–1
Wendler, D. 73–4, 83, 153–4, 303
Whelton, E. 243–4, 303–4
White, B. 91, 304
Williams, D. 14, 64
Wisconsin Medical Society 69
Wolfe, G. 237
Wright, J. 78

Yamtich, B. 30, 45–6, 304
Yoshida, K. 181

Zeliadt, N. 91